The New Eugenics

The New Eugenics

Selective Breeding in an Era of Reproductive Technologies

JUDITH DAAR

Yale UNIVERSITY PRESS/NEW HAVEN & LONDON

Published with assistance from the Mary Cady Tew Memorial Fund.

Yale University Press books may be purchased in quantity for
educational, business, or promotional use. For information,
please e-mail sales.press@yale.edu (U.S. office)
or sales@yaleup.co.uk (U.K. office).

Set in Minion type by Newgen North America.
Printed in the United States of America.

ISBN 978-0-300-13715-6
Library of Congress Control Number: 2016944941
A catalogue record for this book is available from
the British Library.

This paper meets the requirements of ANSI/NISO Z39.48-1992
(Permanence of Paper).

10 9 8 7 6 5 4 3 2 1

For Eric and our four sons,
Evan, Jared, Adam, and Ryan
with continuing love and gratitude

Contents

Preface

On a lovely autumn afternoon in November 2008, I lunched with two women whose personal struggle for parenthood had recently garnered tremendous public attention. The previous August, a much-awaited decision that would clear a procreative path for many was handed down by the California Supreme Court. Like so many high-profile cases, the legal saga endured by this couple, Guadalupe ("Lupita") Benitez and Joanne Clark, began with an ordinary act, a simple visit to the doctor. This fateful medical appointment seemed a logical and practical starting point for Benitez and Clark, who understood that their shared desire to start a family could not be accomplished without reproductive assistance. What they did not realize at the time was that their status as lesbians would stand as a tremendous barrier in their pursuit of parenthood. They likewise did not appreciate that their struggle was not unique; many would-be procreators in the years before and since Lupita and Joanne began their legal journey have been deprived of medical assistance in conception because of personal characteristics unrelated to their capacity to lovingly carry and rear a child.

As the lunch menus were passed, the two women began to tell me their story, just like countless couples who relish reliving their mutual discovery. The women had been together for five years when they decided to start a family, electing for Lupita to carry the couple's child. Venturing, at first, lightly into the world of assisted reproductive technologies (ART), Lupita began trying to conceive using at-home insemination with sperm purchased from a commercial bank. Low-tech and relatively low-cost, this DIY method of assisted conception is also linked to somewhat low success rates. When no pregnancy ensued after months of self-inseminations, Lupita sought medical assistance.

From an access-to-care perspective, Lupita considered herself fortunate because her employer-sponsored health insurance provided coverage for infertility, a rare benefit for insurance plans. The sole ART provider in her insurance network was a fertility clinic in the San Diego area, a reasonable distance from the couple's home. At an initial visit attended by both women, the treating physician, Dr. Christine Brody, performed a history and physical exam on Lupita. At that same appointment, according to court records, Brody also told the patient and her partner that should any procedures beyond simple insemination become necessary, she would be precluded from providing further treatment because of her religious beliefs, which disapproved of invasive assisted conception for individuals occupying Lupita's social situation. At least one other doctor in the group was reported by Brody to hold similar views.

At this point in the story the women smiled at each other, anticipating the shock that would predictably come over my face as they presented a nugget that was not discussed by the California Supreme Court. According to the couple, the San Diego clinic had adopted a nondiscrimination policy that represented its physicians did not and would not discriminate against any patient based on marital status or sexual orientation. Perhaps assured that Dr. Brody and the other physicians in the practice would abide by this policy, Lupita continued to seek treatment at the clinic. After months of unsuccessful inseminations, it became clear that Lupita would require more invasive treatment in the form of intrauterine insemination (IUI), in which sperm is injected directly into the uterus via a catheter. When the treatment plan turned toward IUI, as warned, Lupita was told that the physicians' religious objections precluded further involvement in her care. She recalls this moment as utterly horrifying and humiliating, causing her to question her worth as a potential parent and a woman. As the pair recounted this part of the story, the dynamics of their close relationship came into clearer focus; when a sobbing Lupita returned home to share this news, Joanne became outraged and immediately sprang into action.

The eight-year legal and medical odyssey that followed ultimately yielded a happy ending for the Benitez-Clark family. In a unanimous decision, the California Supreme Court ruled that the state's civil rights laws prohibiting discrimination on the basis of sexual orientation did not contain an exemption for medical providers' assertions of religious freedom. Doctors and other purveyors of public goods and services in the Golden State are governed by California's relatively robust network of anti-discrimination laws, free to voice but not impose their religious-based objections in the course of their professional activities. The favorable ruling thrilled Lupita and Joanne, but its practical impact had been realized several years earlier. After being turned away by the San Diego clinic, Lupita sought treatment with a willing out-of-network provider who recommended she undergo in vitro fertilization (IVF). This treatment proved quite effective, as evidenced by the supply of baby photos Lupita and Joanne proudly paraded around the table. A son, followed by twin daughters, kept the couple very busy and enormously grateful for their cherished clan.

Meeting Lupita and Joanne was both inspiring and troubling. I wondered how many other prospective parents were denied the tools of family formation because of who they were, not whether they were good candidates for medical intervention. After all, having toiled my entire academic career in the ART field, I understood that when an individual or couple cannot reproduce through natural conception, their path to parenthood runs through a medical office in which providers are empowered to accept or turn away treatment seekers largely at their own discretion. This power is enormous and, I believe, mostly wielded in a fair and legal manner. But when outlier behavior results in procreative deprivation, grave harms befall individual patients and, I argue in the pages that follow, providers, children, and society in ways that should be recognized and can be addressed.

Withholding the means of reproduction is not limited to physician behavior. The growth and success of reproductive technologies, accounting for three of every one hundred babies born in the United States today, have prompted lawmakers to introduce and occasionally pass legislation that expressly or indirectly limits access to ART by certain individuals. These formal legal barriers, combined with individual and practice-wide physician conduct, coalesce to suppress access to assisted conception for those who have historically experienced a devaluation of their reproductive worth. These categorical subductions arise from socioeconomic status, race, ethnicity, geography, sexual orientation, gender identity, marital status, and disability, with each finding at least a modicum of support in the prevailing system of ART allocation in the United States. This wholesale, state-sanctioned suppression of procreative opportunity among disfavored groups recalls the practices and tenets of the American eugenics movement, a multi-decade period beginning at the dawn of the twentieth century in which tens of thousands of Americans were forcibly robbed of their reproductive capacity at the hands of misguided genetic enthusiasts certain of the inescapable force of heredity.

The eugenics movement was founded on the now discredited belief that all human traits were passed along to offspring, even improbably those that were entirely situational, including poverty, trauma-induced disability, prostitution, homelessness, and general ne'er-do-well-ness. The social engineering that flowed from this belief in biological determinism invoked a public health rubric that justified individual (and often coerced) sacrifice in the name of societal betterment. The eugenics credo—prevent the unworthy from reproducing while promoting high-order childbearing among the upper echelon—was a two-sided coin deploying positive and negative tactics. In its heyday, the movement was embraced by presidents, lawmakers, academics, scientists, and physicians who would come to rethink its premise only in the wake of Nazi atrocities attributed directly to American support for orchestrating human betterment through reproductive manipulation. The eugenics legacy remains a haunting reminder that human manipulation of natural reproductive forces can be devastating and long-lasting. Thus, it is no surprise that modern reproductive technologies invite critique and caution for their eugenic potential.

The mainstay critique of ART treatment as a eugenic practice focuses on established and emerging technologies that allow prospective parents to view the genetic makeup of their in vitro embryos, imparting decisional authority to transfer or discard potential future children based on parental perceptions of health and other genetic traits. Current embryonic screening technologies can reveal the presence of more than 250 disease-associated genetic anomalies, whose clinical impact ranges from minimal to life-threatening. Parents who seek and act upon this genetic information do so in a manner that is individualistic and voluntary, in contrast to the forced population-based tactics of early eugenicists. Still, this branch of ART has prompted some to cast those who embrace these technologies as modern-day eugenicists, manipulating the birth and non-birth of offspring in service of some normative vision of human value. After all, so goes the critique, there is no difference between the widespread discard of genetically unhealthy embryos and the prevention of unhealthy persons from reproducing their kind. Both find support in contemporaneous scientific knowledge; both suppress the birth of undervalued human beings.

This book charts a different course in the conversation about eugenic aspects of ART. The true eugenic impact of modern-day reproductive technologies is not in their use but in their deprivation. In both number and effect, the uptake of assisted conception, including genetic screening techniques, is relatively small compared with the unavailability of ART to those who could benefit from its use. While tens of thousands of babies are conceived in the United States each year with medical assistance, millions of Americans experience infertility that remains untreated. Infertility can be classified as medical or social, with medical infertility caused by the absence or malfunction of reproductive organs, and social infertility a product of the social structure in which a person lives his or her life. Blocked fallopian tubes and same-sex relationships are equally incompatible with natural conception through heterosexual intercourse. Both conditions manifest in people across all wealth, demographic, and relationship spectra, yet the vast majority of those who seek ART are wealthy, white, married, and heterosexual.

The reasons for this wide service gap are embedded in the myriad barriers to ART access that deprive the less wealthy, less white, less traditional, and less able-bodied of the tools necessary to achieve biologic parenthood. This exercise of procreative deprivation is eugenic to the core. In advancement of this argument, this book is organized to establish the import of ART in modern family formation, juxtapose these reproductive technologies against the historical background of the American eugenics movement, enumerate the specific ways in which physician conduct and formal law create barriers to ART access, and finally advance a set of recommendations to aid in dismantling the inequalities that persist in the otherwise marvelous world of assisted reproductive technologies. As the mother of four sons, I truly appreciate the privilege and joy that parenthood bestows, and experience equal pain for those who have been denied that transformative opportunity. This book is one person's effort to pay it forward, in the hopes that by casting light on what is a complex network of economic, legal, and human factors, a brighter future for those now in the shadows will emerge.

Acknowledgments

I join the innumerable cadre of authors who lament their inexplicably long journey from a book's conception to its completion. As my journey approaches close to a decade, I am exceedingly grateful to those who have encouraged and comforted me along the way. Prominently, my colleague and friend Paul Lombardo has served as a beacon of light from the outset, inspiring me to plumb the modern implications of the eugenics movement in the context of reproductive technologies. As an accomplished historian and legal scholar, Lombardo's groundbreaking work has culminated in several books that guided my way, including *Three Generations, No Imbeciles: Eugenics, the Supreme Court and Buck v. Bell* (2008) and *A Century of Eugenics in America: From the Indiana Experiment to the Human Genome Era* (2011).

I owe many thanks to my acquisitions editor, William Frucht, who has supplied welcome feedback and support, displaying patience and cheer in his stewardship of the publication process. I am grateful that my book landed in Bill's capable hands. Additional thanks to Joyce Ippolito whose careful and thoughtful editing greatly improved the book's readability.

Numerous colleagues from varied disciplines offered needed help along the way. In May 2015, I was privileged to present Chapter 5 at the Ninth Annual Baby Markets Roundtable held at Harvard Law School.

Many of the thoughtful edits suggested have been incorporated into the chapter, including those offered by Noa Ben-Asher, Gaia Bernstein, Mary Pat Byrne, Glenn Cohen, Susan Crockin, Camille Davidson, Martha Ertman, Theresa Glennon, Rosanna Hertz, Kim Krawiec, Browne Lewis, Paul Lombardo (primary commentator), Kathryn Lorio, Holly Fernandez Lynch, Jody Madeira, Kimberly Mutcherson, Doug Nejamie, Radhika Rao, Rachel Rebouché, John Robertson, Rachel Sachs, Julie Shapiro, and Sonia Suter. Members of my Whittier family have been wonderfully supportive beyond the strains of collegiality, most especially long-term friend and ART collaborator Deborah Forman and emerging family law scholar extraordinaire Erez Aloni. Whittier Law School dean Penelope Bryan made sure I had the time and resources to undertake this project, making her contribution invaluable.

The life of a law professor is uniquely rewarding, offering the opportunity to explore the limits of one's legal imagination and the community to share one's discoveries. Included in my community are two extraordinary friends whose willingness to share their path to parenthood with me and others serves as a continuing inspiration for this book's hopeful theme. To Mark Katz and Robert Goodman and their son, Marcus, thank you for all that you do in this world. I want to acknowledge and give thanks to my incredible father, Norton Freedel, who has supplied a lifetime of unconditional love and support. Finally, and most crucially, I am beyond fortunate to enjoy the love, friendship, and wisdom of a cherished husband who spares no effort in making my every wish a reality. For Eric and our sons, Evan, Jared, Adam, and Ryan, each incredible in their own right, you bring the light into my life every day.

The New Eugenics

The Reproductive Revolution

"Give me children, or else I die."[1] Rachel's biblical entreaty to Jacob exudes the anguish and despair that remain pillars in the modern world of infertility. Given the limitations of reproductive medicine in an era when the survival of the human race teetered on the durability of a wooden ark, Jacob could offer little solace to his treasured bride. Committed to thwarting Rachel's suicidal ideations, Jacob followed in his grandfather Abram's reproductive footsteps and agreed to "know" his wife's maid so that a child could be born into the marriage.[2] Although it would take millennia for this procreative pinch-hitting to be styled "surrogate parenting arrangements," the impact of this early biblical tale is as simple as it is profound: People who want to be parents but are unable to procreate naturally will seek assistance from others, often in ways that are medically, financially, emotionally, psychologically, legally, and socially burdensome.

The Rachels of today, though equally distressed by the prospect of involuntary childlessness, can explore a panoply of medical options whose increasing effectiveness often earns them the designation "modern marvels."[3] The marvelous world of assisted reproductive technologies (ART) offers those who cannot reproduce the old-fashioned way a basket of medical techniques aimed at achieving pregnancy by means other than sexual intercourse. Simply put, ART is designed to bypass or substitute for the human processes that produce natural conception. By disaggregating sex from reproduction, ART is the story of both technical sophistication and social liberation.

Wresting the building blocks of human life—the female egg and the male sperm—from the deep recesses of the reproductive tract and exposing them to the light of day and the inevitable frailties of human manipulation invites alignments and configurations that were unimaginable in a pre-ART world. The shakeup of long-established medical, social, and familial norms has been one of ART's hallmarks, a distinguishing characteristic that often places it in the crossfire of contemporary culture wars. For those who view traditional family structures as the backbone of modern society, any slight reconfiguration can evoke fear, resistance, even panic.[4] Though designed as mere medical techniques to overcome infertility, ART's increasing invocation by those historically deprived of reproductive opportunities invites scrutiny into its every use, its very existence.

The use of reproductive technologies for family formation may be quintessentially modern, but the coupling of science and procreation was introduced into the American psyche as early as the dawn of the twentieth century. In 1900, European scientists rediscovered a dormant scientific paper penned in 1865 by German monk Gregor Mendel discussing inherited characteristics of sweet peas. The monk's observation that plant offspring systematically displayed characteristics similar to their parent plants eventually morphed into the robust field of human genetics. This fascination with trait heritability made its way across the Atlantic to be embraced by a cadre of U.S. physicians, politicians, and public caretakers who became enthusiasts of the practice of eugenics, controlled human reproduction for the betterment of society. Selective breeding through a network of laws and policies that prevented so-called undesirables from reproducing dotted the American landscape for decades, garnering true repudiation only after World War II when Nazi concentration camp medical atrocities were ascribed to U.S. eugenical inspirations.[5]

At first blush, the American eugenics practices of discouraging and disallowing reproduction by institutional segregation and surgical sterilization seem to bear little resemblance to the reproductive enthusiasm embodied by modern-day ART. After all, one set of practices actively prevented certain populations from procreating, while the other plainly assists those who lack the physiological or relational capacity to become naturally conceiving parents. But the commonality of reproduction is far too thin a reed on which to juxtapose these contradictory practices. The link lies not in the prevention or promotion of procreation, but rather in the transfer of such a personal and intimate decision into the hands of third parties.

To be functional, both eugenics and ART extract control over reproduction from the closed universe of the progenitors and deliver it to a world of procreative strangers. In retrospect, we can be fairly certain that the third-party strangers in the eugenics movement were unified in their desires and actions to prevent the feebleminded, the insane, the delinquent, and the criminal from reproducing, but we are currently too enmeshed in the burgeoning ART world to fully comprehend the motives and goals of the stakeholders who mediate access to today's field of reproductive medicine. Without the hindsight of history, only contemporaneous evidence gleaned through trends, advocacy, and experiences can help us begin to construct the lens through which future generations will assess the success or failure of ART in twenty-first-century America. Whether releasing reproduction from a closed, intimate setting to an open, negotiated marketplace will ultimately yield a betterment for the human race is an unsettled question, worthy of multidisciplinary exploration.

This exploration can begin with a pivotal U.S. Supreme Court decision that marked the beginning of the demise of the eugenics movement and ushered in an era of procreative protectionism. In *Skinner v. Oklahoma*,[6] thrice-convicted armed robber Jack Skinner challenged the constitutionality of the Oklahoma Habitual Criminal Sterilization Act of 1935, a law passed during the heyday of the eugenics movement. Based on the scientifically unsupported proposition that criminality was a heritable trait, the law permitted state officials to sexually sterilize those convicted two or more times for felony crimes involving "moral turpitude."[7] Writing for a unanimous court in overturning the law, Justice William O. Douglas described the case as "touch[ing] a sensitive and important area of human rights . . . the right to have offspring."[8]

In repudiating the law and protecting Mr. Skinner, and countless others, from forced sterilization, Justice Douglas declared: "Procreation involves one of the basic civil rights of man . . . fundamental to the very existence and survival of the race."[9]

At the time of this broad midcentury proclamation of reproduction as a fundamental right, procreation through means other than sexual intercourse was largely unknown. Justice Douglas's understanding of human conception entailed a single scenario in which one man and one woman privately melded their gametes inside the woman's body to produce a child. By the end of the twentieth century, this simplistic view had shifted dramatically with the birth of reproductive medicine, an amalgam of arrangements requiring collaborations unthinkable in the postwar era. Would Justice Douglas offer the same unfettered protection against state interference to today's reproducers? The question of procreative freedom that engaged the Court seven decades ago is far more complicated today, asking not simply whether a right exists, but to whom it should be assigned.

Would Justice Douglas, for example, defend the right of a legally married same-sex male couple to have children with the aid of an egg donor and a gestational carrier, the latter who happens to be the non-biological father's sister?[10] When the sister changes her mind about the limits of her role in this modern family formation, demanding parental rights to the twin girls born of her womb but not of her blood, to whom would Justice Douglas ascribe the basic civil right of procreation? How about the rights of Thomas Beatie, a female by birth and chromosomes but a transgender male by phenotype and law, and wife Nancy Beatie to become parents through donated sperm injected into Thomas's still-functional reproductive tract? Rebuked as a biological freak by some, Thomas gave birth to three healthy children but later became embroiled in a legal dispute over his identification as a man when the couple sought dissolution of their marriage.[11] Does the "human right" of reproduction entitle Thomas to give birth and then list himself as "father" on the child's birth certificate? What about the 2009 phenom Nadya Suleman, dubbed "Octomom" after giving birth to octuplets conceived in a Beverly Hills fertility clinic?[12] Does this single mother of fourteen children have an unfettered right to access the technology that makes such un-natural multiple pregnancies a clinical possibility?

Sorting through the rights and privileges of modern-day procreation in a constitutional framework is highly challenging. Since the 1940s, reproductive medicine has introduced myriad advances in assisted conception and childbearing, yet *Skinner* remains the only U.S. Supreme Court precedent to consider the right to procreate as an affirmative, intentional act.[13] Every other case to come before the Court in the reproductive realm has involved the right to avoid procreation, through the use of either contraception or abortion.[14] The question of whether reproduction via ART would receive the identical constitutional treatment as natural reproduction has been much debated but remains unresolved.[15] Resolution of the constitutional status of assisted conception has implications beyond academic interest. Increasingly, access to infertility treatment is thwarted by public and private barriers whose validity depends upon the constitutional status assigned to assisted reproduction. The aim of these pages is to reveal the ways in which prospective ART parents face far greater obstacles to reproduction than those who rely strictly on Mother Nature. In some instances, these obstacles take shape as formal legal regulation; in others, the barriers result from private conduct that is arguably outside the reach of law.

Understanding the link between the age-old two-party reproductive arrangement and modern-day ART is best accomplished by tracing the science of assisted conception to its ancient origins. After chronicling nearly three millennia of investigating the mysteries of human conception, we are reminded that our intense desire for biological parenthood knows few boundaries. Against this backdrop of technical advancement, our lens refocuses on the current use of ART in the United States and abroad. Beginning with the birth of Louise Brown in 1978, the first child conceived through in vitro fertilization (IVF),[16] assisted reproduction has grown and evolved, becoming an indispensable player in contemporary family life. In three-plus decades, ART has blossomed from a nascent technology into a multi-billion-dollar industry responsible for the births of over five million children worldwide.[17] Despite this impressive epidemiological accounting, ART remains an elusive luxury for many, namely those who are not wealthy, not married, not heterosexual, not able-bodied, not white.

This chapter presents a brief history of ART, followed by a discussion of its current uptake by those in need of conceptive assistance domestically and abroad. The dramatic swell in utilization, particularly over the past fifteen years, can be attributed to a number of factors, including increased public awareness of infertility, a rise in the number of clinics offering ART services, and the globalization of the reproductive technologies market. In the midst of this growth, however, lie pockets of deprivation in which subclasses of the infertile face significant obstacles in accessing medical assistance in reproduction. The chapter concludes by exploring the issue of access to reproductive technologies in contemporary America, querying whether barriers to reproductive assistance are reminiscent of the practices and tenets of the American eugenics movement, which systematically repressed breeding by those deemed unworthy of dynastic participation in the human race.

A Brief History of ART

Awareness of infertility as a treatable condition can be traced to writings from the fifth century B.C. by Hippocrates, a Greek physician regarded as the Father of Medicine.[18] Hippocrates, who lived from 460 to 377 B.C., prescribed a number of recipes inspired by the Egyptians to diagnose and treat infertility. One such recipe combined red nitre, cumin, resin, and honey, used to open a woman's cervix that was thought to be "closed too tightly."[19] Seven hundred years later, records from the third century A.D. show that Jewish thinkers discussed the possibility of human insemination by artificial means. Such references appear in the Talmud, a collection of Jewish law, which discusses the legal position of women who achieve pregnancy without physical contact.

For the next millennium, physicians postulated about the causes and cures for infertility, instituting treatments that might strike the modern mind as downright hilarious. During the Middle Ages, infertile men were prescribed a steady diet of testicles and livers from young stags, while women were diagnosed as infertile if their breath failed to display a garlicky odor after cloves of garlic were placed in their vagina.[20]

A major breakthrough in medicine generally came in the mid-1600s with the invention of the microscope by Dutch scientist Antonie van Leeuwenhoek (1632–1723). In 1677, Leeuwenhoek observed his own sperm under the microscope, an experiment he "performed without defiling" himself, according to a letter he wrote reporting his findings to the Royal Society of England. Armed with the ability to visualize sperm, scientists began to understand its role in the fertilization of the egg inside the body.

Still, a century went by before any further inroads were made in advancing the field of assisted conception. In 1780, the Italian priest and scientist Lazzaro Spallanzani (1729–1799) developed the technique of artificial insemination, limiting his experiments to dogs. Spallanzani understood that the male ejaculate contained semen, which carried the sperm; he further realized that the process of reproduction required that the sperm-carrying semen unite with the egg inside the body. The scientist used this knowledge to inject sperm-carrying semen into the female canine reproductive tract, producing the earliest mammalian births by artificial insemination. Only a few years passed before this technique was used successfully in humans.

In 1785, the first attempts at human artificial insemination were made by Scottish surgeon John Hunter (1728–1793). In the late 1770s Dr. Hunter was approached by a London cloth merchant who suffered from hypospadias, a developmental anomaly in which the opening of the penis is too low, thus inhibiting the projection of semen into the vagina. Dr. Hunter suggested that he collect the patient's sperm and inject it into his wife's vagina using a warm syringe. In 1785, Dr. Hunter's efforts to separate sexual intercourse and reproduction proved successful, as the first child conceived through artificial insemination was born.[21]

Despite Dr. Hunter's advancement in infertility treatment, medical journals were bereft of information about advances in artificial insemination for the next one hundred years. It was not until 1884 that Dr. William Pancoast of Jefferson Medical College in Philadelphia published the first report of artificial insemination in a modern medical journal. What differentiated Dr. Pancoast's accomplishment from that of his predecessor Dr. Hunter was the source of the gametic material. Instead of using the woman's husband's sperm, Dr. Pancoast relied on a "donor," a man unrelated to the woman patient who produced his sperm to help her achieve pregnancy. The circumstances surrounding Dr. Pancoast's experiment are worthy of inclusion, leaving much for the modern medical ethicist to ponder.

Apparently the story begins with a wealthy, married merchant who complained to Dr. Pancoast of the couple's inability to procreate. The good doctor took this as a golden opportunity to try out a new procedure. The unknowing human subjects were summoned to the doctor's medical facility. At some point during the visit, the patient's wife was anesthetized. Before an audience of medical students, the doctor inseminated the woman using semen obtained from the "best looking member of the class." Nine months later, a baby boy was born. The mother is reputed to have gone to her grave none the wiser as to the manner of her son's provenance. The husband was informed and was reputedly delighted. The son discovered his novel history at the age of twenty-five when enlightened by a former medical student who had been present at his conception.[22]

The technique of artificial insemination by donor (AID) grew in use and success over the next fifty years, with multi-patient studies reporting promising results appearing in medical journals in the mid-1950s. A turning point for AID in terms of practicality came in 1953 following reports of pregnancies using stored frozen semen.[23] With sperm freezing, or cryopreservation, a willing donor could, over a relatively short period of time, produce enough semen to be stored for current and future use. The prospect of a multi-child family replete with whole-blood siblings held tremendous appeal for couples facing male factor infertility. But as the use of AID grew, so too did the social and religious condemnation of this technique that separated marital sex from reproduction, earning it the moniker "mechanical adultery."[24] Despite attempts to criminalize its use and assaults on the legitimacy of the children born therefrom, AID remained a viable alternative to involuntary childlessness, today accounting for approximately sixty thousand births annually.[25]

At the same time physicians were using and improving the technology of AID, scientists wondered whether an embryo could be created outside the body by retrieving eggs from the woman's ovaries and uniting them with sperm in a laboratory test tube. Experiments on this method of in vitro (literally, in glass) fertilization initially focused on animals, yielding success in rabbits in the late 1950s.[26] The transfer of IVF technology from animals to humans seemed an inevitable and beneficial leap to many scientists, but as in the case of AID, opposition mounted. When scientists began to report initial success in the field of human IVF in the late 1960s, critics emerged. One such critic, Paul Ramsey, a professor of religion at Princeton University, wrote a series of articles in 1972 urging against any further advancement in the field of reproductive technologies. He posited at the outset of one piece, "I must judge that in vitro fertilization constitutes unethical medical experimentation on possible future human beings, and therefore is subject to absolute moral prohibition."[27]

Despite this and other dissenting voices, the wheels of science churned, and due largely to the efforts of two British scientists, the world's first "test tube baby," Louise Joy Brown, was born on July 25, 1978.[28] British gynecologist Patrick Steptoe and Cambridge University scientist Robert Edwards met in 1968 and over the next ten years worked to perfect the process in which eggs could be surgically removed from a woman's body just prior to ovulation, mixed with viable sperm in a hospitable petri dish (the so-called test tube), and encouraged to fertilize into an embryo and develop over three days to the eight-cell stage for transfer back to the woman's uterus, where implantation and gestation would hopefully ensue.[29]

Today, this process of IVF, though helped along by significant technical improvements over the past thirty-five-plus years, remains fundamentally the same. IVF and AID combine to produce three of every one hundred births in the United States, playing a far greater role in family formation than domestic infant adoption.[30] ART's functionality and popularity rest in its ability to mimic the natural reproductive process by bypassing impaired structures (as when a woman experiences blocked fallopian tubes), or substituting for nonfunctioning or absent reproductive structures (as when donated sperm is used to treat male infertility or to assist single women and lesbian couples to conceive). The opportunity for biological parenthood outside the bounds of traditional familial and sexual relations continues to provoke wonder and worry as the technology evolves.

Current Use of ART in the United States

In the nearly four decades since the birth of the first IVF baby, considerable energies have been devoted worldwide to tracking the use and yield of this method of assisted conception. As discussed below, in the United States a federal agency is charged with annually compiling detailed data surrounding IVF use, the results of which are analyzed, summarized, and published replete with charts, graphs, and statistics aplenty.[31] While this bolus of data does provide some insight into the current use of ART in the United States, it falls short in providing a comprehensive view of family formation through assisted conception. Identifying what is known, what is conjectured, and what further research could reveal about the use of reproductive technologies in the United States seems a logical starting point for discerning the role of ART in American life.

THE TYRANNY OF DEFINITIONS

Tracking who needs and who uses ART in the United States is highly dependent upon definitions. How one defines the most foundational terms, including "ART" and "infertility," can drastically change statistical outcomes, which in turn can influence perceptions and policy. For example, the federal Centers for Disease Control and Prevention (CDC), which collects data on assisted conception, defines ART as "all infertility treatments in which both eggs and sperm are handled."[32] Technically, and by further admission, the CDC's definition of ART is essentially limited to IVF, and does not include procedures in which only sperm is handled, namely AID.[33]

This limitation on the definition of ART is significant for two reasons. First, the CDC is the only mandated reporter of ART usage in the nation. The mandate arises from a federal law, the Fertility Clinic Success Rate and Certification Act of 1992,[34] which requires the Secretary of Health and Human Services, through the CDC, to "annually thereafter publish and distribute to the States and the public . . . pregnancy success rates reported to the Secretary" by ART programs.[35] As the only repository of epidemiological data surrounding ART, the federal government's exclusive focus on IVF limits study of other forms of assisted conception. Moreover, the CDC's annual publications of two separate reports, *Assisted Reproductive Technology: Fertility Clinic Success Rates Report* and *Assisted Reproductive Technology: National Summary Report,* could certainly give the impression to the uninitiated observer that therein lies the totality of assisted conception in the United States.

The second impact of an IVF-only definition of ART is the potential for skewing perceptions about the demographics of ART users. Since the CDC reports only IVF use, there is no national collection of data surrounding what is reputed, by anecdotal evidence, an equally utilized form of assisted conception—donor insemination. Informal studies suggest that approximately sixty thousand infants are born in the United States each year as a result of AID, rivaling the number of offspring produced through IVF (now at around sixty-five thousand annually).[36] Importantly, and again via informal channels, the profiles of those who use IVF and those who use AID are thought to be quite different in terms of marital status and sexual orientation. While the CDC does not collect data on the marital status of ART patients, assertions abound that the majority of patients patronizing fertility clinics are married Caucasian heterosexual couples.[37]

In contrast, commercial sperm banks report that about half of their clientele—women who order donor sperm for insemination—are lesbian couples and single women.[38] National databases that purport to detail ART outcomes, and neglect to include about half of those who use assisted conception, present an incomplete if not misleading image of reproductive medicine as only available to and utilized by white married couples. The fact that a quarter of all ART use, defined broadly as *all* medical techniques used to achieve pregnancy by means other than sexual intercourse, is attributable to unmarried women stands in contrast to the homogeneous picture painted by the CDC's limited definition. To the extent that law and policy surrounding ART—including such vital areas as access, insurance coverage, and regulation—are based on existing data, definitions matter.

The other definition that shapes our understanding of the current use of ART is that attributable to the term "infertility." In nearly every publication where a definition of infertility is offered, the term is characterized as a medical diagnosis that follows from a specific clinical observation, typically the failure of a woman to conceive and maintain a pregnancy after one year of unprotected intercourse.[39] Defining infertility strictly as a medical condition has both clinical and political implications. Clinically, it is useful for physicians to agree when to begin treating nonconcepting patients who fail to conceive. An agreed-upon definition is particularly important when a clinical syndrome manifests in the absence, rather than the presence, of symptoms.

Politically, casting infertility as a medical condition has been a decades-long goal of patient advocacy groups for two main reasons. First, defining infertility as a medical problem is fundamental to securing health insurance coverage for any treatment thereof. If, for example, state legislators can be convinced that infertility is a medical problem with medical solutions, then they may be more likely to compel insurers to cover nonexperimental treatments for the condition. Second, patient advocates have expressed the view that by deeming infertility a medical condition, some of the blame—usually directed toward women—and stigma associated with infertility will be reduced.[40] While infertility remains largely viewed as a "woman's problem," some movement can be seen in the area of insurance coverage and reimbursement.[41] The perception of infertility as a medical condition is gaining ground among lawmakers, including judges, who have authored statutes and case opinions acknowledging that involuntary childlessness is a medical outcome rather than a social choice.[42]

Defining infertility strictly as a medical condition, though explicable and even essential for certain treatment and financial purposes, does have an exclusionary impact. Limiting, even by definition, the pool of ART users to those who have been diagnosed as medically infertile excludes those whose sexual orientation, gender identity, or social status makes assisted conception essential for reproduction. Prospective parents in this latter category may experience medical infertility, but more likely their use of ART is based on social infertility—the inability to conceive and maintain a pregnancy within a particular social structure without medical assistance. This counterpart definition of infertility is broad enough to include a range of social configurations without delving into questions of how or why one's relationship (or lack thereof) arose. Those poised at the threshold of infertility, whether medically or socially induced, share a common goal of parenthood. Their journey to and through the ART world should be of no definitional significance.

Limiting the definition of infertility to a strictly medical calculus impacts the annual ART data reported by the CDC by excluding social factors as a basis for seeking treatment. In its annual report, the CDC does collect and tabulate data on "the causes of infertility among users of ART."[43] The list of causes contains exclusively medical conditions, including tubal damage, ovulatory dysfunction, and low sperm count. Even the category "other causes" is limited to those of medical etiology, such as immunological problems and chromosomal abnormalities. The data simply do not account for the use of ART for reasons unrelated to biological dysfunction. If inclusion in the CDC database requires a medical indication, are male couples who commission a gestational carrier counted, since no party in the arrangement has a listed diagnosis? Do the statistics include lesbian couples who use one partner's eggs and the other's uterus to produce an IVF child?[44] Though these uses of IVF might be relatively rare, they nonetheless deserve to be counted as part of our annual ART snapshot.

ART BY THE NUMBERS

Despite the limitations on ART data collection in what and who are counted, it is worthwhile to glance at the annual reports, as they reveal strong trends in the utilization of certain assisted reproductive technologies. The period between the mid-1990s and the mid-2000s was one of particularly robust growth for the ART industry, as can be seen in ART (essentially IVF) usage and success rates for fertility clinics that reported data annually to the CDC (Table 1). From 1996 to 2006, there were dramatic increases in usage (up 114 percent), success (as measured by live births—up over 30 percent for both donor and nondonor egg cycles), and third-party assistance (significant increases in the use of donor eggs and gestational carrier services). By comparison, while usage continues to grow steadily every year, the increase in ART cycles for the ten-year period 2003–12 was 28 percent, much lower than the 114 percent growth seen the previous decade. Likewise, the percentage increase in babies born slowed to 34 percent (from 2003 to 2012) compared with

Table 1: ART Success Rates over an Eleven-Year Period (1996–2006)

ART event	1996	2006	Increase
Number of ART cycles performed	64, 681	138,198	114%
Number of live babies born	20,840	54,656	162%
Live births per transfer using fresh non-donor eggs	28%	37%	32%
Live births per transfer using fresh donor eggs	39%	56%	38%
Number of ART cycles using donor eggs	5,162	16,976	329%
Percentage of all ART cycles using donor eggs	8%	12%	50%

Source: *Centers for Disease Control and Prevention,* 2006 Assisted Reproductive Technology Success Rates, National Summary and Fertility Clinic Reports *(Nov. 2008)*

162 percent (from 1996 to 2006).[45] Although the CDC reports document these upticks and trends, they do not analyze or explain the reasons behind such statistics. There are any number of factors that, alone or in concert, could account for the explosion in ART use.

Discerning reasons for the doubling of ART usage in an eleven-year period (as measured by the number of ART cycles performed) can be as much about exclusion of factors as it is about identifying causative forces.[46] Logically, increased use of a medical technology could be linked to increased medical need for such service. Perhaps it is the higher incidence of infertility in the United States that is bumping up ART usage? Not according to published data, which show a decline in infertility rates in the United States over the last quarter-plus century. In 1982, the rate of infertility among married women in the United States aged fifteen to forty-four was 8.5 percent, compared with a significantly lower 7.4 percent in 2002.[47] In 2010, this number dropped to 6 percent.[48] This decline, according to researchers, cannot be explained by changes in the composition of the surveyed population, meaning equal declines were observed across all subgroups.

If the percentage of infertile women of reproductive age has declined rather than increased, perhaps increased ART usage can be attributable to higher treatment-seeking by affected populations. Maybe greater
awareness of infertility and its treatment has prompted more women to
seek treatment, thus fueling the doubling of IVF cycles performed in the
United States. Again, the available data suggest a counter-trend, rather
than lending support. According to the CDC, in 1996 about 15 percent
of women of childbearing age in the United States had, at some point in
their lives, used an infertility service.[49] While the CDC does not define
the term "infertility service" in its 1996 report, it does so in later reports,
including the 2006 report. Infertility service is therein defined as "medical tests to diagnose infertility, medical advice and treatments to help
a woman become pregnant, and services other than routine prenatal
care to prevent miscarriage."[50] Presumably the same metrics applied in
1996 as did in 2006, permitting a one-on-one comparison to identical
services. By 2006, treatment-seeking showed a 20 percent decline, with
the CDC reporting 12 percent of women of childbearing age had used
an infertility service at some time in their lives.[51]

Trends showing declines in overall female infertility and lifetime
treatment-seeking are noteworthy for the study of population demographics, but they probably interact very little with trends in ART utilization. The use of ART—particularly IVF—among infertile women
in the United States represents a small percentage of the overall infertility services documented. For example, in 2002, of the approximately
62 million women of reproductive age in the United States, about
1.2 million, or 2 percent, had an infertility-related medical appointment
within the previous year.[52] Of these 1.2 million medical visits, a little under one-tenth resulted in an IVF cycle, as measured by the 115,392 cycles
performed in 2002. Marginal increases in the percentage of treatment-
seekers who ultimately undergo IVF can be culled from the available
data, but the overall ratio remains small.[53]

Eliminating increases in female infertility and treatment-seeking
as causative factors in the rise of ART use does shift the focus from
changing characteristics within a defined population (medically infertile women) to a range of factors external to this studied control group.

Factors external to the size and behavior of the medically infertile may play an essential, even exclusive, role in explaining the substantial growth in ART use in the United States over the past decade or so. Successfully incentivizing participation in ART both within a static population and by outreaching to previously underserved populations can produce dramatic increases in utilization. Three external factors that likely contributed to the explosion in U.S. ART use are increased public awareness, increased number of ART providers, and globalization of the fertility market.

PUBLIC AWARENESS

One can hardly pass a supermarket checkout without noticing the many high-profile parents who have graced covers of the nation's magazinery with tales of triumph over infertility. Famous-for-being-famous icon Kim Kardashian allowed viewers to keep up with her visits to a Los Angeles fertility clinic when trying to conceive a second child, though whether IVF actually yielded the pregnancy remains a family secret.[54] Beloved diva Céline Dion, mother of an IVF-conceived son, spoke publicly about her "private heartbreak" wrought by four unsuccessful attempts to give birth to another child.[55] Marcia Cross, one of the stars of *Desperate Housewives,* recounted the expense and pain she experienced undergoing IVF to conceive her twin daughters;[56] the timeless Brooke Shields spoke often and candidly of her reliance on IVF to conceive her first child;[57] Courteney Cox of *Friends* fame welcomed a daughter after years of IVF treatment;[58] supermodel Cindy Margolis chronicled her odyssey with IVF in a best-selling book.[59] So routine is the use of ART by those in the public eye, many a website is devoted to tracking the disappointments and successes of star-studded assisted conception.[60]

Even the use of gestational surrogacy is popping out of the Hollywood closet. In recent years, entertainment personalities have talked openly about their use of surrogate mothers, in glowing and grateful terms. In December 2010, pop icon Sir Elton John and his longtime partner (now husband) David Furnish introduced the world to baby Zachary Jackson Levon Furnish-John, born by a California surrogate. The same surrogate birthed the couple's second son in 2013.[61] Celebrity duo Nicole Kidman and Keith Urban announced the birth of their second daughter via gestational carrier in December 2010, to join an older sister who arrived the old-fashioned way. Neil Patrick Harris (of *How I Met Your Mother,* and for the older crowd, *Doogie Howser, M.D.*) and his partner (now spouse) David Burtka welcomed fraternal twins in October 2010, with each dad supplying sperm for the donor eggs that were fertilized and transferred.

In one of the more highly publicized ART uptakes, surrogate mother Michelle Ross gave birth to Sarah Jessica Parker and Matthew Broderick's twin girls in 2009. Pop singer Ricky Martin became the single papa to twin boys with help from an egg donor and surrogate in 2008. Finally, in August 2004, the *Frasier* star Kelsey Grammer and his wife, former *Playboy* model and Real Housewife of Beverly Hills Camille Donatacci, welcomed their second child through a surrogate mother. The couple's relationship later soured, perhaps after Camille confessed she needed four nannies to manage the children. She cited irritable bowel syndrome as her reason for employing a surrogate, providing no explanation for the four nannies.[62] Surrogacy in the news isn't just about celebrities. Cover stories on this human interest relationship have appeared in the popular press, including features in the *New York Times Magazine*[63] and *Newsweek,*[64] the latter revealing the popularity of surrogacy—from the service provider perspective—among military wives whose husbands are deployed overseas.

These public displays of assisted conception can help shape perceptions about infertility and its treatment. Though cause and effect cannot be empirically asserted, one suspects the rise in ART use is attributable in part to the reduction in stigma heretofore associated with the failure to naturally conceive. Knowing that others—notably those whose lives appeared to be so blessed—have endured and survived an infertility diagnosis helps normalize the experience for many onlookers. Moreover, the now routine and lavish praise appropriately heaped on celebrity surrogates likewise nudges the practice into the mainstream, opening hearts and minds to the myriad ways parenthood is achieved in the modern era.

Public interest and awareness about ART may be piqued by celebrity aficionados, but the field does not lack for tremendous interest

among ordinary folk. These days a college-age girl or postgraduate
woman in the workforce can hardly escape the many references to assisted conception in her everyday world. Be it websites for each of the
450-plus fertility clinics in the United States, blogs hosting all manner
of participants and would-be participants in the ART world, best-selling
books documenting the business side of infertility services, marketing
campaigns for egg freezing targeting professional women, or flyers that
appear in college dorms soliciting interest in egg donation, the narrative
of infertility in the American culture is ubiquitous.

Enhanced popular- and cyber-culture references to ART are supported by substantial data, readily available to anyone with Internet
access. Since 1996, the CDC, with the aid of the Society for Assisted
Reproductive Technology (SART), has been collecting and publishing
individual clinics' results, so that prospective patients can assess their
likelihood of success at any given site. The annual *ART National Summary Report and Fertility Clinic Success Rates Report* notes general trends
across the country according to select demographics (age, diagnosis)
while also detailing results of each cycle performed at all reporting clinics. These annual "report cards" seem to have had an impact on patient
awareness and decision making in ART. A study found that the market share clinics enjoyed prior to the publication of their success data
was later affected by their reported results. For example, clinics with
higher birth rates enjoyed larger market shares following adoption of
the report card system, while clinics with a disproportionate share of
young, relatively easy-to-treat patients had lower market shares after
adoption versus before.[65] The study authors concluded that consumers
take into account information on patient mix when evaluating clinic
outcomes. From a public awareness perspective, the study confirmed
that the CDC's collection and publication efforts have raised awareness
among prospective patients. Ideally, this enhanced awareness translates
into more informed decision making surrounding the ART process.

The observed increase in public awareness of ART, especially IVF,
may be somewhat self-generating and self-sustaining, but at the heart of
the phenomenon lies the adage "nothing succeeds quite like success."
What the public is increasingly aware of is that IVF works, or at least
works far better than it used to. This is clear in the trends we saw in

Table 1—a 32 percent increase in live births using the intended mother's eggs, a 38 percent increase in live births using donor eggs, and a whopping 329 percent increase in the number of ART cycles using donor eggs. Improvements in ovulation induction, egg maturation, and embryo enculturation have contributed to increasing success rates when a woman's own eggs are used, while third-party donors have helped increase live birth rates when called into service by those who lack gametes or house impaired ones. Today, when 12 percent of all ART cycles involve the use of donor eggs, and on average over 40 percent of all donor egg cycles result in the birth of a live infant, the term "assisted conception" takes on a true double meaning.[66]

With the combination of celebrity exposure, unfettered Internet access, outreach to gamete donors, official data reporting by the CDC / SART public-private partnership, and improving success rates for both first-party and third-party assisted conception, increasing public awareness of ART emerges as a logical product of these factors. What remains unknown is whether increased public awareness, even acceptance, of the technology has translated into increased access for those who occupy far less privileged social and economic circles. Increased public awareness of infertility and its treatment may pave the way for some to enter the world of ART, but others remain on the outside, some by choice and others by nefarious design.

INCREASING THE NUMBER OF ART CLINICS

The bridge to the twenty-first century was dotted with an increasing number of infertility clinics. In the eleven years spanning 1996 to 2006, the number of medical facilities offering ART services in the United States increased by 50 percent. By 2006, only two states lacked a resident fertility clinic—Montana and Wyoming.[67] States with the largest number of clinics increased their overall offerings substantially, with California jumping from thirty-nine to seventy-one clinics, New York moving from twenty-four to forty clinics, and Texas increasing its clinic population from eighteen to thirty-nine sites.[68] In addition to increases in the sheer number of clinics, services at clinics across the United States likewise expanded, including a 26 percent increase in the percentage

Table 2: ART Clinics and Services over an Eleven-Year Period (1996–2006)

ART clinics	1996	2006	Change
Number of ART clinics in the United States	315	483	53%
Number of states with zero or one ART clinic	15:	11:	−27%
	0 (5)	0 (2)	
	1 (10)	1 (9)	
Percentage of clinics offering gestational surrogacy services	37%	81%	120%
Percentage of clinics offering donor egg programs	74%	93%	26%

Source: Centers for Disease Control and Prevention, Use of Assisted Reproductive Technology—United States, 1996 and 1998, *51 Morbidity and Mortality Weekly Report 97–101 (Feb. 8, 2002); Centers for Disease Control and Prevention, 2006* Assisted Reproductive Technology Success Rates, National Summary and Fertility Clinic Reports, *Appendix C (Nov. 2008)*

offering egg donation services, and 120 percent increase in the percentage offering gestational surrogacy services (Table 2). Thus, in an eleven-year period, ART services became broader and deeper across the nation.

The addition of nearly two hundred ART clinics in an eleven-year period was accompanied by a doubling of the number of IVF cycles performed over that same period, with a 114 percent increase throughout the United States from 1996 to 2006. Applying classical economic analysis, one might conclude that the increased supply of ART clinics was in response to growing demand for services. Certainly the trend of delayed childbearing among professional women, a key demographic in the ART market, played a role on the demand side. In her book *Creating a Life: Professional Women and the Quest for Children,* author Sylvia Ann Hewlett describes the pattern of professional women joining the workforce and delaying motherhood to focus on career advancement, only to discover infertility at the top of the corporate ladder. As to the numbers, Hewlett reports, "Across the board, 33% of professional women are childless at age 40 and yet only 14% of these women had planned lives without children. Many yearn for families and at least some go to extraordinary lengths to bring a baby into their lives."[69]

The data collected and reported by the CDC also support the observation that increases on the demand side are attributable in part to the greater numbers of older women seeking treatment. Comparing just two data points—2000 and 2006—there is a slight increase in the percentage of ART patients age thirty-eight or older in one category (patients using their own eggs for fresh embryo transfers) compared with the overall population in that category.[70] Another indication that the ART-seeking population has grown disproportionately in the older demographic is culled from the data on infertility diagnosis tracked by the CDC. A common diagnosis for a woman of "advanced maternal age" is diminished ovarian reserve (DOR).[71] As a woman ages, the quantity and quality of her eggs for reproductive purposes declines. Though no specific age is identified for the onset of DOR, the American Society for Reproductive Medicine (ASRM) warns that "fertility decreases with age, particularly after age 35."[72]

The creeping incidence of age-induced DOR can be both observed and inferred from published reports. Since 1996, when the CDC began publishing its annual report card for ART, the data included a breakdown of the various causes of infertility for each patient who sought treatment in a given year. A handful of causes, including tubal factor (blocked or damaged fallopian tubes), male factor (low sperm count or functionality), and even unexplained causes, were named. In 1996, the CDC report listed "ovulatory dysfunction" as causative in 12 percent of all reported cases. The report defined this syndrome as when "the ovaries are not producing eggs normally or . . . egg production has diminished with age."[73]

By 2006, the CDC had created an entirely separate category for DOR, retaining "ovulatory dysfunction" as a category but with a more limited definition that included only non-normal egg production. In that year, ovulatory dysfunction accounted for 6.4 percent of all infertility cases. The CDC described the new category of DOR by stating, "The ability of the ovary to produce eggs is reduced. Reasons include . . . advanced age." In 2006, DOR accounted for 9.2 percent of all infertility diagnoses that resulted in ART cycles, up from 8.2 percent just one year earlier.[74] Even if one were to disaggregate the combined category of ovulatory dysfunction in 1996, and then roughly estimate the percentage attributable to DOR based on the 2006 figures, the percentage of age-related infertility appears to have increased in the general ART population.

The increase in the number of ART clinics nationwide may be in response to growing demand, but the industry remains fiercely competitive. As the supply-side part of the economic equation blossomed, so did the creativity surrounding the marketing of assisted reproductive services. During what may now be fondly recalled as the heyday for new ART clinics, one New Jersey site broke into the market with gusto. When Reproductive Medicine Associates opened its doors in Morristown in late 2001, they hired a marketing consultant, started weekly support group meetings for infertile couples, and invited doctors to dinners, including a wine-tasting dinner with a sommelier flown in from France.[75] Marketing, especially on the Internet, has become such a key feature to a clinic's success that a secondary market in ART advertising has sprung up. Doctors, whose training likely did not include a rotation in marketing, can turn to the likes of FertilityMarketing.com, self-described as "an Internet marketing system designed to effectively increase patient volume for high cost, elective medical procedures."[76]

The fact that ART services are marketed as "high cost, elective medical procedures" prompts the query of whether the increased number of ART clinics has translated into greater access for all who require medical assistance to procreate. Eyeballing the way in which IVF is marketed, the targeted audience seems rather homogeneous. According to a 2013 report, the vast majority of websites for U.S. fertility clinics that display photographs feature one of two themes—either a picture of a light-skinned single baby, or a mother-baby image, again with white-appearing models. Where websites displayed only a single image of a baby, in virtually all cases the baby appeared to be white (with Hawaii standing out as an exception with one clinic featuring a single Asian-appearing cherub). Many of the websites also feature opposite-sex couples with a baby, and again those with a single image displayed mostly white-appearing parents (an exception being a New York City university-based clinic with a black-appearing couple on the welcome page). No site featured on its single-entry home page an image of a same-sex couple, or a single man and child pictured as a family.[77]

Is this image of commercial IVF meant to attract or repel a certain type of client? Is the image of a white baby with married heterosexual parents designed to represent the typical IVF patient (it does), or is it subliminally calculated to discourage non-lookalikes from pursuing treatment (it may)? True, some of the websites do feature multiethnic images in their photo-book range of satisfied clients, and some do provide information on "gay couple family planning," as one Boston-area center advertises on a hard-to-locate page. But the overall message seems to be that nontraditional parenting is an afterthought in mainstream ART marketing. In some markets, ignoring or actively dissuading non-white, nonheterosexual couples may be the product of intent. If so, then measuring the impact of increased services in the ART market should take into account the effect, positive or negative, on subpopulations.

Internationalization of the ART Market

The boom in ART use in the early twenty-first century was not just an American phenomenon. Prospective parents worldwide have turned to assisted conception in growing numbers. For proof, see the number of international monitoring agencies that regularly publish data on the use of ART around the world. One such agency is the International Committee for Monitoring Assisted Reproductive Technology (ICMART), which collects data from regional and national ART registries and then publishes results measuring use worldwide. The ICMART studies typically are internally comparative, showing changes in worldwide, regional, and national use from period to period. For example, the 2009 ICMART report analyzed ART use from 2000 to 2002 based on data collected from 1,563 clinics in 53 countries.[78] For the two-year period analyzed, ICMART reported a 25 percent increase in the number of IVF cycles performed worldwide. This compares with a 17 percent increase in ART use in the United States during that same period. Thus, the international data show an even larger percentage gain in ART use worldwide than the gains seen in the United States during the same time.[79]

Although the U.S. data make up part of this international collective, that is by no means the majority contribution. Overall, the U.S. activity accounted for roughly 20 percent of all ART use and births worldwide.[80] Data for the remaining activity were collected from registries (similar to the CDC registry) in Europe, Australia, Japan, and Latin America, as well as individual clinics in the Middle East, Asia, Africa, Oceania, and the West Indies.[81] More recent statements from ICMART indicate that IVF use worldwide in 2012 stands at 1.5 million cycles per year (compared with 950,000 cycles in 2004), producing 350,000 babies annually.[82] Increased interest in ART worldwide is also reflected in the growing number of clinics providing service (at least as measured by the number of clinics reporting their data for ICMART use). In 2002, ICMART reported data from 1,563 clinics in 52 countries; in 2005 the number of reporting clinics grew to 2,973, though the number of reporting countries grew by just one to 53.[83]

Empirical data support the conclusion that the first decade of this century was a growth period for ART, both in the United States and worldwide. But growth does not necessarily mean widespread availability to all who could benefit. From a global perspective, the vast majority of the estimated 80 million people worldwide who suffer infertility live in countries where IVF is unavailable.[84] Even in locales where IVF and other high-tech treatments for infertility are available, they may not be widely accessible to all in need. In fact, the same barriers to ART access that plague the U.S. market also appear, to greater and lesser degree, in most other countries. Saving for later chapters a more in-depth discussion of specific ART barriers, suffice it to note that cost and social status are primary barriers to access in most countries where the technology is available.

The cost of ART is a well-described and long-standing barrier to its use. Even where treatment is available, on average it is prohibitively expensive and thus utilized by only a fraction of those who could benefit from care. The high cost of ART prices many out of the market; even the select individuals who can afford care often incur financial hardship in their quest for parenthood.[85] While the absolute costs of ART are universally high, price disparities among treatment-providing nations do enable some patients to access relatively less expensive care abroad. Thus, cost becomes an incentive for traveling across national boundaries to access infertility treatment, a phenomenon known as cross-border reproductive care (CBRC).[86] CBRC is also incentivized by legal restrictions in many countries that prohibit single individuals or same-sex couples from accessing treatment.[87] The risks, benefits, and impacts of CBRC are only beginning to be studied, but its growing use indicates that the medically and socially infertile will continue to look beyond their own borders for assistance in reproduction.[88]

In sum, over the past decade or so, ART use abroad has rivaled, and in some ways surpassed, use in the United States to create a global market in assisted conception. While the remaining chapters focus primarily on barriers to ART access in the United States, understanding that our set of experiences coexists in a global context can bring both solace and frustration. Whatever limits, indignities, harms, or impasses ART patients face in this country are unlikely to be resolved abroad, and in many instances would be far more severe. Having a system that is better than some, even most, is still unacceptable if it works serious deprivation on selected populations based on long-standing patterns of societal mistreatment. Given our medical and technical acumen, we should strive to be a global model for fair and ample access to infertility treatment.

The Depth and Breadth of ART Barriers

The ways in which would-be parents are denied access to assisted conception are highly varied, with some restrictions being patent, direct, and clear while others are indirect and subtle, revealing themselves as barriers only upon retrospective reflection. In the chapters that follow, we look at several broad categories of barriers, including costs, race and ethnicity, marital status, sexual orientation, domicile, disability, and provider discretion. Within these broad categories we can see that barriers may be multiple and can take on different forms. To create a rubric for further discussions, barriers to ART access are catalogued in six groups: (1) direct barriers, (2) indirect barriers, (3) formal acts, (4) informal acts, (5) intentional acts, and (6) unintentional acts. Further, cross-cataloguing these factors provides a broad overview of the types of conduct that impair an infertile person's opportunity to reproduce.

Examples of the various barriers are discussed according to whether the barrier is direct (a bar to service) or indirect (a deterrent to service), and whether the conduct giving rise to the barrier is formal (positive

Table 3: A Catalogue of ART Barriers

	Direct barrier	Indirect barrier
Formal act	State insurance laws denying coverage to unmarrieds State laws limiting commercial surrogacy to married couples	Laws requiring identification of gamete donors (creating severe shortages of available donor gametes)
Informal act	Physician groups and individual providers refusing service to single individuals or same-sex couples	Past discriminatory practices by health care providers chilling treatment-seeking behavior by racial and ethnic minorities
Intentional act	State and federal lawmakers' and employers' unwillingness to mandate fertility treatment as covered health care benefit	Locating the majority of ART clinics in mostly white, wealthy, urban, and coastal areas
Unintentional act	The high cost of ART services	Lower socioeconomic status and levels of employment among racial and ethnic minorities compared with nonminorities

law), informal (private conduct), intentional, or unintentional (Table 3). What is striking is the range and depth of the panoply of access barriers. Each barrier, whatever its origin, no less grieves the affected populations by depriving them of a highly prized and revered right. Harms from lack of ART access are as deep and diverse as the barriers themselves, and it is these harms that motivate this book's call to action.

Early in this chapter we queried whether the sheer existence of ART and the long-celebrated legal protections afforded reproduction coalesced to create an unlimited right to access assisted conception in every case. Even while authoring a book decrying barriers to ART access, I would answer this query in the negative. I don't believe, nor do I argue herein, that U.S. law and policy should embrace unlimited and unconditional access to ART for all. At the very least, it must be acknowledged that not every person who could benefit from ART supports its use. The detractors and drawbacks to assisted conception are many and varied. Some decry the use of a technology that adds to the world's overpopulation, hindering global efforts at achieving worldwide environmental sustainability.[89] Others lament what they describe as the high failure rates associated with IVF, leaving six of every ten patients with nothing more than disappointment and indebtedness after each attempted cycle.[90] While the average IVF success rate (measured by live-born offspring) hovers around 33 percent per cycle, keep in mind that the chance of a medically or socially infertile individual procreating without ART is essentially zero.[91] While the myriad critiques surrounding ART are worthy of exploration, this book sets a different course. For those who desire access to assisted conception, these pages advocate for equality in the provision of services.

Returning to the question of parity between the rights associated with ART and natural reproduction, one obvious distinction is the necessary presence of third-party actors. As we will see, the provision of medical services for reproduction can affect several stakeholders—including patients, partners, donors, offspring, and providers—any one of whom could be negatively affected by the use of ART in a particular circumstance. Like all rights, the right to access ART is susceptible to the balancing of interests and harms that accompanies that technology's unfettered provision or regulated restriction. Assessing the acceptability of ART infringements is deeply wrenching not just because of the parenthood that is at stake for the individual seekers, but because of the legacy of reproductive repression that serves as a backdrop for modern discussions on the right to procreate. This backdrop, the American eugenics movement of the past century, holds many lessons for current-century assisted reproductive technologies.

Our Eugenics Past

S hould a despised and discredited movement that gained momentum a century ago and faltered after World War II play any role in the discussion of technologies invented long after historians declared the movement "a permanent stain on the national record"?[1] While advocacy abounds urging burial and nonresurrection of the shameful period in U.S. history known as the American eugenics movement (circa 1890s to 1940s), equally compelling arguments suggest that only through contemporary reflection on the factors that enabled the movement's flourishing will we be prepared to guard against history repeating itself.[2] The notion of a 1900s-style eugenics revival is not presented as a concern in any literal sense; few worry that modern-day Americans would respond favorably to scientific assertions about improving the human condition by organizing a web of state-sponsored programs that assess, suppress, deprive, and encourage reproduction according to one's expressed and inherited characteristics. The goal of revisiting our eugenics past is to plumb this half-century period for the motivations, patterns, strategies, and language that drew in so many, so that we might recognize our current selves in the ghosts of our past.

Searching the parameters of a movement that targeted, in the main, natural reproduction for lessons about modern methods of assisted conception is both highly logical and utterly counterintuitive. To the latter point, one can be skeptical that formalized efforts to prevent certain individuals from reproducing (old eugenics) could bear any resemblance to private individualized collaborations to control the production of offspring through sophisticated reproductive technologies (new eugenics?). Put more starkly, what could procreation avoidance at a population level aimed at improving the human race have in common with induced reproduction by autonomous individuals motivated by self-interest to fulfill their personal desires for parenthood? From these base descriptions one might argue that eugenics cares about individual reproduction only as it impacts the population, whereas ART cares about the population only as it assists in individual reproduction.

The common denominator between eugenics and ART, of course, is reproduction. The act of delivering a new human being into the world, whether initiated by the private union of a loving couple or produced by a team of medical, gametic, and gestational collaborators, lies at the heart of both enterprises. More specifically, eugenics and ART are logically tied by their mutual focus on controlling reproduction. Eugenical control over reproduction, described in more detail below, was embodied in a number of state-sponsored programs, including forced sterilizations, believed to be capable of boosting desirable and eliminating undesirable members of the human race. The control that ART exercises over reproduction appears *ab initio* as purely technical in nature. Doctors work to control conception and gestation in concert with an intended parent's desires for parenthood. No hegemonic or macro pursuits are readily detected.

Casting the pursuit of reproductive control during the American eugenics movement and the ART era as, respectively, nefarious and technical defies both history and current practices. Control over reproduction during the eugenics period was more nuanced than its notorious legacy might lead us to believe. While the network of laws and policies that robbed tens of thousands of their reproductive capacity is a documented fact, eugenics can also be understood from a categorical perspective. Studying eugenics in four categories—public (authoritarian), private (liberal), positive (promoting reproduction), and negative (preventing reproduction)—allows assemblage of a broader contemporaneous perspective on the role that reproduction played in shaping the nation's future.

Likewise, ART cannot be viewed as a mere technocratic practice devoid of social influence and statement. The introduction of IVF in the late 1970s inspired emotional commentary about the unnaturalness and immorality of wresting reproduction from the hands of God.[3] Social commentary continued as ART gained a foothold in the reproductive lives of Americans, and grew in volume as collaborative forms of reproduction introduced even casual observers to terms like "gestational carrier" and "egg donor."[4] Today, with ART as a route to family formation readily available for some but equally inaccessible to others, questions about the merits and harms of external control over assisted reproduction are beginning to emerge. New terms are making their way into our lexicon, including "stratified infertility" and "marginalized reproduction."[5] The idea that ART revisits reproduction from a "haves" and "have nots" perspective should concern us enough to investigate the truth of any such claims.

Four questions in particular may be probative of whether the practice of ART today is problematically reminiscent of devastating eugenic practices of yesteryear. Each of the four multipart questions set forth herein takes note of a truism that describes the American eugenics movement and queries whether this same assertion could be made about some aspect of contemporary ART. If so, then the process of asking and answering these questions should equip us to better guard against these particular features further morphing into another regrettable chapter in our human narrative.

The questions are: (1) The eugenics movement was built upon assumptions and expectations about the way newly discovered scientific developments could be used to better society. What role do technical advances in reproductive medicine, and other related disciplines, play in the use and delivery of ART services? (2) Eugenic practices gained support through an orchestrated campaign that used evocative language and images to stir a desired response from targeted audiences. To what extent does ART practice communicate certain messages or themes to its users and would-be users? (3) The utilitarian edict of the eugenics movement that certain individuals must sacrifice for the good of the

population was channeled through celebration of majoritarian institutions, including marriage, white supremacy, and religiosity. Does
ART similarly embrace and extol the supremacy of traditional values?
(4) One rationale for certain eugenic practices was based on economic
logic, promising tax savings and reduced government spending once
undesirables were shed from the public dole. What role do economics
and the expenditure of public funds play in modern-day ART?

With these queries in mind, we now turn to an overview of the
American eugenics movement, ably chronicled and analyzed by a number of prominent scholars. In retelling and summarizing the detailed
accounts of the lives, the lures, and the losses that define the movement,
I'll also keep us focused on the themes that emerge from the four questions posed—science, language, tradition, and economics. As each
theme emerges, we may want to reflect on whether similar themes reso-
nate in the modern ART world.

The Birth of Eugenics

Historians unanimously attribute the term "eugenics" to Sir Francis
Galton (1822–1911), a Victorian aristocrat and half cousin of evolution-
ist Charles Darwin (1809–1882). Galton is best known for his pioneering
work in statistics and its application to problems of human heredity.[6]
In the mid-1860s, Galton's studies of British families led him to observe
that the worthiest individuals seemed to have the fewest offspring, while
"defectives" were reproducing at a much faster rate. As a remedy, he proposed that those "highest in civic worth should be encouraged to have
more children; the stupid and improvident, fewer or none."[7] It would
take two decades before this notion of selective breeding was reduced to
a memorable term. In 1883, Galton coined the term "eugenics" from the
Greek *eugenes,* for "good in birth." He defined eugenics broadly as "the
science of improving stock, which . . . takes cognizance of all influences
that tend in however remote degree to give the more suitable races or
strains of blood a better chance of prevailing speedily over the less suitable than they otherwise would have had."[8] Through his writings and
advocacy, Galton sowed the seeds for a field that would wield enormous
social, political, scientific, and legal power for the ensuing fifty years.

By the turn of the twentieth century, Galton and his colleagues harnessed the growing enthusiasm over the new yet burgeoning discipline of genetics to further advance the concept of controlled human reproduction. The story of human genetics begins with an Austrian monk named Gregor Mendel, whose mid-nineteenth-century experiments with pea plants demonstrated that hereditary traits could be explained by certain factors in the parent plants. By mating plants with different traits (round versus wrinkled seeds, tall versus dwarf size, white versus purple flowers), Mendel noted that offspring plants often resembled one parent, leading him to theorize that each plant inherits one factor from each parent.[9] Mendel's "factors" theorem lay dormant for nearly forty years until 1900, when it gained the attention of several scientists who were working on problems involving hybridization and theories of evolution.[10] By 1908, Mendel's factors would be called genes and the study of human genetics would occupy scientific minds worldwide.[11]

The coalescing of theories of improving the human race by selective breeding with scientific discoveries in genetics had a synergistic effect on the eugenics movement. In fact, the man who is often described as the founder of the American eugenics movement, Charles Davenport (1866–1944), was himself a geneticist by training and profession.[12] In the early 1900s, Davenport was the director of the respected Station for the Experimental Study of Evolution at Cold Spring Harbor, New York. In 1910, he convinced a wealthy benefactrix to fund an institution dedicated to improving human heredity.[13] These funds, and others supplied by the Carnegie Institution of Washington, enabled Davenport to establish the Eugenics Record Office (ERO) on land adjacent to the station. The ERO's mission was to collect, catalogue, and eventually analyze hereditary information from thousands of individuals. Between 1911 and 1924, the ERO dispersed more than 250 field workers to gather the data that would fuel the legitimacy and popularity of the eugenics movement.[14]

The building blocks of eugenics took shape as collections of family records that displayed member traits for several generations. As Paul Lombardo, a historian and law professor who has written extensively on the eugenics movement, recounts, "Data was gathered by field workers acting with the cooperation of asylums, hospitals, and other institutions. Once assembled, family information was displayed in genealogical charts using symbols to denote troubling characteristics that might reappear within related groups, such as criminality, sexual immorality, feeblemindedness, insanity, and infectious diseases like syphilis or tuberculosis."[15] Davenport and other like-minded eugenic enthusiasts presumed that most, if not all, human traits were transmitted genetically. This assumption gave rise to their edict that educated, resourceful, and self-sufficient citizens be encouraged to produce "well-born" children, and correspondingly that socially inadequate individuals be discouraged or even prevented from reproducing.[16] While this rather simple assessment of an area as complex as human nature might strike the modern mind as wholly ill-supported and ill-advised, at the time it was enticing beyond the frailties of its own logic.

The science of eugenics, which in retrospect sounds cruelly oxymoronic, grew in respectability by gaining the imprimatur of mainstream geneticists and prestigious universities. As evidence, every member of the first editorial board of the American journal *Genetics,* founded in 1916, endorsed the movement.[17] Hundreds of colleges and universities in the United States and Europe incorporated courses on eugenics in their curricula, offering instruction on the science of good birth in such diverse disciplines as biology, social work, public health and medicine, and "sex" hygiene.[18] A common teaching in eugenics instruction focused on the image of diseased "germ plasm," later revealed as DNA. Thought to be the source for shunned human characteristics, including criminality, poverty, insanity, chronic illnesses, physical disabilities, and feeblemindedness, faulty germ plasm and its eradication became a rallying cry for eugenicists nationwide.

During its heyday in the first third of the twentieth century, the eugenics movement grew and sustained itself on the basis of three main tenets that intertwined aspects of genetics and public health: (1) that social, moral, physical, and mental qualities are transmitted in predictable patterns by the mechanisms of heredity; (2) that the human race can be improved by selective mating; and (3) that the ills of society can be eradicated by discouraging, or preventing if necessary, the reproduction of socially deviant individuals.[19] Although these tenets were grounded in the science of heredity such as it was, their operationalization depended on public acceptance and cooperation. As history shows, eugenicists were able to harness the coercive power of public health policy and law to activate their ideas on a population basis. Grounded in a utilitarian realm, the public health approach to human betterment called for individual sacrifice, even at great personal risk or deprivation, to promote the health and well-being of society as a whole.[20]

Implementing this public health approach to human betterment involved multiple strategies and tactics. In retrospect, we can better understand and assess the eugenics movement by categorizing the ways in which it played out in early twentieth-century America. As we saw, at least four categories of eugenics are worthy of exploration: public, private, positive, and negative.[21] Each category has its own core definition and examples, but each event that serves as a piece of the eugenics movement puzzle is a blend of two or more categories. Still, deconstructing the movement by stripping it down to its component parts has value. For our purposes, creating discrete categories for investigation now will help us later assess whether current ART practices resemble any aspect of the past eugenics movement.

Public Eugenics

Public eugenics, sometimes called authoritarian eugenics, refers to state-sponsored efforts to improve the human gene pool.[22] The state can exercise its authority in a eugenic manner in a variety of ways, including by (1) enacting laws that directly or indirectly influence human reproduction; (2) adjudicating legal disputes that involve human reproduction; (3) providing or withholding financial benefits for activities that affect human reproduction; and (4) authorizing or prohibiting conduct, through licensing, regulation, and other means, that affects human reproduction. Public eugenics suggests a coercive and formal approach to channeling human behavior in a way that the state desires. Escape from public eugenics by any individual person would likely be perilous and costly; defying a state-sponsored eugenic command risks prosecution, imprisonment, and the range of sanctions available to a governmental body.

In general, the public eugenics tactics associated with the American eugenics movement were negative, meaning they were designed to suppress or prevent reproduction by certain individuals. Discussions of state-sponsored eugenic practices typically focus on the first two activities described above—enacted laws and decided cases that touch on human reproduction. Enacted eugenic laws focused in three areas: immigration, marriage, and sterilization. The eugenics case law likewise centered on these topics as challenges to the constitutionality of enacted eugenic laws. Below we explore the major legislative trends of the eugenics era, as well as the courts' review of these public laws.

LAWS REGULATING IMMIGRATION

Immigration policy in the United States is a matter of federal jurisdiction, a principle recently confirmed in the wake of state efforts to regulate border-crossing activity.[23] Federal undertakings to restrict and curb entry into our borders date back to at least the mid–nineteenth century, long before eugenics added voice to these efforts. Until the end of World War I, immigration restrictions were aimed, in large measure, at laborers from Asia who were seen as a threat to the American labor force.[24] But the Great War shook allegiances and fortunes across the Atlantic, producing a massive influx of immigrants from southern and eastern Europe, most notably Jews and Italians.[25] This immigration wave coincided with the rise of the eugenics movement, prompting federal lawmakers to consider the impact these newcomers would have not just on American jobs, but on our culture and biological future. The ensuing legislation made clear that immigration was viewed as a threat to the country's genetic well-being.

In 1924, Congress passed and President Calvin Coolidge signed the Immigration Restriction Act.[26] In effect, the law imposed numerical quotas on the number of foreign-born individuals of a given nationality permitted lawful entrance into the United States. The act's major provisions were crafted by famed eugenicist Harry Laughlin (who worked alongside Charles Davenport at the ERO), and were praised by others in the movement for their biological wisdom.[27] The law was intended to combat the "rising tide of defective germ-plasm" carried by the suspect Europeans who were noted to reproduce in larger numbers than existing Americans.[28] President Coolidge echoed the eugenic nature and aspiration of the law, declaring, "America must be kept American [be-cause] biological laws show . . . that Nordics deteriorate when mixed with other races."[29] Staving off biological deterioration was a key rally-ing cry for eugenicists, and it played well in the political arena.

Passage of the 1924 immigration law is but one example of the sup-port the "science of selective breeding" received at the federal level. Every president from Theodore Roosevelt to Herbert Hoover was a member of a eugenics organization, publicly endorsed eugenic laws, or willingly signed eugenic legislation.[30] Teddy Roosevelt was particularly outspo-ken in his admiration for procreation controls, referring often to the country's "race destiny," which he feared was doubly threatened by the onslaught of inferior immigrants and the failure of old-stock Americans to reproduce at an adequate rate.[31] On the immigration front, he im-plored Americans to "keep out races which do not assimilate with our own," while working to shore up well-bred natives by casting men and women of good stock who chose not to procreate as "race criminals."[32] As to the third prong of eugenic policy—reproductive restrictions—Roosevelt was no less bold, decrying that "society has no business to permit degenerates to reproduce their kind."[33]

The fear, debasement, and blame cast upon immigrants were, as it turned out, scientifically and empirically unfounded. The foundational scientific thesis of the eugenics movement—that like produced like—fared poorly under observation in the general population and grew even more tenuous as our understanding of genetics improved. Geneticists began to separate themselves from eugenicists, challenging the latter's view that race purity meant salvation for the human species. Instead, the burgeoning field of genetics made clear that "the biological strength of the human race lay in the vast diversity of its genetic makeup."[34] As to the assertion that immigrants to the United States outbred "native" Americans, this also turned out to be false. Although immigrants did generally produce more children than native-born women, succeed-ing generations did not. At the second-generation level, many women delayed or avoided marriage (and correspondingly reproduction in the 1920s and 1930s) in order to work and help support their families during these hard economic times.[35] But the low fertility rates among

Americans coupled with the large foreign presence in cities created the impression that immigrants were far outbreeding the natives.

These two features of the eugenics movement—reliance on faulty science to predict the health and worth of offspring and acceptance of an inaccurate assumption that too many of the "wrong" individuals were reproducing in proportion to the "right" reproducers—may have modern-day analogues. Treatment denials in ART, as we shall see, are often grounded in a professed scientific certainty that assisting a particular individual or couple will produce harm—to the offspring, to the prospective parent, or to society. Today's refusals to provide care add another component not associated with the eugenics period—concern about harm to physicians in the form of legal liability for aiding in the conception of a child born with disabilities. As with reliance on discredited scientific assertions of harm, basing denials on fear of legal liability is likewise suspect.[36] The second factor in the eugenics outlook—too many of the undesirable population reproducing—also has ART ties. Demographic changes have shifted the uptake of reproduction from (mostly) married, heterosexual couples to (increasingly) unmarried individuals and same-sex couples, evoking similar concerns that majoritarian values and institutions need to retain their foothold in American society. Thus, on balance, ART treatment denials echo some of the same sentiments that buoyed the eugenics movement for years.

Suppressing reproduction, whether during the eugenics movement or in the modern era, means preventing people from engaging in activity that will lead to the birth of a child. Today, such suppression is complicated by the myriad methods available to aid in conception and childbirth. In the early 1900s, however, reproductive suppression took the simple form of preventing marriage or preventing conception. It is to these state-sponsored efforts we now turn.

LAWS REGULATING MARRIAGE

Today it is estimated that over 40 percent of U.S. births are to unmarried women.[37] This compares with an out-of-wedlock birth rate of around 1 percent in 1920. Clearly, regulating who could and could not marry in the early twentieth century had a direct impact on who would and would not reproduce during that period. Unsurprisingly, marriage—its encouragement and restriction—was of keen interest to eugenicists whose drive for white supremacy depended upon Caucasians marrying within the race. While aficionados of the American eugenics movement did successfully advocate for adoption of laws banning interracial marriage, legal prohibitions against miscegenation (racial mixing) were in place long before the term "eugenics" was coined in the mid–nineteenth century.

Anti-miscegenation laws in the United States trace back to the colonial period, with Virginia and Maryland enacting laws in the 1690s that prohibited free blacks and whites from intermarrying. By the time of the American Revolution, seven of the thirteen colonies had laws prohibiting interracial marriage. As the nation expanded to the south and west, all of the slave states as well as several free states, including Illinois and California, enacted anti-miscegenation laws. While many states repealed these laws in the wake of the Civil War and Reconstruction period, by the mid-1920s laws criminalizing marriage between whites and blacks (and in some cases, between whites and all nonwhites) persisted in approximately thirty states. In some states, laws barring interracial marriage had been repealed in the late nineteenth century, but were later reinstated during the eugenics movement.[38]

The general dialogue that supported and encouraged anti-miscegenation laws relied on the "scientific" theory that race hybridization produced disharmonies.[39] These disharmonies, according to Charles Davenport, produced certain "incompatibilities" in interracial offspring that manifested in physical, mental, and temperamental maladies. He hypothesized, for example, that if a tall person, with internal organs adapted to his or her large frame, bred with a short person with correspondingly smaller organs, a resulting child could suffer from having organs that were too small or too large for his or her frame. Thus, he argued, characteristically tall Scots were ill-suited to marry shorter Italians, for fear of breeding children with organs incompatible to their bone structure.[40] This physical disharmony would also take shape as unhappiness, restlessness, and rebelliousness, as the hybrid struggled against his or her ill-fitting body and fate.

Framing the potential harm of interracial marriage in the image of a damaged child propelled the anti-miscegenation movement into the public health arena.[41] While the underlying motivation was largely vested in protecting the racial integrity of the white gene pool, dressing interracial marriage in public health garb helped procure a wider base of support. The efforts to codify a contemporary anti-miscegenation law were particularly strong in Virginia, where several state officials welcomed the opportunity to clarify and strengthen the state's colonial-era law.[42] In 1924, lawmakers passed the Virginia Racial Integrity Act, the law that would eventually lead to the undoing of state-sanctioned marriage barriers based on race.[43] The law provided as follows:

> *Intermarriage prohibited; meaning of term "white persons."* It shall hereafter be unlawful for any white person in the State to marry any save a white person, or a person with no other admixture of blood than white and American Indian. For the purpose of this chapter, the term "white person" shall apply only to such person as has no trace whatever of any blood other than Caucasian; but persons who are one-sixteenth or less of the blood of the American Indian and have no other non-Caucasian blood shall be deemed to be white persons. . . .
>
> *Punishment for marriage.* If any white person intermarry with a colored person, or any colored person intermarry with a white person, he shall be guilty of a felony and shall be punished by confinement in the penitentiary for not less than one nor more than five years.[44]

This law, and others like it across the country, stood as a symbol of the American eugenics movement for over four decades until struck down as unconstitutional by the U.S. Supreme Court in *Loving v. Virginia.*[45] Before its ultimate rejection, the law withstood several legal challenges, including one waged by the married couple who would eventually go on to prevail at the highest level. Mildred Jeter, a black woman, and Richard Loving, a white man, were married in the District of Columbia in 1958. Soon thereafter the couple moved to Virginia, where they were charged under the Racial Integrity Act and sentenced to one year in jail. The trial judge suspended the sentence on the condition that the Lovings leave the state and not return together. In his written opinion meting out this "justice," the judge held nothing back in sharing his admiration for the Virginia law: "Almighty God created the races white, black, yellow, malay and red, and he placed them on separate continents. And but for the interference with this arrangement there would be no cause for such marriages. The fact that he separated the races shows that he did not intend for the races to mix."[46] Never mind that "the interference" the trial judge spoke of was nothing short of the millennia-long march of human progress, this judicial snippet provides deep insight into the unshakable prejudice and discrimination that ebbed into and flowed from race-based marriage laws. The Lovings went on to appeal their conviction, eventually gaining review by the Supreme Court. In a unanimous opinion that experienced a second wind in the contemporary debate over same-sex marriage, the Court struck down the Virginia law, and by result the fifteen other state laws that punished marriage on the basis of racial classification. In sweeping language, the Court declared:

> Marriage is one of the "basic civil rights of man" fundamental to our very existence and survival. . . . To deny this fundamental freedom on so unsupportable a basis as the racial classifications embodied in these statutes, classifications so directly subversive of the principle of equality at the heart of the Fourteenth Amendment, is surely to deprive all the State's citizens of liberty without due process of law. . . . Under our Constitution, the freedom to marry or not marry, a person of another race resides with the individual and cannot be infringed by the State.[47]

The Court's decision in *Loving* nullified the remaining antimiscegenation laws across the country, but it would take until the year 2000 for the last state to officially amend its constitution to remove language prohibiting interracial marriage.[48] Clearly for some, shedding the trappings of a bygone era comes only by force and with great reluctance. The eugenics fixation on marriage as a way to control procreation was practical in its day, given that the vast majority of children were born in wedlock. Thus, as a tactical matter, leaders in the movement embraced, even glorified, the institution of marriage as a path to achieving their foundational goal of race purity. For our purposes, this raises the question of whether regulation of the institution of marriage, or other social institutions, could be used to suppress reproduction by undesirables via assisted conception. The short answer is that marriage can and has been used as a wedge to separate those who can and those who cannot access ART.

Manipulating reproduction as a by-product of marriage regulation in an ART era can take one of two forms. First, formal law can regulate who can and who cannot marry. We know from recent debates over marriage equality and the rights of same-sex couples to marry that many of the arguments, for and against, focus on reproduction.[49] Interestingly, despite the fact that a near majority of U.S. children are born to unwed parents, social policy still inexorably links reproduction with marriage. The second way that reproduction is formally linked to marriage is through law and policy that investigate marital status as a credential for accessing ART. Marriage is privileged in many ways in the ART market, and can provide unique access to desired services. In some cases, the status of being unmarried stands as an active barrier to ART care, as discussed more fully in Chapter 5. Knowing how and why eugenicists focused one of their three main regulatory prongs at marriage may be instructive in deciphering whether modern-day policies and practices have eugenic underpinnings.

The final regulatory prong of the eugenics movement—joining immigration and marriage regulation—typically garners the most revulsion and is wielded as the most shameful symbol of the half-century crusade. Of course we are speaking of the forced sterilization laws that authorized the surgical sterilization of tens of thousands of Americans over a several-decade period. In the arena of public eugenics, the bevy of forced sterilization laws stands out as a particularly misguided, prejudicial, and cruel exercise of state power. How these laws came to be and what their meaning is in today's world are explored below.

LAWS REGULATING REPRODUCTION

Historians generally agree on the numbers: the state of Indiana enacted the nation's first sterilization law in 1907;[50] during the eugenics movement, compulsory sterilization laws were enacted in thirty-two American states;[51] between 1907 and 1979, approximately sixty-five thousand state-mandated sterilization surgeries were performed in the United States;[52] nine states did not repeal their sterilization laws until the 1980s or later, while one state's law remains intact.[53] The story behind these numbers is one of collaboration among eugenicists, lawmakers, and physicians who earnestly believed that society's ills could be effectively addressed by the dual approach of segregating undesirables from the general population and surgically ensuring they never reproduced. Lest we comfort ourselves that such barbarism could never occur in today's era of informed consent and patient autonomy, our delusions fall away in the wake of occasional news reports documenting involuntary sterilizations. Exhibit A: in August 2013 the California Legislature held hearings to investigate why 150 female prisoners were sterilized without authorization over a recent four-year period[54]—segregation followed by unauthorized sterilization in our modern midst.

Recalling the eugenicist trilogy of truths, (1) that all traits and behaviors are heritable, (2) that selective mating (including no mating) is in humanity's best interest, and (3) that socially undesirable individuals should be prevented from reproducing, it is no surprise that interest swelled in compulsory sterilization of certain trait-bearing individuals. Practically speaking, such interventions were more direct and more effective than the indirect methods that merely held undesirables at bay or staved off mixed-race marriages. If immigration laws kept undesirable non-Americans from reaching our shores and breeding with our "native" population, and marriage laws prevented the dilution of race (that is, Caucasian) purity by forestalling the birth of interracial offspring, forced sterilization provided assurance to a surgical degree that socially, physically, and mentally "defective" individuals would not reproduce their own kind. Like the paths to eugenic immigration and marriage laws, the road to sterilization laws was paved with junk science, unabashed prejudice, and deceit.

The first step toward "cutting off the human strain"[55] carried by biologically undesirable outcasts was to segregate them during their reproductive years, ensuring distance from the socially fit with whom they might procreate. Eugenicists began to contemplate and organize a nationwide plan for mandatory, long-term custodial care to house the socially inadequate, particularly the feebleminded, as a way of "controlling the rapidly growing defective germ-plasm."[56] Such plans for custodial institutions were ambitious in both infrastructure and scope. As to the latter, one leading figure in the eugenics movement, Harry Laughlin, maintained that the socially inadequate classes were defined as follows:

> *The socially inadequate classes,* regardless of etiology or prognosis, are the following: (1) feeble-minded; (2) insane (including the psychopathic); (3) criminalistic (including the delinquent and wayward); (4) epileptic; (5) inebriate (including drug-habitués); (6) diseased (including the tuberculous, the syphilitic, the leprous, and others with chronic, infectious and legally segregable diseases); (7) blind (including those with seriously impaired vision); (8) deaf (including those with seriously impaired hearing); (9) deformed (including the crippled); and (10) dependent (including orphans, ne'er-do-wells, the homeless, tramps and paupers).[57]

The idea of segregated living quarters for the unfit took shape at the turn of the twentieth century. The colony movement, as it is now known, envisioned institutional shelters for problem individuals and families. Physicians supported such efforts, confirming that "degenerates," whose growing numbers were seen as "a menace to the well-being of the state," should be segregated.[58] Colonies began to dot the U.S. landscape, first in the northeast and eventually making their way south and west. Once the designated undesirables were taken out of the societal mix, attention shifted to assuring their inability to reproduce, either while institutionalized or upon release. While "colonization" was effective, it was also costly. Thus, efforts at segregation were coupled with a growing campaign for sterilization of residents to prevent their reproducing upon rejoining the general population.

Eugenicists lobbied for two decades for the enactment of compulsory sterilization laws. Initial efforts were met with skepticism, and early attempts either failed at the legislative level or were shuttered by the governor's veto pen.[59] Eventually, as noted above, the campaign to enact forced sterilization laws—pertaining to the feebleminded and their ilk, the criminal element, or both—succeeded in great measure. Despite these legislative victories, eugenicists continued to meet resistance in the courts, where several of the state laws were declared unconstitutional.[60] It would take one state's law and the perfect test case for these enactments to gain judicial approval. That law was the Virginia Eugenical Sterilization Law of 1924,[61] enacted just in time for the arrival of a young woman at the Virginia State Colony for Epileptics and Feeble Minded. The woman's name was Carrie Buck.

The story of Carrie Buck and the role she played in the American eugenics movement is elegantly and painstakingly recounted by Paul Lombardo in his book *Three Generations, No Imbeciles,* from 2008, and other, shorter works. Lombardo met Carrie Buck in December 1982, three weeks before her death. This meeting would inspire and propel Lombardo's work for many years, leading him to uncover photos and documents that tell the true saga of a girl and a family locked in a political and moral whirlwind far beyond their ability to react or comprehend. The 1927 Supreme Court decision that forever cast the Bucks as "three generations of imbeciles"[62] served as ground zero for Lombardo's thorough exploration of the people and events that define the American eugenics movement.

Born into poverty, Carrie Buck was separated from her family at an early age. While in the care of foster parents, she was raped by a relative of her appointed caregivers and sent away to the Virginia Colony when her pregnancy became obvious. Carrie was sixteen years old when she arrived at the now infamous state institution, which also housed her mother, Emma Buck, accused of being a prostitute and a pauper. Soon after the birth of Carrie's daughter, Vivian, deemed "below average" and "not quite right," a small but avid group of eugenicists seized the Buck family's plight as an opportunity to inaugurate a newly enacted eugenical sterilization law aimed at ridding society of hereditary defects.[63] The law authorized the sexual sterilization of "mental defectives" on the theory that "many defective persons who if now discharged would become a menace but if incapable of procreating might be discharged with safety and become self-supporting with benefit to themselves and to society."[64]

The records that Lombardo discovered reveal that the attorney who represented Carrie in her constitutional challenge to the Virginia law was far from a zealous advocate on his client's behalf. The lawyer, Irving Whitehead, was a founding member of the Virginia Colony's board of directors and major supporter of the campaign to enact the sterilization law. According to Lombardo, "The evidence presented [by the State] at Carrie Buck's trial was transparently weak. . . . But the defense never materialized; in large part because Carrie's lawyer had no intention of defending her. He offered no rebuttal to the state's arguments for surgery; he called no witnesses to counter the experts who had condemned the Buck family; he never explained that Carrie had not become a mother by choice, but that she had been raped."[65] Moreover, no one attempted to show that Carrie's daughter Vivian was quite normal, even above average, as later school records would show.[66]

The case reached the Supreme Court in 1927, landing in the hands of Chief Justice (and former president) William Howard Taft, himself an active member of the national eugenics movement. He assigned the case to Justice Oliver Wendell Holmes Jr., whose father had instructed him on the merits of eugenic policies that the jurist came to enthusiastically embrace.[67] Justice Holmes's opinion for the Court, which voted 8–1 to uphold the law (Justice Pierce Butler dissented without opinion), is dismaying, if not shocking, to the modern reader, but is unabashed in its certainty that a program of state-mandated sterilization is justified and beneficial as a public health measure.

> The judgment finds . . . that Carrie Buck "is the probable potential parent of socially inadequate offspring, likewise afflicted, that she may be sexually sterilized without detriment to her general health and that her welfare and that of society will be promoted by her sterilization." . . . We have seen more than once that the public welfare may call upon the best citizens for their lives. It would be strange if it could not call

upon those who already sap the strength of the State for these lesser sacrifices, often not felt to be such by those concerned, in order to prevent our being swamped with incompetence. It is better for all the world, if instead of waiting to execute degenerate offspring for crime, or to let them starve for their imbecility, society can prevent those who are manifestly unfit from continuing their kind. . . . Three generations of imbeciles are enough.[68]

The decision in *Buck v. Bell,* with its factual errors and misanthropic spirit, remains a valid precedent in American jurisprudence. Although a later case, *Skinner v. Oklahoma,*[69] overturned an Oklahoma law authorizing state-mandated sterilization of certain repeat criminals, the case never explicitly overruled *Buck.*[70] The 1927 case paved the way for Carrie's sterilization and seemed to break down any lingering objection to forced sterilization. By the mid-1930s, a majority of U.S. states had laws permitting unconsented surgeries to eradicate the unfit from society. Even at the time, we understood that the reach of the American eugenics movement was international, inspiring like-minded laws in Canada, Switzerland, and Japan, and throughout Scandinavia. But it was the American-inspired eugenics program in Nazi Germany that would eventually lead to its demise and disrepute.[71]

In 1933, Germany enacted a law "For the Prevention of Hereditarily Diseased Offspring," a statute that would justify the forced sterilization of four hundred thousand Germans during Hitler's regime. The law would later serve as the backdrop for the horrendous surgeries performed on prisoners in Nazi death camps, all under the rubric of "medical experimentation." The true horror of Nazi medicine and its genocidal goals would be revealed at the Nuremberg doctors' trial beginning in 1946.[72] When lawyers defending the Nazi doctors read from the *Buck* opinion during the trial, offering the U.S. precedent in their clients' defense, it was clear that eugenics was experiencing a devastating—but not fatal—blow.[73] The shadow of the Third Reich loomed large over the United States and much of the world during the postwar period, prompting a rethinking and reform of relations between physicians and patients.[74] Eugenics was discredited as a matter of social, legal, and medical policy, but its extraction from the hearts and minds of those who truly believed in the certain heritability of all human traits would prove a long-term challenge.

The breadth and depth of public eugenics during the first three decades of the twentieth century reflect the political power and appeal of the proposition that majority populations should be isolated and insulated from minority influences. Having eugenicists occupy the White House, the Supreme Court, Congress, and various state houses ensured enactment and entrenchment of formal law authorizing state-sponsored eugenic practices. The government's imprimatur of xenophobia, segregation, and sterilization could be understood as approval for private individuals to act in a like manner. Private eugenics, though less formally documented and studied, did play a role in the American eugenics movement. The study of private eugenics is particularly important to our study of eugenic aspects of reproductive medicine because many of today's ART activities are under the control of private parties.

Private Eugenics

Eugenic practices were not entirely the product of authoritarianism. That is, in addition to being the subject of legal directives, eugenics was taken up voluntarily as part of America's prevailing social institutions. Logically and inevitably, eugenics' social acceptance was fueled by decades of formal support exuded by elected officials and judicial officers that flowed from its embrace among this empowered populace. These nondirected displays of support for eugenics, organized under the term "private eugenics," took shape in various forms. For example, as previously noted, colleges and universities embraced eugenics in their curricula, offering courses across multiple disciplines. Classes in eugenics were available in a wide range of university departments, including biology, genetics, sociology, education, and physical education.[75] Integration of eugenic ideology at the highest level of education helped to normalize, if not elevate, the wisdom of race betterment through reproduction regulation. At a less elite, more populous level, scholars describe how the tenets of eugenics were internalized by many, even those whose lives had been forever changed by sterilization. Wendy Kline documents the sentiments of dozens of individuals who were surgically sterilized during the eugenics period, some of whom viewed their personal sacrifice as a public service. One patient, writing to her doctor, beams, "My general health is ten times better. . . . I couldn't feel any better." On the larger benefits of the procedure, she writes, "I think such operations is just the finest thing there is for people that are not normally or physically healthy: not only for them, but for all those women who are bearing unwanted and uncared for children."[76]

Another lens through which to view the private propagation and acceptance of eugenic principles is the practice of medicine. Though physicians are hardly a monolithic group, history suggests that their widespread support for eugenic ideals and practices contributed significantly to the movement's credibility and durability. An interesting microcosm of the medical profession's relationship with eugenics emerges in the early history of the birth control movement. Briefly, beginning in 1873, access to contraception in the United States was criminalized under the federal Comstock Law, so named for nineteenth-century anti-vice crusader Anthony Comstock. During his reign, Comstock orchestrated the arrest of more than three thousand individuals in the name of public morals, believing as he did that "anything remotely touching upon sex was . . . obscene."[77] A quarter century later, attitudes toward sexuality and reproduction began to transform, with some feminist activists advocating greater sexual freedom for women. In part, this freedom depended upon access to birth control—which disaggregated sex from reproduction.[78]

Initially, organized medicine joined the mainstream groundswell against freer access to contraception, concerned that it would lead to a breakdown of sexual morality. A major shift began in 1920 with the election of Dr. Robert Latou Dickinson as president of the American Gynecological Society. A eugenics and birth control advocate, Dickinson advanced his ideology that contraception should be viewed as an enhancement of family health and racial stability rather than an endorsement of female reproductive independence. By casting birth control as a vehicle for human betterment, Dickinson won hearts and minds among his colleagues, who were, after all, the gatekeepers of women's reproductive health. Transitioning from birth control in general to sterilization in particular, Dickinson's passion for eugenics guided a natural path from preventing pregnancy to thwarting reproduction. Eventually persuaded by Dickinson and others that it was the doctor's role to control women's reproductive capacity, physicians aligned to form the clinical backbone of the eugenics movement. Physician support for clinical eugenics boosted public acceptance, helping transform sterilization from a suspect radical procedure to a legitimate medical practice.[79]

With the broad support of these private actors, be they university professors, physicians, or as described below, citizens who organized to promote "better babies and fitter families," the eugenics movement was able to reach a large swath of the American public. While the number of souls actually touched by a surgeon's scalpel or the reach of the immigration and anti-miscegenation laws was relatively small compared with the general population, the movement thrived because its purpose was embraced by majoritarian institutions. As noted, the practice and pace of eugenics in the private sphere are less easily assessed than public eugenics, but they serve as signposts suggesting that support and adherence pepper the social, medical, and educational landscape of the time. In addition to a desire for hereditary betterment through segregation and reproductive suppression, eugenics enthusiasts also favored a positive approach that celebrated the best bred.

Positive Eugenics

Eugenic law and policy aimed at thwarting and preventing reproduction by "undesirables," while a major component of the movement, had an important counterpart. Eugenicists likewise encouraged those considered of "good stock" to procreate so as to populate society with children (and eventually adults) of superior heredity.[80] As we saw already, President Theodore Roosevelt exhorted the benefits—if not the urgent need—for well-bred natives to reproduce if for no other reason than to outbreed the newly arriving immigrants and assorted misfits who seemed to be replacing themselves at alarming speed. While Roosevelt's message of selective pronatalism was couched in negative and menacing language, including warning of "race suicide" by those of superior breed, the intent of these efforts was to encourage targeted reproduction.[81] In addition to this push for affirmative or "positive" re-production, the eugenics movement also supported a variety of health-related measures aimed at promoting the well-being of certain children and families. Thus, positive eugenics took shape as a combination of formal and subtle inducements, channeled to certain subpopulations, designed to encourage and reward selective childbearing and child caring.[82]

The story of positive eugenics is often told through the rise and popularity of "Better Baby" and "Fitter Family" contests that were held at state fairs across the country. These competitions were aimed at showcasing ideal offspring and parents for community admiration and imitation. Modeled after contests assessing better livestock, the better human competitions encouraged parents to bring their children to the annual gathering to be judged according to physical health, anthropo-metric traits, and mental development.[83] The first Better Baby contest was held in 1911 at the Iowa State Fair after an organizer challenged the gathering crowd, exhorting, "You are raising better cattle, better horses, and better hogs, why don't you raise better babies?"[84] Within a few years these contests became all the rage, appearing in every state except West Virginia, New Hampshire, and Utah. As the contests grew in popular-ity, the methods used to judge the finest baby at the fair evolved, helped along by significant input from the pediatric medical community. To bolster the contests' credibility, organizers incorporated a scoring sys-tem based on recommendations by the American Medical Association.

As told by Alexandra Stern, the medical community's involvement and investment in the Better Baby contests nudged these crowd-pleasing exhibits from pure eugenical displays of the virtues of race betterment (only white babies were eligible to enter the contests)[85] to public health–minded efforts to promote infant and child health. In Indiana, for ex-ample, the state's Division of Infant and Child Hygiene inaugurated the Better Baby contest at the 1920 Hoosier state fair, with the goals of "child saving" and maternal education. For the next twelve years, with mothers and their children crowded into booths and makeshift build-ings, nurses and an occasional physician spoke about and demonstrated techniques for improved infant nutrition, milk, bottle and food steril-ization, and other child-rearing necessities. Health officials examined some 77,000 babies, enrolled 55,000 mothers in instructional classes, and showed health films to over 600,000 viewers. Attributable in part to these measures, the state's infant mortality rate dropped by one-third over a ten-year period, from 8.2 percent in 1920 to 5.7 percent in 1930.[86]

Adults were also swept up in the celebration of heredity and hygiene through Fitter Family contests. First held in 1920 at the Kansas Free Fair, the Fitter Family contests followed from the Better Baby contests as a recognition that superior children could only hail from and be reared by superior parents.[87] The agrarian venues that housed these human competitions set the backdrop against which "fitness" was measured. Promotional materials accompanying the Fitter Family contests explained the competition's object was "to apply the well-known principles of heredity and scientific care which have revolutionized agriculture and stock breeding to the next higher order of creation—the human family."[88] These words were written by the American Eugenics Society and published in its periodical, *Eugenical News*. In addition to stressing heredity, contest organizers emphasized each person's duty to maintain a healthy lifestyle.

Contestants for the prize of "Fittest Family" underwent a rigorous series of examinations, focusing on physical, mental, familial, and moral characteristics. Just as Better Baby contests relied on medical professionals to evaluate the health and well-being of their pediatric population, Fitter Family judges included local physicians who performed thorough medical checkups on all contestants. In an era when routine medical exams were a luxury in which few could afford to indulge, particularly in rural America, the contests provided an opportunity for both intervention and education. In large measure, the messaging of the Fitter Family contests was that while heredity played a role in human well-being, environmental factors such as nutrition, recreation, and social interactions also affected one's overall fitness. The contests increasingly attracted people interested in controlling and improving their own health status.[89]

Combining eugenical celebration with public health outreach was the hallmark of the American eugenics movement. Motivating and validating self-improvement and self-sacrifice for the good of society was the movement's trope as it worked to stave off changes in the nation's racial, ethnic, and sociological makeup. Clinging to the perception of a bygone era, eugenicists paraded an image of the ideal American that they assiduously hoped to maintain. As proof, the Fitter Family winners were invariably white, native-born, married, Protestant, well educated, and middle class.[90] Rewarding those who contributed to race betterment—or more accurately race stasis—was at the heart of efforts to promote selective reproduction, or what we might call positive eugenics.

Studying the Themes: Science, Language, Tradition, and Economics

The eugenics movement was powered by a number of factors that co-alesced across the public and private spheres to produce widespread acceptance of reproductive control in the name of human betterment. As explained in this chapter, eugenics succeeded in deed and thought because it was able to harness the force and credibility of the emerging science of genetics, the fear and suspicion engendered by waves of immigration, the desire to preserve a dissipating majoritarian society, and the appeal of a public health trope that promised those targeted a brighter and richer future. In the chapters that follow, we will track these themes of science, language, tradition, and economics as they affect and emerge in the public and private ART arena. As in the American eugenics movement, we will see that reproductive control via ART is fueled by each of these factors, though they present in different ways. Just as eugenics glommed on to the early science of heredity, construing its meaning and import to support an established social agenda, we will see that, at times, barriers to ART access are defended by reference to expert opinions and published works that ultimately fail to survive scientific scrutiny. The language and imagery of ART, like the eugenics legacy, is often highly celebratory of majoritarian values, messaging that minority populations and their offspring are less deserving of access to fertility care.

The desire to preserve traditional values likewise influences access to ART. In the public realm, selected state laws limit insurance coverage to married individuals, while a surprising number of clinical practices continue to refuse service to single individuals and same-sex couples. Other more subtle factors suppress access for those who fall outside certain favored demographics, making ART harder to come by depending on where one lives and whether one works. Lastly, the economics of assisted reproduction are a dominant force in the battle over access. Popularly and accurately regarded as a costly and unreimbursed medical expense, ART earns its reputation as a luxury item inaccessible to many who could benefit from its use. As the next chapter explores, cost as a barrier to ART is a pervasive impediment to reproduction by select populations. What's more, its deprivation turns out to have enormous public health ramifications, ironically and perversely affecting many of those fortunate enough to afford its high financial cost.

The High Cost of Assisted Reproduction

"The best things in life are free. The second best things are very, very expensive," mused iconic French fashion designer Coco Chanel. Though the purveyor of haute couture no doubt had material goods in mind, the same can be said of family formation in the modern era. Those fortunate enough to enjoy a combination of reproductive tract health and a social orientation that embraces heterosexual intercourse are literally free to procreate without incurring any expense. But those who are infertile, whether medically or socially induced, face an expensive path to parenthood that many are simply unable to ultimately navigate. The facts are clear: the steep cost of reproductive medicine coupled with little or no underwriting by private health insurance creates the most significant barrier to ART access.

The high cost of ART has become a staple in discussions about the field, owing in part to widespread coverage of the debt burden infertility can engender. *New York Times* reporter Gina Kolata, in documenting the case of one woman who spent four years and $300,000 to have a baby, starkly sums up the ART financial picture. "Most couples cannot afford what she spent: she charged the bills for her treatment on her husband's credit card. But more and more women are entering the fertility vortex and finding that despite themselves, they will go as far as needed, spend whatever they can scrape up, take out second and third mortgages on their home, and travel across the country and even overseas for tests and treatments, all in the hope of becoming pregnant."[1] In the ART market, involuntary childlessness gives rise to voluntary impoverishment.

Cost as a barrier to ART access is more complex than just the high price of medical goods and services transacted in the pursuit of parenthood. Reportedly, assisted reproduction generates annual revenues of over $4 billion in the United States, much of it paid out-of-pocket by patients who are woefully underinsured for this aspect of health care.[2] One estimate pegs the patient share of IVF costs at 85 percent.[3] At first blush, it is clear that the synergy between high-priced treatments and low levels of reimbursement produces a world of stratified reproduction in which wealth status determines entrée into the procreative marketplace. A deeper analysis does not refute this impression, but also reveals that socioeconomics alone do not fully explain how ART funding works to suppress reproduction by certain "lower resource" individuals. While early twentieth-century eugenicists targeted the poor as less worthy of reproducing than the rich, twenty-first century ART is more subtle but no less impactful in its sorting of prospective parents. This chapter explores the complex web of ART economics, ultimately making the case that the U.S. approach to financing infertility violates public health norms while promoting eugenic values.

Financing Intimate ART

Let us begin our exploration of ART costs with the simplest treatment configuration—an IVF-seeking male and female who intend to use their own gametes. This patient profile is likely to be composed of two people who are either married or cohabitating, and who plan to jointly rear any resulting child. We can refer to this scenario as "intimate IVF," meaning that no third-party donors or surrogates need be involved—that is, compensated. This couple can expect to pay between $10,000 and $14,000 for a single round of IVF, with the average cost per cycle hovering around $12,000.[4] This "no frills" treatment likely does not include extra (and often medically necessary) services such as intracytoplasmic sperm injection (ICSI—a fertilization-enhancing technique used in well over half of all IVF cycles),[5] genetic testing of preimplantation embryos, and freezing costs for extra embryos to be preserved for later use. In addition, the cost of a single round of IVF needs to be considered in the context of the "likelihood of success." While averages can be defied, a patient undergoing IVF can expect the chances for live birth to be only 33 percent in any given cycle.[6] This average varies widely according to a host of clinical factors, but the message is that most patients will not succeed on the first attempt.

Thus, for anyone facing the prospect of IVF treatment, a legitimate question arises: How much can I expect to pay to give birth to a live baby? That question looks beyond the cost of a single IVF cycle to take into account the probability of achieving a delivery as a result of that cycle. In a study published in the *New England Journal of Medicine,* researchers investigated the average cost of a successful delivery with IVF. The study examined the costs associated with IVF, including the fees for initial consultation, laboratory tests, medications, ultrasonography, egg retrieval, gamete culturing, embryo transfer, and physician and nursing services. The cost assumptions also included calculations for time away from work, maternal complications associated with the procedure, and neonatal complications due to multiple births. On average, researchers concluded that the cost incurred per successful delivery with IVF increases from $66,667 for the first cycle to $114,286 by the sixth cycle. For couples in which the woman is older and there is a diagnosis of male-factor infertility, the cost rises from $160,000 for the first cycle to $800,000 for the sixth.[7]

These eye-popping figures can discourage even those with means from hitching their parental hopes to an ART wagon. Intuition and empirical data confirm that money matters in the market for fertility services. In Chapter 1 we discussed the statistics surrounding the incidence of infertility in the United States and corresponding treatment-seeking by those afflicted. To recap, the incidence of medical (versus social) infertility among women in the United States is fairly well tracked by periodic surveys conducted by the National Survey of Family Growth, a large, ongoing women's health study carried out by the U.S. Department of Health and Human Services (HHS) and the Center for Health Statistics. The survey concludes that 6 percent of married women of reproductive age (ages fifteen to forty-four) experience infertility (defined as lack of pregnancy after twelve months of unprotected intercourse).[8] This means that around 1.5 million married women are thought to be infertile.[9] An additional 12 percent of married women (around three million in number) experienced impaired fecundity, or difficulty in getting pregnant or maintaining a pregnancy to live birth.[10] Data published by the CDC peg the total number of Americans who experience infertility at around 10 million, a figure that includes men and women regardless of marital status. Another epidemiologic marker estimates that approximately 12 percent of U.S. women of reproductive age have sought fertility care at some point in their lives, with around 1.2 million women seeking treatment each year.[11] Crunching these numbers at a level of extreme generality, it is estimated that less than half of all U.S. women who experience difficulty getting or staying pregnant seek treatment.[12] Of the treatment-seekers, only half proceed to treatment, and of this cohort only a very small proportion undergo IVF.[13]

Later discussions in this book will reveal that financial means is not the only factor to affect ART treatment-seeking, but it is likely the primary culprit for untreated infertility. Research confirms that which is intuitive—ART utilization increases as the cost per cycle decreases.[14] Cost limits access to intimate IVF and correspondingly stratifies the medically infertile along socioeconomic lines. Stratified reproduction—in which demographic features create a hierarchy that determines one's ability to access infertility treatment—has been described as the "eugenic logic of IVF" because cost barriers disparately affect low-income individuals and couples who are primarily of color.[15] As discussed in Chapter 2, early eugenicists were not particularly discerning in targeting groups for nonbreeding, and poverty was as good a reason as any other to suppress reproduction. Of course, in the early 1900s the means of procreation were free even to those with no other resources, so suppression methods took on other forms. Today, the high cost of ART works to stratify assisted reproduction along socioeconomic lines, suppressing procreation at and near the bottom rung. To the extent this stratification plagues intimate IVF, it is an overwhelming feature of collaborative ART, a far more costly family formation endeavor.

The Unaffordability of Collaborative ART

The underlying cause of a person's infertility will typically suggest its treatment. In cases of medical futility—such as blocked fallopian tubes in women or low sperm counts in men—treatments like IVF and intrauterine inseminations (IUI) that bypass structural or physiological anomalies can be highly effective in helping the patient or the patient's partner conceive. But in some cases of medical infertility and virtually all cases of social infertility, patients must rely on third parties to provide reproductive services needed to birth a child. The cost of these services adds considerably to the already staggering price of the basic treatment required to address the patient's inability to reproduce "the old-fashioned way." Collaborative reproduction, through the use of sperm donors, egg donors, embryo donors, and gestational carriers, includes the fees paid to the sponsoring individuals as well as a host of legal, medical, and business professionals who aid in orchestrating these complicated arrangements. As a result, collaborative reproduction is accessible only to those of the highest wealth status.

The three most widely used ART collaborators, in order of lowest to highest expense, are sperm donors, egg donors, and gestational carriers. As an aside, it must be acknowledged that use of the word "donor" in the context of collaborative reproduction is a misnomer since virtually all non-relative gamete providers are compensated for aiding in another's reproductive enterprise. Despite the fact that the literal and plain meaning of the word "donor" implies a purely altruistic act, when paired with "sperm" or "egg" the term is widely understood to reference a commercial transaction. While the amount each collaborator is paid varies depending on a host of factors, including geography, phenotype, genotype, professional status, and educational achievement, certain generalizations can be made.

THE COST OF COMMERCIAL AND ALTRUISTIC SPERM DONATION

Let's look first at the cheapest form of collaborative reproduction—engaging a paid sperm donor.[16] While men who "donate" sperm receive an average of $125 per donation (or a maximum of $1,500 per month), buyers can expect to pay at least $2,000 for a single attempt of at-home insemination using sperm purchased from a commercial bank. One such entity, the California Cryobank (CCB), opened its doors in 1977 and today boasts centers in four university-adjacent locations—Los Angeles (UCLA), Palo Alto (Stanford), Cambridge (Harvard), and New York (Columbia)—presumably to recruit donors of ample intellectual endowment. According to the extensive menu of services and accompanying prices set out in CCB's website, the cost for a single vial of sperm for home use is $595, with two to three vials per insemination recommended for maximum effectiveness. Assorted additional costs include access to donor information ($145 to see a childhood photo, $250 for an adult facial feature report), storage fees ($275 for six months), and delivery fees ($235 for overnight delivery). Women who want an "open donor" who is willing to be contacted when any resulting child turns eighteen can expect to pay more at the outset.[17]

Even bargain hunters who convince a friend or stranger to truly donate his sperm can face steep fees in this most low-tech of ART processes. The costs of this arrangement, dubbed "directed donation," are linked to legal regimes that can heap hefty, and sometimes hidden, expenses on top of a seemingly altruistic arrangement. Directed donation can be costly in two ways. First, if a patient elects or needs to engage a physician to conduct the insemination, the sperm will generally need to be processed according to federal tissue guidelines set out by the Food and Drug Administration (FDA). FDA requirements for sperm of a non-sexually-intimate partner typically mean the gametic material will be tested for infectious diseases and then quarantined in frozen storage for up to six months pending retesting of the donor to rule out any diseases that were too early to detect in the first sample.[18] CCB fees for directed donation range from $3,200 to $4,000, outpacing the cost of a single attempt at anonymous donation.[19] While there are opportunities for sperm recipients to request a waiver of the FDA requirements, the clinic's willingness to process and release fresh sperm from a known donor varies across practices and across jurisdictions.[20]

The second way in which directed donation can be costly is best described through the saga of William Marotta, a Kansas man who answered a Craigslist ad seeking a sperm donor in 2009. The ad posters, a lesbian couple without the financial resources to patronize a commercial sperm bank, felt blessed to find Mr. Marotta, who provided the sperm that led to the birth of their daughter later that year. The donor, moved by the couple's plight, declined to accept the $75 offered in the ad. All went well until the women split up and the birth mother sought assistance for her child from the state. The Kansas Department for Children and Families became involved, pursuing Mr. Marotta for thousands of dollars in child support despite a written agreement signed at the time of donation releasing him from any parental rights or responsibilities. Since the mothers did not regard Mr. Marotta as a parent, why did the State of Kansas pursue him in this role? The answer lies in the Kansas Family Code, which, like the law in over half of all U.S. jurisdictions, declares that a donor is not a parent so long as he "provides semen to a licensed physician."[21] Since this was a private arrangement accomplished without medical assistance, the law did not protect the donor from being roped in as a duty-bound parent.[22] Thus, the cost of sperm donation can begin in the thousands of dollars, even when the parties try to avoid any monetary exchange. As the Kansas saga reveals, an act of altruism can produce a lifetime (or at least eighteen years) of parental expense.

PAYMENTS TO EGG DONORS

Visit almost any college campus and you will spot the ads. "Pay Your Tuition with Eggs," reads one insert in an Ivy League campus newspaper. Another promises $50,000 to an "intelligent, athletic egg donor" who "must be at least 5–10 and have a 1400 SAT score."[23] The recruitment and perceived lavish compensation of female egg donors is much discussed in the popular press, but less well studied in the clinical realm. While sperm donors are generally paid the same amount per sample, payments to egg donors vary depending upon a woman's location, age, looks, health status, and family history. While ads may boast of fees in the tens of thousands of dollars, in truth the average egg donor in the United States earns around $5,000 for her trouble. This figure derives from a 2007 survey of several hundred fertility clinics that offer egg donation services. The survey authors found the national average for egg donor compensation settled around $4,200, with regional variations.[24]

On the buying end, as with sperm donation, the egg purchaser can expect to pay far more than the donor's fee to procure the surrendered gametes. One Southern California egg donation agency tells prospective parents that they can expect to pay up to $20,000 for donated eggs, $5,000 to $10,000 for the donor's fee, up to $5,000 for the donor's medical expenses, and $6,000 for administrative costs, including psychological screening of the donor and legal fees.[25] Also keep in mind that once purchased, eggs must be manipulated by an IVF specialist to be reproductively useful. In some cases, the infertile patient will gestate the resulting embryo; in other cases, the intended parent(s) will seek a gestational carrier to bring the child to term, another exorbitant expense discussed below. Whether the donor egg ends up in a patient's uterus or that of a gestational carrier, someone will have spent a lot of money to place the precious cargo in that locale.

As we have seen, the ART world has been experiencing tremendous growth in the egg donation sector despite its high cost. In 2013, more than one in every ten ART cycles involved a donor egg (12 percent of all ART procedures involved either a fresh or frozen embryo created with a donor egg).[26] The reason for the widespread use of donor eggs has little to do with a couple's desire to birth a lanky, intelligent, musical, and athletic child, but more to do with the pregnancy success rates using donor eggs. Overall, a woman has a 56 percent chance of delivering a live baby if she uses a fresh (nonfrozen) donor egg. This rate is considerably higher than the 33 percent average success rate for IVF using the patient's own eggs. Most importantly, donor egg success rates hold up even for older women, who experience the highest rates of ART failure.[27] This latter demographic—older women (in fertility terms generally over the age of thirty-seven)—are more likely to be financially able to enter the egg market than their younger infertile colleagues. Still, for the overwhelming number of patients who could benefit from the process of egg donation, affordability is an impossibility.

THE SKY-HIGH PRICE OF SURROGACY

The precise number of children born via gestational surrogacy in the United States (or the world, for that matter) is not widely reported, but estimates peg the figure at around two thousand each year.[28] This is a small fraction of the total number of infants born each year through IVF—nearly 68,000 in 2013—but measured in terms of parental expenditure, the numbers become far more aligned. Surrogacy is extravagantly expensive, open to only those privileged few who can afford its six-figure price tag. The cold, hard facts are difficult to locate, but a good estimate is that the cost for a typical surrogacy birth in the United States ranges between $75,000 and $150,000. The costs include the surrogate's fee (on average, $25,000), medical expenses (some health insurance policies explicitly exclude coverage for surrogacy pregnancies), psychological testing, legal fees, agency fees (for the brokers who match surrogates and intended parents), pregnancy-related expenses (often surrogates get a monthly allowance from the time the contract is signed), life insurance for the surrogate, plus additional fees if an egg donor is used.[29]

For the medically infertile, resorting to gestational surrogacy may come at the end of a long and expensive clinical road dotted by numerous rounds of IVF and several attempts at egg donation. It is easy to see how this path could cost upwards of $500,000 or more. For the socially infertile, gestational surrogacy may be the first and only alternative to biological family formation. Such is the case for same-sex male couples who lack the "equipment" to reproduce as a two-person team. For a male couple to have a child who is genetically related to one member, surrogacy is the only option.

The high cost of surrogacy has, perhaps not surprisingly, given rise to pockets of corruption that threaten to tarnish the field as a whole. In 2006, a Sacramento-based surrogacy agent pled no contest to seven counts of grand theft and served six years in prison for duping intended parents into paying thousands of dollars for promised, but never delivered, surrogacy services. In August 2009, clients at a Modesto, California–based surrogacy agency filed a class action lawsuit after the owners abruptly closed the agency doors, shutting down access to hundreds of thousands of dollars in fees paid by hopeful parents. Dozens of expectant parents and pregnant surrogates were left without recourse for services and moneys promised by the agency's owner. Yet another Golden State agency owner was sentenced to eighteen months in prison in 2015 for converting fees paid by intended parents for surrogacy and egg donation services to her own personal use.[30]

Perhaps most egregiously, in August 2011 Theresa Erickson, a prominent legal expert in ART with her own radio program on the subject, pled guilty to federal fraud charges for what is described as an international baby-selling ring. An FBI investigation revealed that Erickson and two co-conspirators solicited U.S. women to travel abroad to be implanted with donated embryos. When the would-be surrogates reached the second trimester of pregnancy, the trio would recruit prospective parents who were falsely told that the women were gestational carriers for other couples who had backed out of the deal. Upon a payment of $100,000 to $150,000, Erickson would submit false documents to the local court seeking a pre-birth order allowing the substitute parents to be named on the child's birth certificate. After one surrogate grew nervous because she was due to deliver with no intended parents in sight, she sought advice from another lawyer who quickly sized up the situation and notified authorities.[31]

Having established the absolute and relative costs of intimate and collaborative ART, a logical question follows: Are any of the costs associated with assisted reproduction covered by insurance? After all, most health care in the United States is expensive, yet it is accessible to many through a web of public and private insurance schemes that make treatment closer to a right than a privilege. As the next section discusses, the relationship between ART and insurance does not mirror the same terms and coverages provided in the general health care market.

Infertility and the Struggle for Insurance

For many patients, a diagnosis of infertility works a double blow. First, the patient learns she will need high-priced medical assistance in order to have a child, and a quick review of whatever health insurance she carries will almost certainly reveal she is not covered for any of the associated expenses. Health insurance coverage in the United States is a complex web of public programs (primarily Medicare, covering those sixty-five and older, and Medicaid, covering mostly the indigent) and private insurers that are largely accessed by individuals through their workplaces. In fact, over half of all Americans under the age of sixty-five receive health insurance through their employers, meaning that employment status joins with wealth status to affect access to ART.[32] Even under major health reform enacted by the Patient Protection and Affordable Care Act of 2010 (ACA),[33] responsibility for health insurance remains primarily with individuals, rather than the government. The government provides little or no coverage for infertility services,[34] so any reimbursement for services will necessarily be accessed through private health insurance policies.

Whether an individual's health insurance policy covers infertility services may depend upon whether the state in which the policy is issued requires insurers to provide such coverage. According to the National Conference of State Legislatures, fifteen states have passed laws that require insurers to either cover (known as a "mandate to provide" or "hard mandate") or offer coverage ("mandate to offer" or "soft mandate") of fertility diagnosis and treatment. Thirteen of the states have laws that require insurance companies to cover infertility treatment (hard mandate states), while two states have laws that require insurance companies to offer coverage for treatment (soft mandate states). That said, the level of coverage in each state is highly variable.

For example, Massachusetts and Rhode Island have the most comprehensive statutes, mandating health insurance companies to provide coverage for diagnosis and treatment of infertility. But the Massachusetts law actually provides wider coverage because the Rhode Island statute is limited to married couples. In 2007, the governor of Rhode Island vetoed a bill that would have extended infertility insurance coverage to unmarried women. Texas and California are both "soft mandate" states and require insurers to offer coverage to employers, which they may accept or decline. Even if employers in both of these states elect to offer coverage, Californians will see less benefit because the state law specifically excludes coverage for IVF (as do laws in New York and Louisiana).

In Texas, coverage applies only to married couples with a five-year history of infertility who do not require a gamete donor. The law in Hawaii is similarly restrictive, imposing a five-year waiting period to begin treatment in most cases. Since aging is the chief cause of female infertility, linking insurance coverage to a five-year waiting period negates its usefulness in many cases. A woman who discovers she is infertile in her mid- to late thirties would not be advised by her physician to wait five years to begin treatment. Thus, access to insurance coverage in those jurisdictions provides no real economic benefit; those who can afford fee-for-service care will seek it out, those who cannot will be unlikely to achieve parenthood via assisted conception. Relevant portions of the Massachusetts and Texas statutes are set forth below. Various state laws related to infertility insurance coverage, including the date of original enactment plus significant amendments, are gathered in Table 4.

A further limitation to access to infertility care is a 1974 federal law designed to standardize pension benefits for American workers. While it remains the case in the United States that the regulation of health insurance is largely left to the states, an astute student of the law of insurance will be quick to point out that federal law does significantly impact the insurance industry through the Employee Retirement Income Security Act of 1974 (ERISA), 29 U.S.C. § 1001 et seq. Briefly stated, ERISA is a federal statute regulating employee benefit plans, including health benefit plans. The importance of ERISA to infertility insurance coverage is that in some cases, particularly when employers self-insure their health insurance coverage, the federal law preempts (or makes void) state laws that relate to employee benefit plans. Thus, even if a state requires insurers to cover infertility treatments, ERISA may preempt such a state law and allow health insurance providers to decline to offer infertility coverage.[35] In fact, according to the National Academy for State Health Policy, between 33 and 50 percent of all employees are covered by self-funded health insurance plans, a significant blow to state-mandated fertility coverage.[36]

A final note on insurance coverage for infertility explains why recent changes to our national health care insurance labyrinth had almost no impact on reimbursement for infertility-related expenses. The ACA, enacted in March 2010, directs the U.S. HHS to establish a minimum level of health benefits, called the essential health benefits, that must be offered by certain health plans, including all plans participating in the individual and small group health insurance markets. While there was initial hope that the ACA would require coverage for at least some fertility treatment,[37] ultimately the law basically deferred to existing protocols

Table 4: Summary of Legislation Related to Infertility Insurance Coverage

State	Coverage
Arkansas	**Ark. Stat. Ann. §§ 23−85-137 and 23−86-118 (1987, 2011)** require health insurance companies to cover the expenses of IVF procedures at licensed facilities.
California	**Cal. Insurance Code § 10119.6 (1989)** requires insurers to offer coverage of infertility treatments, except for IVF. Infertility may be a result of a medical condition or may refer to the inability to carry a pregnancy during a one-year or more period of time. Infertility treatment refers to diagnosis, diagnostic tests, medication, surgery, and gamete intrafallopian transfer (GIFT).
Connecticut	**Conn. Gen. Stat. § 38a-536 and 38a-509 (1989, 2005)** require health insurance organizations to provide coverage for medically necessary expenses of the diagnosis and treatment of infertility, including IVF. Infertility refers to an otherwise healthy individual's inability to retain a pregnancy during a one-year period.
Hawaii	**Hawaii Rev. Stat. §§ 431:10A-116.5 and 432.1−604 (1989, 2003)** require health insurance policies that provide pregnancy-related benefits to include a one-time-only benefit for outpatient expenses arising from IVF. In order to qualify for IVF, the married couple must have a history of infertility for at least five years or prove that the infertility is a result of specified medical conditions.
Illinois	**Ill. Rev. Stat. ch. 215, § ILCS 5/356m (1991, 1996)** requires certain insurance policies that provide pregnancy-related benefits to provide coverage for the diagnosis and treatment of infertility. Coverage includes IVF, uterine embryo lavage, embryo transfer, artificial insemination, GIFT, zygote intrafallopian tube transfer, and low tubal ovum transfer.
Louisiana	**La. Rev. Stat. Ann. § 22:1036 (2001)** prohibits the exclusion of coverage for the diagnosis and treatment of a medical condition that results in infertility. The law does not require insurers to cover fertility drugs, in vitro fertilization, or other assisted reproductive techniques, or reversal of a tubal litigation, a vasectomy, or any other method of sterilization.

Maryland	**Md. Insurance Code Ann. § 15–810, Md. Health General Code Ann. § 19–701 (2000)**, prohibits health insurers that provide pregnancy-related benefits for outpatient expenses arising from IVF. Law requires a history of infertility of at least two years' duration and infertility associated with one of several listed medical conditions. An insurer may limit coverage to three IVF attempts per live birth, not to exceed a maximum lifetime benefit of $100,000. An insurer or employer may exclude coverage if it conflicts with the religious beliefs and practices of a religious organization. Infertility care is included in the definition of health care services.
Massachusetts	**Mass. Gen. Laws Ann. ch. 175, § 47H, ch. 176A, § 8K, ch. 176B, § 4J, ch. 176G, § 4, and 211 CMR 37.00 (1987, 2010)**, require health insurance policies that provide pregnancy-related benefits to also provide coverage for diagnosis and treatment of infertility, including IVF. Infertility is defined as the condition of a presumably healthy individual who is unable to conceive or produce conception during a period of one year if female is thirty-five or younger, or six months if the female is over thirty-five.
Montana	**Mont. Code Ann. § 33–22-1521 (1987)** revises Comprehensive Health Association, the state's high-risk pool, and clarifies that covered expenses do not include charges for artificial insemination or treatment for infertility.
	Mont. Code Ann. § 33–31-102(2)(v), et seq. (1987), requires health maintenance organizations (HMOs) to provide basic health services on a prepaid basis, including infertility care.
New Jersey	**N.J. Laws, Chap. 236 (2001)**, requires health insurers to provide coverage for medically necessary expenses incurred in diagnosis and treatment of infertility, including medications, surgery, IVF, embryo transfer, artificial insemination, GIFT, zygote intrafallopian transfer (ZIFT), ICSI, and four completed egg retrievals per lifetime of the covered person. The law has a religious exemption for employers that provide health coverage to less than fifty employees.

(*continued*)

Table 4 (*continued*)

State	Coverage
New York	**N.Y. Insurance Laws §§ 3216 (13), 3221 (6), and 4303 (1990, 2002)**, prohibit individual and group health insurance policies from excluding coverage for hospital, surgical, and medical care for diagnosis and treatment of correctable medical conditions otherwise covered by the policy solely because the condition results in infertility. The law does not require coverage for IVF.
Ohio	**Ohio Rev. Code Ann. § 1751.01(A)(7) (1991)** requires insurers to offer basic health care services, including infertility services when medically necessary.
Rhode Island	**R.I. Gen. Laws §§ 27–18-30, 27–19-23, 27–20-20, and 27–41-33 (1989, 2007)** require any contract, plan, or policy of health insurance, nonprofit hospital service, nonprofit medical service, and HMO to provide coverage for medically necessary expenses of diagnosis and treatment of infertility. Co-payments for infertility services may not exceed 20 percent. Infertility is defined as the condition of an otherwise healthy married individual who is unable to conceive or produce conception during a period of one year.
Texas	**Tex. Insurance Code Ann. § 3.51–6, Sec. 3A (1987, 2003)**, requires health insurers to offer and make available coverage for services and benefits on an expense incurred or prepaid basis for outpatient expenses that may arise from IVF procedures. In order to qualify for IVF services, the couple must have a history of infertility for at least five years or have specified medical conditions resulting in infertility.
West Virginia	**W. Va. Code § 33–25A-2 (1995)** requires health insurers to offer "basic health care services," which include infertility services. Applies to HMOs only.

Source: National Conference of State Legislatures

surrounding infertility care in each state.[38] As written, the ACA disincentivizes states from adding additional mandates, so expansion is not anticipated in the immediate future. As a result, the most far-reaching health care reform legislation since the establishment of the Medicare program in 1965 did little to assist the plight of the uninsured infertile.

Mandate to Offer
Texas Insurance Code § 1366.003–005
Offer of Coverage Required

(a) An issuer of a group health benefit plan that provides pregnancy-related benefits for individuals covered under the plan shall offer and make available to each holder or sponsor of the plan coverage for services and benefits on an expense incurred, service, or prepaid basis for outpatient expenses that arise from in vitro fertilization procedures.

(b) Benefits for in vitro fertilization procedures required under this section must be provided to the same extent as benefits provided for other pregnancy-related procedures under the plan.

Conditions Applicable to Coverage

The coverage offered under Section 1366.003 is required only if . . .

(2) the fertilization or attempted fertilization of the patient's oocytes is made only with the sperm of the patient's spouse;

(3) the patient and the patient's spouse have a history of infertility of at least five continuous years' duration.

Mandate to Provide
Mass. Gen. Laws Ann. ch. 176A, § 8K
Infertility diagnosis and treatment benefits

Any contract . . . between a subscriber and the corporation under an individual or group hospital service plan which is delivered, issued for delivery or renewed in the commonwealth while this provision is effective and which provides pregnancy-related benefits shall provide as a benefit for all individual subscribers or members within the

commonwealth . . . , to the same extent that benefits are provided for other pregnancy-related procedures, coverage for
medically necessary expenses of diagnosis and treatment of
infertility. . . . For purposes of this section, "infertility" shall
mean the condition of an individual who is unable to conceive or produce conception during a period of 1 year if the
female is age 35 or younger or during a period of 6 months if
the female is over the age of 35.

The Eugenics of Cost

The high cost and low reimbursement of ART services combine to effectively stratify access to fertility care along socioeconomic lines. One
could declare the economics of ART eugenic in nature because they
work to permit reproduction by more favored groups (the well insured,
the wealthy) while suppressing reproduction by less favored groups (the
uninsured, the poor). But is it fair to compare today's market for procreative goods and services to a long abandoned orchestrated effort to
enact laws and establish policies that actively robbed individuals of their
reproductive capacity? After all, one argument avers, the contemporary
ART market derives not from state coercion but according to the laws
of supply and demand. Without proving some conspiratorial conduct
on the part of lawmakers and providers to actively make ART services
unavailable to the poor, the current market structure would seem to
deflect application of the eugenic label. A deeper analysis, however,
suggests that stratifying access to ART along socioeconomic lines has
a more pernicious impact than just separating the rich from the poor.
Wealth status, it turns out, scores for more than one's ability to pay for
fertility treatment.

INCOME SOURCE AS A BARRIER TO TREATMENT ACCESS

In the competitive world where ART providers vie for the patronage of
(mostly) cash-paying patients, one would surmise the source of a person's wealth would be of no concern or interest to a treating physician.

Survey data suggest this is not the case. It turns out that patients who derive some or all of their income from public sources are highly likely to be turned away by ART providers. In a survey of fertility clinic directors conducted in 2001, the surveyors sought to discover the screening practices and beliefs of the gatekeepers of reproductive medicine. A major tenet of American health law is that "the physician-patient relationship is . . . a voluntary and personal relationship which the physician may choose to enter or not for a variety of reasons."[39] While negotiated contracts and civil rights laws do limit a doctor's ability to refuse treatment, in general the principle of physician autonomy allows providers to pick and choose among prospective patients with impunity. Given this wide discretion, researchers set out to discover provider practices for screening candidates. By "screening," the researchers refer to "the assessment and consideration of factors other than those that impact fertility and treatment success or ability to pay in decisions about the provision of ART services."[40] While patients might have the ability to pay, how those resources are amassed seems to matter.

Physician attitudes and practices were solicited by questionnaires presenting a variety of hypothetical candidates that asked the programs' likelihood of turning away a prospective candidate in each of the categories. When asked the likelihood of refusing treatment when "the couple is on welfare, and want to pay for ARTs with social security checks," 38 percent of respondents said they were "very or extremely likely to turn away" this hypothetical candidate.[41] On the other hand, nearly half (47 percent) said they were "not at all or slightly likely to turn away" this couple. Thus, it appears a majority of ART providers are slightly, very, or extremely likely to refuse treatment to a patient whose income derives from public sources. Why is that? Since no follow-up questions were posed as to the reasons for a particular answer, we can only speculate.

Could it be that providers worry that public benefits are insufficient to cover the treatment costs and thus these patients would ultimately be unable to pay the bill? Perhaps, but similar concerns could apply to any patient whose source of wealth is unknown or insecure. In this regard, about half of all survey respondents stated that as part of their screening process, they collect information on the candidates' "financial stability."[42]

Linking these two queries, it must be that some providers seek out information from prospective patients about their financial health not just to assess whether they *can* pay but to judge whether they *should* be using their resources for this purpose. Denying a low-resource person ART because she receives public benefits while treating another low-resource patient who is supported by her family, consumer debt, or in some other private manner cannot be justified on economic grounds and may suggest a more pernicious, pretextual motivation.

INCOME SOURCE AS A BARRIER TO DONATION

Low-resource prospective patients are not the only ART stakeholders to face barriers because of cost. Individuals who want to become ART collaborators by supplying their gametes or gestational services are screened, either directly or by proxy, based on their financial status. In the case of sperm donors, while most commercial programs do not inquire about a man's income or assets during the screening process, they do require that all applicants be enrolled in a four-year university (thus excluding community college students) or hold a bachelor's degree.[43] While this educational requirement is not explicitly linked to a donor's socioeconomic status, it is well known that men with a college degree earn significantly more over their lifetimes than those without such a credential.[44] Women who wish to be egg donors can expect to be screened for certain markers that give a glimpse into their financial health. For example, one egg donor agency requires all applicants to have "reliable transportation," presumably to be able to arrive timely at the many medical appointments involved in the donation process.[45] Another queries prospective donors on the online questionnaire, "Do you receive welfare payments or public assistance from any city, state or federal agency?"[46] While the questionnaire does not indicate that respondents who answer "yes" will be disqualified, one wonders what other purpose such an inquiry might serve.

Poverty is an express barrier to service as a gestational surrogacy. Women who want to become gestational carriers need not apply if they receive public assistance. One surrogacy agency, in describing a "typical" surrogate on its website, explains that the woman:

Must be financially secure. Since money should not be a major motivating factor in deciding to become a surrogate mother, anyone on welfare or receiving state assistance, is excluded from our program. (On occasion a surrogate mother who goes back to college for further education and receives state assistance, will be considered for participation in our program.) Financial consideration should not be the major motivating factor.[47]

The reason most often given for this exclusion is that the woman could be rendered ineligible to receive further aid, including health coverage through Medicaid, if she is paid for her services as a gestational carrier. Employing a gestational carrier who receives government aid is dubbed "state-funded surrogacy" and is highly disfavored by agencies. Commentators warn against a woman trying to "skirt the law" by conspiring with intended parents to evade reporting her surrogacy compensation to government authorities. To do so is fraud. As one former surrogate exclaimed, "Doing this is fraud against the United States Government. I cannot think of a worse entity to attempt to cheat! Don't do it! Using state funded surrogacy is one of the absolute worst things you can do."[48] Other reasons given for wholesale rejection of women receiving government aid include the presumed absence of a stable and secure home situation. As one commentator said in response to why a surrogate cannot be on public aid of any sort, "Surrogates need to live in a stable environment to foster a healthy pregnancy."[49] Does this mean that women on state or federal assistance do not have healthy pregnancies? As a general matter, they do. Recall that one concern of eugenics enthusiasts was that the poor had too many healthy pregnancies, and thus were outpacing the rich in terms of birthrates.

A final rationale for avoiding the engagement of women on public assistance as surrogates evokes the oft-argued critique that commercial surrogacy exploits poor women. The nature of a surrogacy exchange is such that an infertile person (and often his or her partner) with resources negotiates with a woman (and sometimes her partner) who is desirous of compensation for the service of gestating the intended parent's (or parents') child. The exploitation argument highlights that the surrogate is typically (far) less wealthy than the intended parent(s), and thus the practice is called out as expressly and dangerously exploitive of women who are coerced into the arrangement because of their dire economic circumstances. In rejecting this argument as a reason to declare commercial surrogacy void against public policy, the California Supreme Court acknowledged, "Although common sense suggests that women of lesser means serve as surrogate mothers more often than do wealthy women, there has been no proof that surrogacy contracts exploit poor women to any greater degree than economic necessity in general exploits them by inducing them to accept lower-paid or otherwise undesirable employment."[50] Rejecting a potential surrogate because she is "too poor" will do little to convince critics that the practice is less exploitive. Refusing to accept a public-supported candidate in order to combat the perception of exploitation may breed far more reputational harm, likening the rejection of poor women as surrogates to the eugenic practices that deprived so many Americans of their procreative potential.

Cost as a Public Health Factor

As discussed in Chapter 2, the American eugenics movement steeped itself deeply in the language and architecture of public health. The rallying cry that society would be better off as a whole if certain individuals did not reproduce and thus sully the gene pool helped sustain the heinous practices that now symbolize that regrettable period in American history. Today, as argued throughout this book, barriers to ART display worrying similarities to the reproductive suppression advanced during the eugenics period, even if unaccompanied by such an express and celebrated agenda. While explicit appeal to public health as a rationale for discouraging selective procreation is not a central theme in ART availability, there is an important public health component to the high cost of assisted conception. Those who can afford to access ART do so in ways that often produce significant health hazards for women and children, while those who cannot access ART often remain childless, but otherwise healthy.

The greatest public health impact of ART is the persistently high rate of multiple births associated with IVF. On average, nearly one in every three IVF deliveries are twins or greater. Thankfully, the number of high-order multiple births (triplets or greater) has decreased significantly in recent years, falling from 2.6 percent in 2004 to just under 1 percent (of all ART live births using fresh nondonor eggs or embryos) in 2013, but the rate of twins remains staggeringly above the 3 percent average seen in natural conception.[51] Multiple birth in ART is responsible for costly maternal and fetal morbidity, producing dangerous pre-term deliveries and long stints for infants in neonatal intensive care units.[52]

The reason for the high multiple birth rate in ART is attributable to two main factors. First, ART remains an art and not a science, such that we are still unable to predict with absolute certainty whether an embryo will progress to a live-born infant. Thus, physicians often transfer more than one embryo in a cycle to boost or maximize the chance that a live birth will occur. In 2008, for example, each IVF cycle in patients under age thirty-five involved transfer of 2.2 embryos on average, despite a recommendation by the American Society for Reproductive Medicine that this cohort receive only one or two embryos per cycle.[53] The second and related reason for the high multiple birth rate in ART centers on the high cost of IVF, which prompts patients to press their physicians to transfer more embryos than recommended because they cannot afford to pay for another treatment cycle.

The high cost of unreimbursed IVF inevitably influences patient and physician behavior. As Deborah Forman observes, "Patients . . . seek to maximize their chances in any given cycle, even at the risk of increasing the odds of a multiple birth. Indeed, some patients . . . may actively seek twins as a cost and stress saving measure. . . . Physicians are also under pressure to post high success rates, which may influence their decisions about the number of embryos to transfer."[54] Data from outside the United States support this observation that the greater the financial pressure on patients, the greater the pressure they exert on physicians to transfer more embryos. In 2010, when lawmakers in Australia reduced IVF reimbursement by $1,500, clinics reported "more pressure from cash-strapped patients to implant multiple embryos to boost chances of pregnancy in one cycle."[55]

Surveillance of IVF practices internationally shows that countries that include infertility treatment as part of their national health service have managed multiple births far better than the United States. In Britain and Sweden, for example, countries that cover IVF as part of a national health system, the rates of multiple births are 27 percent and 5 percent, respectively, compared with 32 percent in the United States.[56] In these European countries, embryo transfer numbers are regulated by the national health authorities. Our neighbors to the north have likewise succeeded in dramatically reducing the incidence of multiple birth by including fertility care as a funded health benefit. In the province of Quebec, lawmakers instituted a system of universal public funding of IVF. After one year, Quebec's rate of elective single embryo transfer rose from 1.6 to 31.6 percent of transfers, and its rate of multiple births dropped from 29.4 to 6.4 percent, although pregnancy rates also declined from 39.9 to 24.9 percent.[57] Data make clear that in these universal health care countries, rates of multiple births are reduced when coverage for ART is increased. Whether coverage is paired with mandatory or voluntary reductions in embryo transfer, such behavior is easier to inspire when patients do not have to mortgage their homes in order to seek treatment.

The relationship between insurance coverage and multiple births is also well documented in the United States. Researchers at Harvard Medical School conducted a study to determine whether coverage for IVF services is associated with increased use of services and improved outcomes for patients and offspring. The Harvard team reviewed the annual data published by the CDC reporting ART success rates and divided the clinics into three groups according to the state in which the clinic was located: (1) states that mandate complete insurance coverage for IVF (31 clinics), (2) states that mandate partial coverage for IVF (27 clinics), and (3) states that did not require any coverage (302 clinics). The results were intuitive: States that do not require insurance coverage have the highest number of embryos transferred per cycle, the highest rates of pregnancy and live birth from IVF, and the highest rates of births of multiple infants (especially three or more).[58]

From an economic standpoint, the researchers argue, the net savings of health insurance dollars by not covering IVF is more than nullified by a greater expenditure of dollars to care for multiple birth newborns. For example, "In 1991, hospital charges for the delivery of twins were 4 times as high and charges for triplets were 11 times as high as charges for a singleton delivery."[59] Moreover, the lifetime health costs to care for multiple birth infants can be staggering due to the higher risk of respiratory distress syndrome, cerebral palsy, blindness, and other physical and developmental disabilities associated with higher-order multiple birth. The other side of the equation—the added cost for including IVF in health insurance—supports the cost/benefit argument in favor of coverage. In Massachusetts, the state reputed to mandate the most generous coverage for infertility care, data show that the law has only minimally affected insurance premiums.[60] "The cost of insurance premiums has risen only between 0.2 percent and 0.5 percent annually, or about $1 a month extra for an average policy, because of the coverage of in-vitro fertilization."[61] Other studies confirm that mandating coverage for infertility care, including IVF, increases premiums only a few dollars a year.[62]

The traditional public health model encourages individual action, even sacrifice, for the greater good. This equation spurred and sustained the eugenics movements for several decades. Now into its fourth decade, the practice of ART seems to be defying, even inverting, this public health model. ART cost barriers mean that individuals are forced to make choices that harm the greater good. What's more, such harms could be alleviated by collective action that demands widespread coverage for infertility care. Since costs to society are low for increased coverage and harms are high due to the lack of coverage, why isn't there a groundswell of support to cover fertility care like other health care benefits? Perhaps, as advocates suggest, there are misperceptions about the costs to individual policy holders and the inability to envision one's own future need for services. Or perhaps there is a more concerning philosophy that continues to stratify assisted conception along socioeconomic lines. Those who form families in nontraditional ways are less worthy of society's support for their parental aspirations; only those wealthy enough to overcome their infertility should be privileged to enter the ART market. Procreative suppression along wealth lines may seem a relic of a bygone era, but the economics of assisted reproduction revive it as an active barrier to ART access.

F • O • U • R

Race and Ethnicity as
Barriers to ART Access

B
y global standards, the United States is an unhealthy place to
live. According to a study released in January 2013, among
seventeen countries studied, Americans live sicker and die
younger than similarly situated people residing in every other
developed nation. America's unenviable last-place position among sister nations stems from our high rates of death by heart disease, diabetes,
lung disease, accidents, and gun violence.[1] Even when researchers controlled for specific demographic features, including socioeconomic status and access to health insurance, the U.S. population remained at the
bottom, health-wise. It may come as a surprise to some that Americans
experience such health disparities on an international level, but even the
most casual observer of our nation's health care system is aware of the
uneven allocation of health and health care among our diverse population. For as long as we have been a nation, access to medical care, the
quality of that care, and the health outcomes experienced by Americans
have stratified along racial and ethnic lines, with people of color persistently populating the bottom rungs of the health hierarchy. This chapter
explores the impact of race and ethnicity in the ART world.

Suspicions about disparities in health and health care along racial and ethnic lines are routinely confirmed by research that measures
a variety of health-related factors. In 2003, the prestigious Institute of

Medicine (IOM) released a comprehensive study documenting difference in health status, available treatment, and clinical outcomes according to patient race and ethnicity.[2] The IOM report summarized data from
more than one hundred studies addressing racial differences in health
care, concluding that racial and ethnic disparities are consistent and extensive across a range of medical conditions and health care services. As
health law scholar Dayna Matthew laments, even after controlling for
differences in socioeconomic status, health insurance, and geographic
differences, "Blacks and Latinos receive fewer and inferior clinical services than whites."[3] Unfortunately, but unsurprisingly, research reveals
that similar disparities plague the provision of ART care, with racial and
ethnic minorities experiencing a greater incidence of infertility, a lower
rate of treatment-seeking, and overall worse health outcomes.

After reviewing the data demonstrating the racialization of infertility care in the United States, we will endeavor to understand why
ART stratifies along race and ethnic lines. Researchers and scholars have
advanced several theories, including lower income levels and access to
insurance in minority populations, social factors that make women of
color less likely to seek treatment for infertility, historic factors that give
rise to a continuing aura of mistrust in the doctor-patient relationship,
and express and implied discrimination by doctors who view minority populations as less deserving of parenthood than white patients.
Whether one, some, or all of these factors explain the racial and ethnic
disparities in infertility care, the fact remains that the circumstances of
one's birth can be an impenetrable barrier to one's ability to procreate.
These new eugenics, like the old eugenics, can persist only so long as
political power structures support and advance their agenda. At the end
of the chapter, we consider whether structural changes along political
lines could be the key to equalizing reproductive opportunities along
racial and ethnic lines.

Racializing Infertility and Its Treatment

Disparities in infertility care access and treatment outcomes along racial
and ethnic lines began to appear almost as soon as the Centers for Disease Control started collecting success rate data from fertility clinics in

the early 1990s. Mandated by the Fertility Clinic Success Rate and Certification Act of 1992, in 1997 the CDC began what is now an annual collection and publication of ART data, including clinic-specific and national summaries on patient diagnosis, number of embryos transferred, and pregnancy and live-birth rates.[4] While the annual CDC ART report does not contain a section on the racial and ethnic makeup of clinic patients, such demographic information can and often is reported to the Society for Assisted Reproductive Technology (SART), the professional organization that oversees national ART data collection. From this SART database, as well as other research efforts undertaken over the past decade or so, we have learned a great deal about the existence of racial and ethnic disparities in infertility care.[5] Understanding the epidemiology of infertility care helps us puzzle through why such wide disparities exist and how we might address the existing barriers going forward.

DIFFERENCES IN THE INCIDENCE OF INFERTILITY

Disparities begin with causation. Women of color experience medical infertility at higher rates than white women. According to the 2002 National Survey of Family Growth (NSFG), infertility is higher among married couples when the wife is nonwhite, compared with couples in which the wife is white. The incidence of infertility is highest, 20 percent, among black women, followed by Hispanic women at 18 percent, and lowest among white women at 7 percent.[6] Infertility among other demographic groups, measured in the 1995 NSFG, was reported at 13.6 percent. This group was defined as married women categorized as "non-Hispanic other," including Asian, Pacific Islander, Alaskan Native, and American Indian women. Minority men also experience infertility at higher rates than white men. Male infertility in men aged twenty-five to forty-four is reported at 12 percent, with white men having the lowest rates of infertility, followed by Asians, Hispanics, and then blacks.[7] What factors account for these fertility disparities? Several researchers have posited theories.

Marcia Inhorn and Michael Hassan Fakih conducted research on the infertility experience among Arab Americans and African Americans who, according to the researchers, share similar risks of infertility, poverty, and discrimination. In assessing why these minority groups suffer greater infertility compared with whites, the doctors explain:

> Both groups are likely at increased risk for infertility problems because of environmental and lifestyle factors. Both groups tend to be concentrated in urban industrial centers, where they are exposed to reproductive toxins, particularly lead, through occupational exposures, ambient air pollution, and toxic waste disposal in their neighborhoods. In addition, their infertility problems might be linked to lifestyle factors, including heavy smoking, caffeine consumption, and drug use, as well as nutritional deficiencies and female obesity, which disrupts ovulation.[8]

In addition to environmental and lifestyle factors, other explanations for the disparate presentation of infertility along racial and ethnic backgrounds look to medical and cultural factors. On the medical side, doctors note that women of color, particularly black women, are more commonly affected by fibroids—benign tumors in or around the uterus that can play a role in infertility. Moreover, according to Mark Sauer, a renowned professor of obstetrics and gynecology and chief of the Division of Reproductive Endocrinology at Columbia University Medical Center in New York City, fibroids in black patients "tended to be larger and more persistent than white women's."[9] Another medical factor may be the increased presence of obstructions in the fallopian tubes, typically referred to as "tubal factor infertility." A 2005 study found that African American and Hispanic women had tubal factor infertility in far greater numbers than white women—24 percent, 27 percent, and 5 percent, respectively.[10] Tubal factor is often associated with a history of sexually transmitted diseases, which the CDC has documented as being more prevalent in minority women than white women.[11]

Cultural factors that increase the incidence of infertility among minority women are interwoven with treatment-seeking behavior, discussed below. Studies show that women of color wait longer to recognize and seek treatment for infertility, which can exacerbate any biological factors.[12] Untreated uterine or tubal disease, over time, could convert from a highly treatable condition with low impact on the woman's infertility to a severe condition with devastating impacts on fertility. In addition, time is not a friend of the infertile. Waiting to seek a diagnosis and treatment for infertility means the woman experiences reproductive aging in the interim. According to the American Society for Reproductive Medicine, a woman's best reproductive years are in her twenties. Fertility gradually declines in the thirties, particularly after age thirty-five.[13] Since a woman's reproductive capacity falls off sharply as she ages, successful treatment depends upon timely presentation to a medical professional. The next part looks at the factors that motivate and intimidate individuals from seeking treatment once they suspect they may be infertile.

DIFFERENCES IN TREATMENT-SEEKING BEHAVIOR

Coming to terms with the inability to naturally conceive and carry a pregnancy to term can be a long and painful journey. For those with medical infertility, recognizing a link between periods of unprotected intercourse and infertility takes time and access to at least some rudimentary medical sources that flag the potential diagnosis. For those with social infertility, the road to a medical appointment is altogether different but may still provoke some of the same anxieties and concerns about exploring the possibility of assisted conception. As noted in Chapter 3, treatment-seeking in the United States is relatively low compared with other developed nations, largely because our health care system does not generally cover or reimburse for infertility-related expenses. Only about half of all American women who are classified as infertile ever seek medical assistance for the condition. Scored along racial and ethnic lines, treatment-seeking among minority patients declines significantly.

Peer review research and data collection at the national level reveal that treatment-seeking, measured according to whether a woman ever sought medical assistance for infertility, is highest among white women (15.8 percent), then Hispanics (12.2 percent), and then blacks (10.7 percent).[14] When minority women do seek treatment, they typically wait longer on average than their nonminority counterparts.[15] Measured from a user perspective, data reveal what some have labeled the "white-ness" of ART in the United States. The vast majority of IVF patients are white, owing in part to the lower levels of treatment-seeking by women of color. For example, statistics culled from a 1999 database show the following breakdown of IVF users by race: Caucasian (85.6 percent), Hispanic (5.4 percent), African American (4.6 percent), and Asian (4.5 percent).[16] So if women of color experience infertility at a greater rate but seek treatment at a lower rate than white women, what are the factors that produce this mismatch between disease prevalence and quest for cure?

Those who study patterns of treatment-seeking suggest that four categories of inquiry can reveal a person's likelihood of pursing medical assistance in the face of clinical infertility. Theories of help-seeking are based on the assumption that moving from symptoms to medical treatment is a complex process. To help explain this process, researchers Lynn White, Julia McQuillan, and Arthur Greil aver that prospective patients typically interact with four factors, in a prescribed order, that help determine whether a person will ultimately seek help in the medical arena: symptoms, perception of a problem, consideration of alternative responses, and behavioral responses.[17]

Symptoms of infertility, unlike a heart attack, which causes acute pain, present in the negative. Because infertility is heralded by the absence of conception after a prescribed period rather than the presentation of an abnormal state, perception of a problem is particularly problematic. Failure to conceive can be attributed to a host of factors other than infertility, including stress, mistimed intercourse, or normal variation. Once symptoms are recognized and infertility is perceived, a range of alternatives need to be considered. Prospective patients may consider medical help along with other options, including adoption, childlessness, and self-care. Whatever behavioral response an individual manifests will reflect influences from her social network, her cultural and religious background, as well as her ability to afford treatment. The ways in which a patient perceives and chooses among her options are linked to her race and ethnicity, as discussed below. Even when a woman of color does seek treatment, her chances of delivering a healthy infant are lower than those associated with ART use by white patients.

DISPARITIES IN FERTILITY TREATMENT OUTCOMES

Across all age categories, minority women have worse outcomes after infertility care than nonminority women. These disparities are seen in lower fertilization rates, lower pregnancy rates, increased miscarriage rates, lower live birth rates, and higher incidence of preterm delivery.[18] Studies that compare outcomes across racial and ethnic lines routinely show that African American women have the lowest success rates after IVF, followed by Hispanic women, then Asian women, and then whites.[19] What is perhaps most troubling about this is that outcomes do not seem to improve in equal-access settings. That is, when women have equal access to ART services—so that affordability levels are the same for all patients—black women still experience more miscarriages and fewer live infant deliveries than white women.[20]

We know from our discussion of disparities in the incidence of infertility and treatment-seeking that the reason for differences in health outcomes can be explained, at least in part, by medical factors. Higher incidence of infertility in minority women is partly the result of increased tubal and uterine disease. Doctors do report that treating infertility in women with large fibroids (which are two to five times more prevalent in black women than white women)[21] is very challenging. In addition, we also know that minority women wait on average eighteen months longer than white women to seek treatment for infertility. This gap could explain exacerbated, less treatable symptoms in women of color who have also experienced reproductive aging while contemplating their treatment options.

These medical factors are useful in explaining ART disparities in minority populations, but they don't tell the whole story. Yet to be explored are questions such as: Why is treatment-seeking for fertility care lower among minority women in general, even when adjusted for affordability? When they do seek treatment, why do minority women wait so much longer than white women to set up a medical appointment? What role, if any, do physicians play in incentivizing or discouraging patients of all races and ethnicities to seek fertility care? In the section below, we explore a few areas that, combined with the medical data, help explain the disparity story.

Understanding Stratification by Race and Ethnicity

Dorothy Roberts was one of the first scholars to bring attention to racial disparities in ART, particularly as they affect black women. Her basic thesis is that reproductive technologies "reflect and reinforce the racial hierarchy in America."[22] She notes the racial differences in infertility prevalence and treatment-seeking, opining that the "reason for the racial disparity in fertility treatment appears to be a complex interplay of financial barriers, cultural preferences, and more deliberate professional manipulation."[23] Each of these factors, along with a few others, has been highlighted as giving rise to the stratified assisted reproduction that is a part of our American health care system. Below we explore the economic, social, cultural, historical, political, and provider-related components that align to create racial and ethnic barriers to ART.

THE COST PUZZLE

The most frequently cited reason for disparities in treatment-seeking is affordability. In ART, we can measure affordability by two features— insurance coverage and income. As to the insurance factor, we already know that very few Americans have access to insurance reimbursement for fertility treatment, and those that do receive coverage mostly through their employers. Moreover, we know that 85 percent of ART care is paid out of pocket, so income is highly indicative of one's ability to afford the high cost of infertility care. Measuring access to insurance and income levels along racial and ethnic lines, we know that minority populations are less well insured and have lower incomes than whites. According to the Kaiser Family Foundation, "Nonelderly Hispanics have the highest uninsured rate, with nearly one in three lacking coverage (32%), followed by American Indians/Alaska Natives (27%), Blacks (21%), and Asians/Pacific Islanders (18%), who are all more likely than Whites (13%) to be uninsured."[24] These figures, according to the foundation, are mostly attributable to lower rates of employment among workers of color.

Income and wealth levels in the United States also stratify according to race and ethnicity. According to the Pew Research Center, the median wealth measured in white households is twenty times that of black households and eighteen times that of Hispanic households.[25] The racial wage gap is persistent in American life. Asian Americans have the highest average income, followed by whites, typically next by blacks, Native Americans, and finally Hispanics. The median black male worker earns 74 percent as much as the median white male worker, while the median Hispanic male worker earns only 63 percent of what the median white male worker earns.[26] These differentials in insurance coverage and income levels would seem to correspond to each group's ability to access infertility care, and they usually do.[27] But some interesting research shows that when affordability is mediated by systems that provide equal access to all patients, ART disparities in race and ethnicity persist.

The two venues in which insurance and income can be removed from the access picture are in states that mandate broad coverage for infertility care and in the U.S. military, which provides wide access to infertility care regardless of rank or income. Research on disparities in states that mandate insurance coverage for ART reveals that racial and ethnic minority women continue to be underrepresented in the pool of patients accessing care. That is, racial and ethnic disparities in the use of ART remain even in states that mandate coverage for all potential users, regardless of socioeconomic status. In one study looking at ART use in Massachusetts, a state with a very generous mandate, researchers hypothesized that patients accessing infertility services in the state with mandated and comprehensive insurance coverage for such services would demographically be a close representation of the state's general population. They were proved wrong by the data. The study revealed that African Americans had lower levels of treatment-seeking than would be expected based on their population in the state. This result, the researchers noted, was also at odds with the higher levels of infertility that African Americans experience compared with other ethnic groups.[28] Hispanics also had lower usage than their proportional population would dictate, while Asian Americans actually sought treatment in numbers greater than their demographic percentage.

The Massachusetts study was not the only one to find that state mandates have little or no impact on racialized treatment-seeking within each jurisdiction. Another group of researchers, looking at data on ART usage in states with IVF insurance mandates, concludes, "We find no evidence that these mandates have mitigated the disparities in treatment by race, ethnicity or SES [socioeconomic status]."[29] Perhaps this result is attributable to aspects of coverage provided in each state. We know that even in the most generous mandate states (often cited as Connecticut, Illinois, Maryland, Massachusetts, New Jersey, and Rhode Island), certain restrictions apply that could disparately impact patients according to race and ethnicity. For example, some states require a long waiting period before benefits are available.[30] For a population that is already likely to wait longer to seek treatment after symptoms emerge, an extended waiting period could further disincentivize minority patients who may feel after a long period of infertility they are beyond medical help. Other states require covered patients to be married, a demographic feature that skews Caucasian.[31] Given that state mandates cover only those with private health insurance and often contain limitations that further suppress coverage, it should be no surprise that this system does not appreciably change the treatment picture for minority women.

A bill introduced in the Maine legislature in 2015 stands as a clear example of the disparate usefulness state-mandated infertility coverage offers racial and ethnic minorities, particularly women. An Act to Provide Access to Infertility Treatment, introduced as LD 943, would have become the nation's sixteenth state mandate, requiring health plans operating in the state to provide coverage for infertility treatment, including IVF. The limitations were both interesting and unique. In addition to a marriage requirement ("the covered individual must be married"), the bill also excluded patients whose infertility was "the result of a sexually transmitted disease."[32] While the bill failed to gain passage, the morality clause did provoke negative commentary—mostly condemning the attempted codification of a lifestyle police.[33] Absent was any outrage over the disparate impact such a limitation would have on minority women, who as earlier noted tend to remain single more often than white women and experience sexually transmitted disease–induced infertility at greater rates than their nonminority counterparts.

If ever there was a health system that could improve infertility care among racial and ethnic women and men in the United States, it is the military health care system. The Department of Defense (DoD) beneficiaries include service members and their families who are racially diverse and span all socioeconomic classes. In addition, infertility care is a covered benefit, including evaluations, medical management, and affordable ART cycles.[34] This equal-access-to-care setting presents a unique opportunity to study the incidence and care surrounding infertility in a U.S. population that includes representatives from all demographic cohorts. In one study at a military health center, utilization among African American women increased dramatically compared with their ART usage in the general population. While black women represent 4.6 percent of the total U.S. ART population (compared with whites at 85.5 percent, Hispanics at 5.5 percent, and Asians at 4.5 percent), their usage within the DoD rose to 19.1 percent, a near fourfold increase.[35] Increased usage was also observed within the Hispanic population (to 9 percent of all ART patients) though it was less dramatic than the surge in black patients. Asian military patients actually declined as a percentage of overall users. These findings differ from the studies conducted in insurance-mandated states (in which treatment-seeking among minority women generally remained lower than their proportional representation in the population), suggesting a need for further research.

Crunching the numbers, the study authors concluded that economics plays the most significant role in infertility treatment access in minority populations. But the authors acknowledge that other factors may be at play. Some of these factors apply more generally to health care–seeking in general, while others are specific to infertility. As a general barrier, the authors cite studies suggesting that African American patients are reluctant to seek care because of mistrust of the U.S. medical system, stemming from historic wrongdoings, such as the Tuskegee syphilis experiments conducted by the U.S. Public Health Service in which black men were intentionally untreated over a forty-year period (1932–72) so that the government could study the natural progression of the disease.[36] Fertility-specific barriers are suggested to include a greater sense of infertility stigmatization among minority populations, less supportive social networks, a reluctance to seek high-tech solutions to treat a natural process, and discrimination and stereotyping among physicians who are less likely to refer minority patients for specialty care. These and other factors combine with economic barriers to provide a clearer view of the impact race and ethnicity have on assisted reproduction.

CULTURAL AND SOCIAL IMPACTS

Involuntary childlessness, whether wrought by medical or social factors, affects individuals in ways that are both highly personal and extensively interpersonal. Research into the psychological aspects of infertility confirms this bifurcated assault, with studies highlighting the personal suffering and societal repercussions endured by the infertile. The infertility experience is often marked by distress, depression, anger, loss of control, stigmatization, and a disruption in the developmental trajectory of adulthood.[37] Numerous studies investigate and confirm the correlative and causative relationship between infertility and psychological distress.[38] While aspects of the infertility experience may be universal, each person responds and reacts to the inability to reproduce unaided in a manner that is unique to that individual. How a person feels and acts in the wake of any life-affecting discovery, including medical or social infertility, is shaped by numerous influences, including the individual's values, experiences, and aspirations. Importantly, cultural and social factors also play an important role in a person's infertility journey, as family building is by definition a collaborative activity. As this chapter's theme suggests, a person's race and/or ethnicity figures prominently in his or her ART narrative.

Social and cultural factors that influence a person's infertility journey can be both internal and external. As used in this context, internal factors focus on the way in which the infertile person sees him- or herself vis-à-vis the ability to procreate. Self-identity among minorities who experience infertility is inextricably linked to their identity as a member of the minority community. Minority women in particular internalize their infertility as an individual as well as a community shortcoming. Dorothy Roberts reports one black woman's reaction to her infertility: "Being African American, I felt that we're fruitful people and it was shameful to have this problem. That made it even harder."[39] Shame, of course, can provoke other emotions that affect one's infertility course. If shame, for example, translates into denial or fear, then treatment-seeking becomes far less likely. We already know that minority women seek infertility treatment far less often than their nonminority counterparts. A related observation, suggested by one researcher, is that African Americans are more apt than other groups to resolve infertility through formal or informal adoption and more likely to seek spiritual solutions.[40]

Personal accounts in the popular culture press likewise reflect this perception that minority women experience a greater sense of responsibility for their infertility because of their membership in the community. Writing on infertility among black women for *Essence* magazine, one reporter observes, "In a culture that often portrays Black women as stoic earth mamas and baby-making welfare queens, this myth may be especially potent among African-Americans."[41] In a *New York Times* article in 2014 covering infertility and race, one minority patient pointed out, "With women of color, specifically Hispanic and African-American women, the stigma attached to us is that it's not hard to have kids, and that we have a lot of kids." She added, "And when you're the one that can't, you feel like, 'I've failed.' "[42]

The myth of the hyperfertile black or brown woman has transitioned from a hushed reference to an openly acknowledged feature of minority infertility thanks to the modern-day public square, affectionately known as the blogosphere. Visit *TheBrokenBrownEgg.org* and you will encounter numerous stories and voices reflecting on "infertility-ville" among women of color. Founded by Regina Townsend, a ten-year veteran of involuntary childlessness, the by-day librarian started the blog so that "no one else will have to feel like the lone wolf of their family." Infertility is lonely enough, Townsend laments, without feeling like a "minority inside of a minority."[43] Visitors to this blog reflect on their own diagnoses, treatment cycles, or fears about seeking medical help. A common theme is the significance of race as a part of their infertility experience. As one writer shares, "Stereotypes about Black sexuality make Black infertility invisible."

Racialized perceptions about the inability to conceive aren't merely internal; they are also visited upon certain populations by external forces. Research suggests men and women of color express distrust of the U.S. health care system based on a long history of racism and discrimination in the delivery of reproductive health care in general. The accompanying stereotyping about the reproductive lives of minority Americans has, many argue, created a significant external barrier to care. In one study surveying barriers to infertility care among African American and Arab American men, researchers describe the racial stereotyping these two groups face:

> Caricatures of Arab American and African American men include images of male hypersexuality and hyperfertility. Arab American men and Muslim men in general are seen as polygamous fathers of children from multiple wives, harkening back to Western Orientalist fantasies of the harem. Similarly, African American men are often portrayed as "informal" polygamists, spawning offspring with multiple, unmarried sexual partners (as well as spreading HIV/AIDS to them). If Arab American and African American men are portrayed as hypersexual, hyperfertile polygamists in the Western popular imagination, then the very possibility that they might suffer from real infertility problems within stable, monogamous unions can be ignored and can lead to the convenient denial of their legitimate reproductive health needs.[44]

The clinical impact of racial stereotyping is a complex, at times circular loop that melds patient and physician attitudes and actions. Speaking to the role of physician conduct in acknowledging and treating infertility among black patients, Roberts writes, "There is evidence that some physicians and fertility clinics may deliberately steer Black patients away from reproductive technologies." She cites the tendency of physicians to diagnose white professional women with infertility problems such as endometriosis that can be treated with IVF. Black patients who fail to conceive are more likely to be diagnosed as having pelvic inflammatory disease (PID), often treated with sterilization. In one study, 20 percent of black patients diagnosed with PID actually suffered from endometriosis.[45]

In addition to disparate diagnoses among white and minority patients, racial differences are observed in the form of lower referral rates of minority patients to infertility specialists from primary care physicians.[46] These clinical observations serve to increase suspicion among prospective patients about their health care providers' ability to deal with their reproductive complaints effectively and without prejudice. If women of color anticipate a physician will respond to their infertility by either subtly or explicitly suggesting that they do not "need" to birth any more children, one can understand why these women shy away from seeking treatment. On the other hand, physicians report that minority women with signs of infertility, particularly African American women, seek out treatment less often than white women. Writing on the blog for infertile women of color mentioned earlier, one patient noted, "My own doctor has told me how hard it is to not only get women of color to admit to the issue, but also to follow-through with just the preliminary testing."[47]

The reticence of racial and ethnic minorities to seek out infertility care seems clearly bound up with the historic and harmful stigmatization of people of color and their reproductive lives. Stigma in this arena produces both internal and external barriers to accessing care, resulting in the breadth of epidemiological disparities discussed earlier in this chapter—greater incidence of infertility, lower treatment-seeking, and poorer health outcomes when treatment is sought. While some degree of stigma may arise from self-perception within the community that "we're a fruitful people and it [is] shameful to have this problem," other sources of reproductive stigma can be traced to a series of mishaps, wrongs, and outright criminal conduct that played out over decades across the United States. Even after rejection of the eugenics movement and its debunked tenets, American history continued to build a legacy of discrimination and mistreatment of minority populations. This legacy is particularly shameful in its quest to disrupt reproduction by people of color, a combined physical, psychological, and dignitary trauma that helps further explain the racial and ethnic disparities in today's ART world.

HISTORIC EXPLANATIONS FOR CONTEMPORARY MISTRUST

If past is prologue, then mistrust of the health care system among minority patients is easy to understand and explain. American history is sadly replete with notorious incidents in which the health, particularly the reproductive health, of minority men and women was ignored, abused, and worst of all—intentionally damaged—by medical experiments and protocols often sponsored by government authorities. Perhaps no one event in particular deters today's patient from seeking treatment, but the totality of these repeated degradations of the health status of people of color have contributed to a generalized race- and ethnicity-based suspicion of the practice of medicine. While some may argue that conducting oneself according to distant events is itself an unhealthy approach to today's medical setting, others point out that the disparate and disparaging treatment of minorities, particularly poor women of color, is hardly a relic of history. A brief review of well-documented events provides the historic timeline upon which contemporary mistrust rests.

In Chapter 2 we explored the tenets and manifestations of the American eugenics movement and its obsession with controlling human reproduction to promote a social agenda. Vital among eugenics tactics were laws and policies that inhibited, and often prevented, procreation by racial and ethnic minorities. The fear of "race suicide" by favored procreators (that is, mostly well-to-do U.S.-born whites) inspired myriad laws regulating immigration and interracial marriage, enacted with the aim of staving off the birth of "undesirables." The racist legacy of the eugenics period persisted even after many aspects of the movement were discredited by their Nazi embrace during World War II. But race prejudice in America is embedded in our nation's founding, gaining strength as an institution during our long acceptance of slavery—a practice that was barely in the past when eugenics first emerged on the scene. In fact, the short chronologic link between slavery and eugenics is joined on the other end by a forty-year assault on the reproductive health of African American men known as the Tuskegee syphilis experiment.

In 1932, the U.S. Public Health Service (PHS) initiated a clinical study to observe the natural course of untreated syphilis in a group of black men. Scientific thinking at the time was that race played a role in the effect and natural progression of the disease. The PHS solicited participation by the Tuskegee Institute, a well-known historically black college in Alabama. The study began during the Great Depression by recruiting poor black men—four hundred diagnosed with syphilis and two hundred control patients—to receive free health examinations, rides to and from the clinic, hot meals, and treatment for minor ailments. The observation study continued even after the discovery of penicillin as a safe and effective treatment for syphilis in the late 1940s.[48] More shocking to today's medical ethics sensibilities, the study persisted until 1972, when a whistleblower recounted the horrifying details to the national media.[49] By that time, nearly 130 of the original subjects had died of the disease or related complications, forty of their wives had been infected, and nineteen of their children were born with congenital syphilis.

Public outrage over the revelation shut down the Tuskegee experiment in one day, but the impacts have been long lasting.[50] Numerous studies, reports, and personal narratives document Tuskegee's damaging impact on the black community's trust of U.S. public health efforts, including outreach to encourage preventive care and recruitment for medical research.[51] One commentator, reflecting on the "egregious missteps in U.S. history" in the medical realm visited upon African Americans, starkly concludes, "Some black folks just don't trust the core institutions that are created to serve the public good, and chief among them may be our health care system."[52]

The forty-year Tuskegee study is now more than four decades past, meaning that the vast majority of men and women of color experiencing infertility today were not even alive when the events were taking place or being contemporaneously discussed. Yet contemporary studies documenting disparities in infertility care along racial and ethnic lines continue to highlight Tuskegee as a factor in minority health-related behavior today.[53] In the ART context, Roberts surmises, "Considering the history of sickle-cell screening, the Tuskegee syphilis experiment, and other medical abuses, many Blacks harbor a well-founded distrust of technological interference with their bodies and genetic material at the hands of white physicians."[54] The sickle-cell screening to which Roberts refers is a 1970s program that screened blacks for the sickle trait, ultimately leading to employment and insurance discrimination as well as restrictions on reproductive decision making among the black community.[55] While Roberts does not elaborate on "other medical abuses" in this particular piece, she and others have amply documented the ways in which women of color disproportionately experience the degradation of their reproductive freedom.

One such scholar, Michelle Oberman, notes the historic link between the aforementioned governmental reproduction-related policies and contemporary efforts to regulate the reproductive lives of women of color. She offers as evidence the uneven enforcement of pregnancy-related substance abuse laws against poor women of color. "Long after being discredited on medical and public health grounds, criminal justice officials have persisted in prosecuting 'pregnant addicts,' focusing on public hospitals used disproportionately by poor women of color who use street drugs," she writes.[56] The statistics are telling: at the national level, 70 percent of criminal cases involving prenatal drug exposure also involved black defendants. And despite a higher rate of drug use among white women, black women are ten times more likely to be reported to authorities.[57] This culture of criminalization around the behavior of poor minority pregnant women has invaded the physician-patient relationship, creating a chilling effect on drug-dependent women's willingness to seek prenatal care. Physician conduct is affected as well, reducing doctors "to the role of drug informants or snitches and the physician-patient relationship is reduced to nothing higher than candy-shop owner-consumer relationship."[58] The perception of physicians as law enforcement rather than health enhancement is instructive in understanding the community of color's reticence to entrust their reproductive futures to the practice of medicine.

From forced sterilizations during the eugenics movement to the intentional deprivation of known cures for sexually transmitted diseases to heightened policing of the womb, minorities who experience infertility are reasonably haunted by a history of medical professionals devaluing and outright abusing their reproductive desires. This legacy "draws upon and reinforces dominant ideals of motherhood, which include ideas about who is and is not fit to be a mother, and about whose offspring are a social benefit and whose are not."[59] History cannot be rewritten, but it can be understood and heeded in contemporary practice. So the question arises, how do today's ART providers regard the fertility treatment needs of minority men and women? Since physicians often occupy a gatekeeper role in the provision of infertility care, knowing their attitudes and practices with respect to distinct patient cohorts would be useful in further understanding race and ethnicity as a barrier to ART care.

GATEKEEPER FACTORS

As a general matter, setting aside for now matters of contracted obligations and anti-discrimination laws, physicians are free to treat or refuse to treat a prospective patient in search of care. Thus, fertility clinics and the providers who operate them can play an essential role in controlling access to ART in their local communities and, collectively, at the national level. At least three factors can be plumbed for impacts on access to care stratified by race and ethnicity: (1) the location of fertility clinics vis-à-vis minority populations, (2) clinic and physician outreach to people of color who may be experiencing infertility, and (3) clinic and physician policies and practices as applied to prospective minority patients in search of care. Let's briefly consider each factor.

Approximately five hundred ART clinics are operating in the United States today, with at least one clinic located in every state except Wyoming.[60] Despite the presence of at least one clinic in almost every state, the geographic distribution of ART centers does not provide equal access to service for every patient who could benefit from fertility care. Disparities in treatment opportunity abound due to geographical factors, with clinics clustering in regions and areas that attract mostly middle- and upper-middle-class patients.[61] In one study investigating the spatial disparity of ART centers based on their location in relation to the population of reproductive age, researchers found that many areas in the United States were either significantly under- or over-served by existing clinics. Using a measure of sixty minutes' driving time to a clinic, the study revealed that as many as six states were under- or poorly served (including Alaska, Montana, Wyoming, and West Virginia), while five states were over-served, with greater than 95 percent of the reproductive-age population living within sixty minutes of an ART center (including Connecticut, New Jersey, and Washington, D.C.).[62]

The above study did not investigate the role of population, race, or ethnicity in relation to clinic location, so any conclusions from the reported data would be entirely speculative. An admittedly less academically rigorous investigation via a few Google searches does shed some light on the relationship between clinic location and stratified access along racial and ethnic lines. A website tracking ART clinics across the country offers links to specified geographic areas. A search for clinics in Los Angeles County displays eight ART establishments with clinics in thirteen locations.[63] Those clinics are clustered in the west Los Angeles and southern San Fernando Valley areas (Beverly Hills, Santa Monica, Encino, Tarzana), which are inhabited by a majority white population (85 percent). In contrast, there are no fertility clinics located in South Los Angeles (57 percent Latino and 38 percent black) or Southeast Los Angeles (70 percent Latino, 7 percent black, and 14 percent white).[64] Given that engaging in fertility treatment involves numerous trips to a medical facility for tests, treatments, and follow-ups, geography matters to patients. Having to travel even thirty miles from South or East Los Angeles to a clinic on the Westside (traversing that epic parking lot otherwise known as the L.A. freeways) is an ordeal that could intimidate even the most determined patient. Never mind that a woman would have to arrange significant time away from work or, heaven forbid in the City of Angels, take public transportation. The point can be comfortably made—clinic location likely contributes to lower access to ART care for minority patients.

Even if clinics are not located in areas where prospective minority patients reside, clinics could devote resources and efforts to outreach in these underserved communities. In the main, we know that fertility clinics actively market their services in an attempt to gain market share.[65] Kimberly Krawiec describes the "elaborate marketing efforts" ART clinics engage in to attract patients. "These efforts include hiring high-priced marketing consultants; advertising on billboards, the radio, newspapers, and magazines; and assiduously courting physician referrals by 'wining and dining' doctors and hosting dinners and parties at medical meetings."[66] Do these efforts include outreach to minority patients? At least one measure—clinic websites—suggests ART clinics do little to attract patients of color.

Since at least the dawn of the twenty-first century, the majority of patients and potential patients from all socioeconomic levels have used the Internet to research their infertility issues.[67] Knowing that generally the first place a person experiencing infertility goes is online, Jim Hawkins conducted an empirical assessment of the advertising displayed on fertility clinics' websites. One of his queries centered on the racial and ethnic diversity, or lack thereof, of images shown on the home pages of clinic websites. Hawkins viewed nearly three hundred ART clinic websites, finding that 63 percent presented pictures of only white babies on the home page, while 1 percent presented images of only black babies, or only Asian babies, or only Latino babies.[68] Looking for pictures with babies of different races, 97 percent of all websites visited contained an image of at least one white baby in the group. What does this mean? As a preliminary response, Hawkins discusses the possibility that the image disparities help explain usage disparities because "pictures of white babies give social proof to white individuals considering fertility care but not to people who are of other races, driving up the number of white patients and driving down the number of patients from other races."[69]

Thereafter, Hawkins suggests a deeper, darker theory; clinics are purposefully using the race of babies to draw in white patients, "confirming the charge of some academics who argue that fertility treatments entrench racist norms."[70] Relying on the social psychology theory that people are inclined to like people who are similar to them, Hawkins surmises that clinics' tendencies to advertise with a high percentage of white-only baby images is designed to create a "halo effect" for the clinic in the minds of white patients. Correspondingly, minority patients find it harder to imagine themselves patronizing a "whites only" clinic, even sensing an abjectly dismissive attitude toward their infertility. Other researchers who have noted the "whiteness" of fertility clinic advertising and the homogeneity of infertility depiction in general as a Caucasian-only issue charge that such behavior imposes an invisibility and marginalization on infertile minority individuals and couples. The lack of pictorial representation of people of color in the infertility narrative makes them invisible, unimportant, and shunned, sending a message that their childbearing is unwelcome in the ART world.[71]

The final feature of our gatekeeper analysis interrogates whether individual physicians or ART practices evince an unwillingness or reticence to treat minority patients. In Chapter 3 we noted that access to fertility treatment is highly correlated with a person's wealth status and that even a prospective patient's source of wealth can serve as a barrier to obtaining care. Survey data suggest that nearly half of all physician respondents said they would refuse to treat a couple whose income source is some form of public assistance. Interestingly, the survey did query physicians about whether they would turn away a "biracial couple," and 100 percent responded that they were "not at all or slightly likely to turn away" such a couple. But can public assistance serve as a proxy for race and ethnicity such that physicians and clinic policies that refuse service on the basis of income source are in effect turning away patients on the basis of race or ethnicity? Statistically, minorities represent a larger percentage of Americans receiving public assistance than their overall representation in the population. These numbers suggest that public assistance could be a pretext for discrimination on the basis of minority status.

Another aspect of the role that individual physicians might play in suppressing access for patients of color centers on the charge that providers steer minority patients away from fertility treatments. Earlier we noted lower referral rates of minority patients to infertility specialists from primary care physicians, as well as a tendency for physicians to diagnose nonconceiving women of color with conditions other than treatable infertility. When a minority patient does get referred to an infertility specialist for treatment, how welcome is she likely to feel? Chances are, her physician will neither look like her nor, in some cases, talk like her. Another portion of Hawkins's study looked at the demographic profile of ART providers. First, he reviewed clinic websites to see how many practices advertised multilingual capacity. He found only 16 percent of clinics offered services in multiple languages.[72] For non-English-speaking patients, the inability to communicate with clinic physicians and staff would certainly pose huge barriers to access.[73]

Hawkins was also interested in determining the racial and ethnic makeup of fertility care providers. He discovered that racial and ethnic diversity among ART physicians is low. Using pictures and last names to identify the race of doctors featured on each clinic's website, Hawkins was able to determine the race of 1,124 reproductive endocrinologists on clinics' websites. His data showed that 80 percent were white, 8 percent Asian, 4 percent Latino, and 2 percent black.[74] These figures are quite disparate from the racial and ethnic makeup of the U.S. population (12 percent black, 16 percent Latino, for example), as well as the percentage of minority women (among all women of reproductive age) who experience infertility. Such a demographic disconnect between patients and providers could be a deterrent for women seeking greater familiarity and comfort with the person with whom they will interact on such an intimate and personal level.

The Road Ahead: Destratifying Assisted Reproduction

The stratification of assisted reproduction along racial and ethnic lines has recently come into clear view, with initial suspicions that infertility among people of color was addressed far less often than it was among white populations confirmed by numerous research protocols. Studies published over the past decade uniformly show that minorities experience infertility at proportionately greater rates than nonminorities, seek treatment later and less often, have poorer outcomes when treatment is sought, and are more challenged to afford and access available care. Placing infertility into a larger health care context, we also know that "disparities related to race, ethnicity and socioeconomic status pervade the American healthcare system."[75] According to the *National Healthcare Disparities Report,* "African American and Hispanic individuals hav[e] worse access to care 40% and 90% of the time, respectively, compared to Caucasians." These two groups also have worse quality of care, 66 percent and 50 percent of the time, respectively. Investigation into the reasons for these disparities reveals a combination of physiological, environmental, cultural, historical, and structural factors that coalesce around the fact that minorities face significantly greater barriers to ART than whites.

Numerous and varied solutions have been proposed to remedy disparities in health care in general and ART in particular. As to general health care disparities, Ruqaiijah Yearby observes that racially unequal access to health care is attributable to three factors: (1) interpersonal racial bias (conscious and/or unconscious racial prejudice exhibited by physicians toward minority patients that influences treatment decisions), (2) institutional racial bias (closing and relocation of health care facilities away from minority communities), and (3) structural racial bias (a health care system based on ability to pay rather than need for treatment).[76] Yearby traces the racial stratification of health care in the United States from the Civil War to the enactment of the Affordable Care Act in 2010, lamenting that despite its mentioned concern for disparities in health care, the ACA may only serve to exacerbate existing inequalities by relying on individual and community rather than systemic solutions.[77] Yearby proposes a host of reforms, including education efforts aimed at physicians (to expose and sensitize them to their racial prejudice in the medical setting) and patients (to provide coping strategies to minimize the stress of perceived racial bias) and enhancements to civil rights frameworks that detect and punish discrimination in the health care setting.[78]

Are education efforts and enhanced regulatory enforcement of racially biased conduct suitable or advisable in the context of assisted reproduction? As to education, logic and experience dictate that knowing more about ourselves and others better informs our decisions and actions. Teaching physicians, ideally early in their training, about the cultural and historic background that accompanies minority patients' medical decision making may pave the way for a better, healthier relationship at the bedside. Reproductive endocrinologists graduating into the ART workplace today may know little or nothing about Tuskegee, sickle-cell screening, the treatment of pregnant substance abusers, or the myriad other examples of racial harm in the medical setting. Particularly if physicians are raised outside the United States, their exposure to these pieces of American history and practice may be quite limited. But this lack of knowledge is likely not as prevalent among today's minority patients. Even if a prospective patient never formally studied history or had any negative interactions in the health care arena, the story of racial bias in medicine has probably been conveyed as part of the community's history. As members of whatever community we hail from or join, an aspect of that membership is being exposed to the group's history, traumas and all. Today's minority Millennials should be regarded to be as sensitized to their forebearers' experiences as their parents and grandparents.

The second prong of education—educating infertility patients—is equally vital to remedying racial disparities in ART care. Teaching teenage girls about gynecologic health and its implications for future fertility would seem a good and noncontroversial idea. The American Society for Reproductive Medicine certainly thought so in 2001 when it launched a public health campaign to create awareness of certain preventable causes of infertility, including smoking, obesity, and sexually transmitted diseases.[79] Imagine ASRM's surprise when it was criticized for focusing too much on the small percentage of infertility that is preventable, arguably causing greater stigma to infertility attributable to congenital conditions.[80] The public awareness campaign was further derailed when shopping malls and movie theaters (where young women congregate) refused to post the ads, judging they were neither family-friendly nor entertaining.[81] While ASRM still maintains a fact sheet on its website detailing the causes of—and possible steps to avoid—infertility, patients must be proactive in accessing this information.

Despite the backlash ASRM received for its attempt to educate the public about preventable infertility, targeted educational outreach still strikes me as a good idea. Since we know that minority women wait on average eighteen months longer than nonminority women to seek treatment for infertility, why not create and distribute pamphlets (and Internet equivalents) about the risks of delaying care if one desires to have a child? These efforts may be especially important in states that mandate insurance coverage or near military installments where reimbursement is fairly robust. The fact that treatment-seeking among minority patients in some equal-access-to-care settings (where affordability is mediated) is lower than their proportional population in the community suggests that educational outreach could have an impact.

Regulatory reforms to address racial disparities in assisted reproduction raise a different set of concerns than educational outreach. Regulating access to ART may touch upon the individual's right to procreative liberty, described by John Robertson as "a negative right against state interference with choices to procreate or to avoid procreation."[82] Procreative liberty, according to Robertson, is not "a positive right to have the state or particular persons provide the means or resources necessary to have or avoid having children."[83] Thus, regulation that aims to increase or provide the means of reproduction to some individuals, even in an attempt to equalize access to all, could infringe on others' procreative liberty and thus face constitutional challenge. As Dorothy Roberts reminds us, giving in to government regulation of an individual for the betterment of a group "was the rationale justifying eugenic sterilization laws enacted" in the early twentieth century.[84] "Governments," she warns, "have perpetuated as much injustice on the theory that individual interest must be sacrificed for the public good as they have on the theory that equality must be sacrificed for individual liberty."[85] For this reason, we are wise to eschew regulatory solutions that, even if well-meaning efforts to adjust maldistribution of fertility services, have the potential to limit or diminish individual access to lawful ART.

Even though the causes and explanations for stratification of assisted reproduction along racial and ethnic lines are a complex matrix of historic and contemporary factors, the single most achievable solution is greater affordability for all. While the Affordable Care Act, as it stands today, can be considered a missed opportunity to address disparities in access to ART, other avenues remain open. Efforts should include a broad-based approach, including educating lawmakers about the racial impact that lack of state-mandated coverage imposes, explaining in public forums the low cost and public health benefits achieved through statewide coverage, urging Congress to allocate greater public spending on combating infertility through prevention, detection, and treatment, just as they have done in the military, lobbying insurance companies and self-insured employers to offer broader coverage, and even opening a dialogue with physicians about fee structures that increase overall access to treatment. Any one, and certainly all, of these efforts combined could begin to break the logjam that now stands between too many patients and parenthood.

Social Infertility and the Quest for Parenthood

Central to this book's theme is the notion that lovemaking is overrated as a method of procreation. Overrated may be an overstatement, but for many couples, their physical expressions of love will never yield a baby. The largest faction of this cohort consists of the medically infertile—those who lack the physical capacity to accomplish the reproductive cycle of conception, gestation, and childbirth through heterosexual intercourse. We know that roughly 10 million Americans suffer from medical infertility, of which only a small percentage ever seek medical assistance.[1] The other faction of the "nonproductive lovemaking" cohort includes those with social infertility—the inability to conceive and maintain a pregnancy within a particular social structure without medical assistance. People with social infertility may or may not be medically infertile, but the structure of their intimate social relationships, or lack thereof, make sexual reproduction an impossibility. The socially infertile include single and transgender individuals and same-sex couples who lack natural access to the necessary ingredients of reproduction in their intimate associations.[2] Who and whether we love can significantly affect our paths to family formation.

The more senior among us might recall that iconic pop culture moment when Vice President Dan Quayle chided fictional television personality Murphy Brown for choosing to become a single mother. In her namesake show, the always articulate and confident yet unmarried news anchor gave birth in 1992, provoking the Veep to admonish Ms. Brown for "mocking the importance of fathers by bearing a child alone and calling it 'just another lifestyle choice.'"[3] Gone are the days when single motherhood could provoke a national debate—or are they? Today over 40 percent of U.S. births are to unmarried women, suggesting a certain routineness, or perhaps even acceptance, of a child being born to and reared by only one parent.[4] In addition to the growth in single parenthood, the nation has witnessed a seismic shift in the civil and marital rights of gay and lesbian Americans, rights that are enmeshed in these individuals' procreative aspirations. But survey data, case law, and statutory enactments tell us that so-called nontraditional parenthood via ART is not as easily achieved as demographic statistics might suggest.

Children conceived and born outside our deeply rooted comfort zone of traditional marriage and heteronormative behavior stir concerns even when such happenings are no longer isolated. While current trends in the legal and policy arenas provide hope that the dignity and desire surrounding single and LGBT parenthood will soon enjoy recognition equal to that accorded traditional family formation, setbacks remind us that a long journey remains. In November 2014, a federal appeals court bucked a several-year trend among sister courts by upholding same-sex marriage bans in several states.[5] While the ruling was later reversed by the U.S. Supreme Court in a 5–4 decision upholding the constitutional liberty of same-sex couples to marry, for our purposes the lower court's reasoning is evidence that procreation outside traditional marriage continues to provoke deep suspicion. In upholding the states' ban on same-sex marriage, the court explained:

> By creating a status (marriage) and by subsidizing it (e.g., with tax-filing privileges and deductions), the States created an incentive for two people who procreate together to stay together for purposes of rearing offspring. That does not convict the States of irrationality, only of awareness of the

biological reality that couples of the same sex do not have children in the same way as couples of opposite sexes and that couples of the same sex do not run the risk of unintended offspring. That explanation, still relevant today, suffices to allow the States to retain authority over an issue they have regulated from the beginning.[6]

The "biological reality" the court references has long been overcome by single individuals and same-sex couples through ART. For these parents, their reality is that reproductive medicine enables them to "have children in the same way as couples of opposite sexes"—via conception, gestation, and childbirth. The only difference is the technique used for combining the egg and sperm that initiates the procreative process. As this chapter explores, this difference is the source of disparate treatment by physicians and lawmakers whose alliance perpetuates a significant barrier to ART access for those who experience social infertility.

The Clinical Landscape

Treatment for social infertility dots a wide spectrum, from simply requesting a friend or relative supply sperm for do-it-yourself (DIY) insemination to enduring the physical and financial difficulties of egg donation, IVF, or gestational surrogacy. Even when a simple DIY insemination will suffice, single women and lesbian couples are often advised to involve a licensed physician for both medical and legal reasons.[7] Thus, ART providers play a significant role in the treatment of social infertility. By virtue of their unique expertise and state-issued medical license, reproductive medicine specialists occupy a powerful gatekeeping role in the lives of the socially infertile. This gatekeeping role, coupled with the American health care system's deference to physician autonomy, imbues ART providers with enormous discretion over who can and cannot access the tools to biological parenthood. Research and anecdotal evidence alert us to the ways in which this power has been wielded in response to treatment requests from those outside traditional family paradigms.

BEWARE THE PERILS OF GAMETE FRIENDING

Not everyone with social infertility needs medical assistance to reproduce. Today a single woman or lesbian couple can procure sperm without parental attachment of the donor from at least two sources. First,
women can purchase sperm from the comfort of home through any
number of online commercial sperm banks. It is estimated there are
seven hundred such banks in the United States, and business is boom-
ing. One estimate pegs the sperm procurement and distribution industry revenue at $320 million annually and growing.[8] In Chapter 3
we discussed the risks, benefits, and economics of at-home insemination using sperm purchased from a commercial bank. For women who
want the security of (hopefully) thorough FDA-guided screening and
no interaction with the gamete provider, DIY insemination with commercially purchased sperm is a good option. A second route is through
directed donation in which a known male agrees to provide sperm for
the woman's reproductive purposes, typically waiving any claim to future parenthood of the resulting offspring. While this type of "gamete
friending" can be less expensive, it carries distinct drawbacks.

Barriers to DIY insemination with purchased anonymous sperm
are low. Commercial sperm banks report that about half of their clientele are single women and lesbian couples,[9] most of whom report satisfaction with the services and outcome they experienced.[10] While usage
and subsequent births are not measured in any formal way (in contrast
to IVF usage, which federal law mandates be collected and published
annually), it is estimated that artificial insemination by donor accounts
for sixty thousand births annually—roughly the same as the number of
infants born each year via IVF.[11] The main limitations are cost and efficacy. As we have seen, a single cycle of AID with sperm purchased from
a commercial bank can run around $2,000. For some women, this price
tag strains or exceeds their financial resources, causing them to either
forgo the reproductive opportunity or turn to a known donor who may
be willing to truly donate his sperm. Even if a woman has the resources
to purchase sperm for several attempts, she may not be able to conceive
in this fashion. Studies suggest that success rates for at-home insemination hover at around 13 percent per cycle, lower than the 20 percent

chance of conceiving through timed intercourse.[12] The inability of a person with social infertility to conceive is not rare, given the incidence of medical infertility in the general population.

Insemination using sperm from a known donor can be less expensive at the outset, but may generate enormous financial, medical, and legal costs down the road. The initial attraction for single women and lesbian couples is obvious—ask a relative, friend, or even stranger (perhaps solicited online) to donate for no or minimal remuneration. If proffered medical records assure the donor's health, many proceed to the agreed-upon exchange. Published stories detailing these exchanges reveal questionable hygienics, with donors tendering plastic cups assembled for use in the back of campers or at a Starbucks restroom.[13] A more cautious recipient might seek to establish the man's suitability, paying for semen analysis that yields information about the donor's potential infectious and genetic makeup. While extremely rare, instances of disease transmission from donor sperm have been reported.[14]

In such informal exchanges all may end well, but too many of these casual arrangements have gone awry, weaving an unmistakable cautionary tale. We already met the lesbian couple that placed an ad for a sperm donor on Craigslist. A Good Samaritan came forward and agreed to provide his sperm at no cost, helping the women have their much desired child. Trouble visited the happy family three years after their daughter's birth when the mothers separated and the State of Kansas successfully pursued the donor for child support, reasoning that because the women had not used a licensed physician for their "treatment," the law regarded the man as the child's father.[15] Needless to say, the women's initial thriftiness ended up costing them dearly—not to mention reifying the adage "no good deed goes unpunished."

Kansas is not the only state in which self-help for social infertility can spring hidden costs and unwelcome parentage awards on unsuspecting participants. At least ten states with laws on the parentage of sperm donor–conceived children require the presence of a licensed physician to relieve the man of potential parental responsibility.[16] These laws, in effect, pose a structural barrier to parenthood for single women and lesbian couples who lack the resources or desire to involve a medical provider in their reproductive lives. In these cases, and in cases of unanticipated medical infertility, a physician's expertise is essential to family building for unpartnered women and same-sex female couples. The group of parenthood-seeking, medically dependent socially infertile grows when single men and same-sex male couples are added to the mix. Considering the diffuse medical needs of the socially infertile, a skilled ART provider is critical to these would-be parents' success. Whether and under what circumstances physician specialists agree to treat patients in varying social structures reveals much about barriers to ART based on marital status and sexual orientation.

PHYSICIANS AS THE RELATIONSHIP POLICE

Once a person without an opposite-sex spouse is thrust into the ART world, how likely is it that person will be turned away by a provider based on her relationship status? For better or worse, the answer is occasionally. Despite the prevalence of marriage-less parenthood and the legality of same-sex marriage, a subset of ART providers expresses discomfort in aiding unmarried women, men, or same-sex couples to achieve their parental dreams. Two sources reveal this minority, but extant, physician attitude and subsequent refusal to treat: attitudinal surveys and a smattering of lawsuits brought by patients who challenged their treatment denial as a form of unlawful discrimination. The most well known case in this latter category made its way to the California Supreme Court in 2008. In *North Coast Women's Care Medical Group, Inc. v. San Diego County Superior Court*,[17] we meet Guadalupe ("Lupita") Benitez and Joanne Clark, a lesbian couple in need of reproductive medical assistance after Lupita failed to conceive following several home insemination attempts using commercially acquired sperm. As it turned out, Lupita suffered from both social and medical infertility; she was diagnosed with polycystic ovarian syndrome, a condition associated with irregular or absent ovulation.

In 1999, the couple made an appointment at the North Coast facility, meeting with Dr. Christine Brody. At their initial meeting, Dr. Brody told the female pair that should Lupita require invasive treatment for her infertility—referencing intrauterine inseminations (IUI)—the doctor's "religious beliefs would preclude her from performing the procedure."[18]

Dr. Brody added that another physician in the practice shared her religious objection, but at least one other doctor in the practice could assist. After numerous months of simple insemination failed, Lupita sought IUI from the medical group. Ultimately, the physicians at North Coast refused to offer treatment, referring her to another provider outside the practice.

In August 2001, Lupita sued North Coast and two of its physicians for sexual orientation discrimination in violation of California's Unruh Civil Rights Act. As an aside, throughout the litigation the parties disputed whether Dr. Brody's treatment refusal was on the basis of the patient's marital status (as alleged by the physician) or sexual orientation (as alleged by the patient). At the time the events transpired California law did not prohibit discrimination in the provision of medical services on the basis of marital status, thus each party's pleading strategy is apparent. Since the case reached the California Supreme Court before a trial on the merits was held, the court deferred to the plaintiff's pleading as a claim for sexual orientation discrimination.[19]

The physicians defended their actions as a protected exercise of their constitutional rights of free speech and religious freedom. They argued these rights exempted them from complying with the Unruh Civil Rights Act's prohibition against sexual orientation discrimination.[20] Thus, the case weighed a patient's right to access nondiscriminatory treatment against a physician's right to assert a professional objection based on a personal religious belief. In a unanimous decision, the court ruled that the rights of religious freedom and free speech, as guaranteed in both the federal and state constitutions, do not exempt physicians from complying with the state's civil rights laws' prohibition against discrimination based on a person's sexual orientation. Citing U.S. Supreme Court precedent, the California high court explained that the First Amendment right to the free exercise of religion does not relieve an individual of the obligation to comply with a valid and neutral law of general applicability on the ground that the law is contrary to the objector's religious beliefs. The Unruh Act was deemed such a law of valid and neutral character.

At the end of the opinion, the court offers some practical advice to the objecting physicians. To alleviate any internal conflict between their religious beliefs and state law, the objecting physicians can simply refuse to perform ART medical procedures for *any* patient, or can refer any objectionable patient to another physician in the group.[21] Essentially, the court acknowledges that physicians can "discriminate" against a procedure—as is widely done by providers who refuse to perform abortion or dispense certain types of contraception—but cannot discriminate against a person. Depriving someone of a needed medical procedure because of who they are sits at the very heart of eugenic practice.

Lupita and Joanne's odyssey eventually took them through several rounds of costly and unreimbursed IVF with a willing provider, yielding a son and twin daughters.[22] Nine years after the case was brought, the parties settled the litigation for "an undisclosed sum of money."[23] In reflecting on the case, Lupita described "the indignity of being turned away." As she succinctly stated, "It does do a great deal of damage to a person when you tell them they aren't worthy of having a child or having a family."[24] Lupita and Joanne's journey of indignity was quite public and, fortunately for them, ended well. But such happy endings are not necessarily common, as these deprivative policies often remain in the shadows. Only through the sporadic lawsuit, or mention of a "married only" policy in reported cases, do we learn the extent of deprivation in the legal domain.[25] A more robust source for understanding the clinical landscape surrounding treatment for those with social infertility can be found in surveys conducted among ART providers. One oft-cited study provides some interesting and disturbing findings.

In 2005, researchers at the University of Pennsylvania conducted a survey to determine the screening practices and beliefs of ART providers in the United States.[26] Their work was motivated by a set of observations that remain true today: (1) U.S. ART providers operate in a relatively low regulatory environment, leaving individual practices and physicians at liberty to set their own boundaries; (2) private restrictions can intrude on fundamental freedoms by placing an unfair burden on those not fortunate enough to be able to have children without medical assistance; (3) imposed barriers can result in a dual standard for parenthood as applied to fertile and infertile prospective parents; (4) without national or consistent guidelines, infertile individuals face the prospect of unequal treatment among ART practices; and (5) the unintended consequences of allowing providers to dictate the qualifications for parenthood could translate into discriminatory or eugenic practices. Giving physicians the power to control the reproductive lives of the less powerful was certainly thematic in the American eugenics movement.

The survey asked about a wide range of topics, including physician attitudes toward their role in assisting a person to have a child. When asked whether "everyone has a right to have a child," 59 percent agreed or strongly agreed with this sentiment. Yet when asked whether it was "acceptable for me to consider a parent's fitness before helping them conceive a child," a full 70 percent agreed or strongly agreed with this position.[27] Nearly the same percentage ratcheted this consideration to a duty, agreeing that ART providers have "the responsibility to consider a parent's fitness before helping them conceive."[28] In an effort to discern the providers' definition of parental fitness, the researchers posed a series of hypothetical scenarios and queried whether the physician was likely to treat or decline to treat in each case. While a host of patient features were included in the survey, we will limit our discussion here to the results dealing with social infertility.

In the marital status category, one in five respondents (20 percent) said they would be "very or extremely likely to turn away" a woman who does not have a husband or partner. Over half (53 percent) said they would be very or extremely likely to turn away a man who does not have a wife or partner. Note the obvious gender stereotyping about parental fitness embedded in these responses. In the sexual orientation category, nearly one in five (17 percent) said they would not treat a lesbian couple who wanted to use donor insemination, and 48 percent answered they would decline service to a gay male couple wanting to use a surrogate, with one of the men serving as the sperm source. Follow-up research has confirmed this extreme discrimination against gay men in search of reproductive assistance, despite companion studies that show this cohort gives the idea of parenthood "much more thought than do heterosexual men and are more likely than heterosexual fathers to express 'the higher status accorded to parents than non-parents' as a motivation for having children."[29]

Granted, the Penn survey discussed above is now over a decade old and might look very different today, but in all likelihood some portion of the respondents would remain steadfast in their beliefs. While the Penn survey has not since been updated and no similarly robust survey has been published, the CDC does collect annual data on ART clinic policies on providing fertility care to at least one social infertility cohort—single women. The good news is that the number of clinics that report a willingness to service single women (undefined—so it could include partnered but unmarried women) has steadily risen since publication of the Penn data. In 2006, 90 percent of the 426 reporting clinics answered they do provide service to single women (compared with 80 percent in the 2005 Penn survey).[30] By 2013, that number rose to 96 percent of 467 reporting clinics.[31] The bad news is that there remain any clinics that refuse to treat single women, and the lack of data collection on the availability of service to other cohorts including single men, gay male couples, lesbian couples, or same-sex married couples.[32] Further, in any given reporting year around 10 percent of operating ART clinics decline to report their data to the CDC; thus, the number of physicians withholding service could be much greater.

These data points setting out the clinical landscape on access to ART for unmarried and LGBT patients tell us *what* is happening, but they don't tell us *why*. Delving into a provider's beliefs and motivations is a far more difficult task, but one that several researchers have undertaken. As the next section shows, treatment denials for social infertility are usually explained by provider concern for the welfare of offspring and deeply held views about parental entitlement in this community. Alone or in combination, these factors create significant barriers to family formation for those whose only route is via a medical provider.

REASONS FOR TREATMENT DENIALS

Why does a segment of ART doctors refuse to treat social infertility? Provider decisions to withhold fertility services dwell in the interlocking worlds of physician autonomy, paternalism, contractual obligations, and anti-discrimination legal regimes. Saving for later a more in-depth discussion of each of these factors, let's proceed by assuming that a physician is under no contractual duty to provide care (such as in a health maintenance organization [HMO] or managed care arrangement) and that the authentic, non-pretextual reason for treatment refusal does not trigger liability under prevailing federal or state anti-discrimination laws. In that case, the likely foundation for a treatment refusal is the physician's belief either that: (1) any child born to the inquiring individual(s) will be harmed by their rearing, or (2) the prospective parents are not suitable for parenthood and should not be assisted in bringing a child into the world. Both rationales are rooted in protectionism, with the former professing concern for the health and safety of a child born to particular parents, and the latter expressing concern for society's well-being should a child of these particular parents be born. Child welfare and parental entitlement justifications for ART treatment denials are equally problematic, yet research suggests both are prevalent in contemporary practice.

Turning first to child welfare concerns, social science research reveals some members of society in general and providers in particular harbor concerns that children born outside of married, heterosexual relationships will suffer from a lack of "normal upbringing." These concerns hover over unpartnered women who are single parents by choice, over lesbian couples who wish to raise fatherless children, over single and partnered gay men whose motherless environment garners particular suspicion. Much of these concerns arise from entrenched stereotypes that continue to suppress social acceptance of so-called nontraditional families. Commonly expressed concerns include that children of single or lesbian mothers will lack essential male role models; that children of gay and lesbian parents will experience social isolation and gender-identity or sexual-orientation problems; that children of gay fathers are more likely to become gay themselves; and that gay males are likely to be sexual predators who may molest their own children.[33]

This notion that children thrive only in a family dynamic with a married father and mother, and correspondingly that children are harmed by being reared in alternative environments, has been studied and rejected by decades of research. In its recent assessment of the rights of LGBT and unmarried persons to secure fertility care, the ASRM

Ethics Committee noted the stated child welfare concerns expressed by opponents and concluded, "The evidence to date, however, cannot reasonably be interpreted to support such fears."[34] In fact, reliance on these stereotypic characterizations is of dissipating value and persuasiveness, as numerous studies continue to reveal that unmarried individuals and same-sex couples produce the same parenting outcomes as their married opposite-sex counterparts, and that children of these "nontraditional" parents fare equally well (and equally badly) as children of wed heterosexual parents.[35] These findings are supported by numerous leaders in the child psychology field, including the Child Welfare League of America, the American Academy of Pediatrics, the American Academy of Family Physicians, the American Psychiatric Association, and others.[36] In contrast, earlier studies suggesting LGBT parenting was harmful to children have been repudiated as based on flawed study methodologies.[37] Like the eugenic reliance on assuredness of complete trait heredity, today's ART world must endure missteps and misrepresentations in the scientific certainty surrounding parental fitness.

Assuming that providers are aware of the data making clear that a parent's marital status or sexual orientation does not, on its own, negatively impact child welfare, what other rationales would a physician have to decline treatment on this basis? Here we turn to physician discomfort with the entitlement of every person to pursue parenthood as an individual right. As reported in the Penn survey, ART providers express a variety of perspectives on the question of parental fitness and the provision of fertility services. In addition to parts of the survey discussed above, it is noteworthy that less than half of all physician respondents (44 percent) believed they did "not have the right to decide who is and is not a fit parent."[38] What the survey did not specifically probe was whether the providers believed a patient's marital status or sexual orientation interacted with that person's prospective parental fitness. While most clinics do collect information on this demographic data (95 percent ask about marital status and 66 percent inquire about sexual orientation), there was no empirical data linking these features with the respondents' definition of parental fitness.

We may not be able to cite substantial empirical data proving that ART denials for the treatment of social infertility arise from physician discomfort with an unmarried or gay person's entitlement to be a parent, but anecdotal evidence suggests this might be true in some cases. In 2010, the ASRM Ethics Committee published its report titled *Access to Fertility Treatment by Gays, Lesbians, and Unmarried Persons*, urging ART programs to "treat all requests for assisted reproduction equally without regard to marital/partner status or sexual orientation."[39] After the report was published, the hosting journal received letters in response, at least one of which it published. The letter's physician author expressed his disagreement with the report's nondiscrimination admonition, arguing that physicians should only "treat, and, if possible, correct, the deviations, alterations, or pathologies of nature." Since, the author asserted, "reproduction cannot be accomplished in a natural way in the case of a single individual or a same-gender couple," there is no duty to offer fertility care to these patients.[40] This viewpoint that those who cannot reproduce within their intimate relationship should not be aided to do so by the medical profession is a strong indictment of single and gay individuals' worth as contributors to the future of the human race.

Recall Lupita Benitez's sentiment after being turned away by her treating physician, who asserted that her religious beliefs precluded her from assisting in this lesbian patient's reproductive desires. In describing her indignity over this devastating rejection, Lupita added, "It does do a great deal of damage to a person when you tell them they aren't worthy of having a child or having a family." The notion of restricting reproduction in the name of advancing only the most worthy among us is, of course, dangerously reminiscent of the tenets of the American eugenics movement. These same child welfare and parental fitness arguments occupied much of the eugenic playbook, justifying forced sterilization of women on welfare and women with disabilities because they were thought not fit to be proper mothers. The anti-miscegenation laws that barred mixed-race marriages were enacted on the majoritarian assumption that being born of mixed race was unfair to children.[41] A hundred years ago, fears about inadequate parenting based on shaky proof gave state actors the power to prevent parenthood among the disenfranchised. Today, those same ill-supported fears influence the availability of reproductive assistance to those who have no other route to biological parenthood.

Vesting the power to control who procreates and who does not in the hands of a powerful few is just as wrong and dangerous an idea today as it was a hundred years ago. Today's "eugenicists" are likely to be just as inaccurate in their powers of predicting a child's future welfare or a parent's future fitness as were their predecessors. With these similarities looming, we must hope that today's laws are better suited to prevent the type of abject discrimination and harm that earlier befell our nation in the name of improving the species.

The Legal Landscape

Under prevailing health law principles, physicians are free to treat or turn away prospective patients as an exercise of their professional autonomy so long as their conduct does not violate anti-discrimination laws. Our nation's laws against discrimination in the provision of medical services (which include treatment for infertility) are contained in federal and state statutory schemes that delineate protected demographic categories. As explained below, federal anti-discrimination laws set a floor below which states cannot venture in their protection of individual civil rights. At the same time, federal law does not prohibit states from increasing protections within their borders based on categories not covered under federal law. As a result, the national checkerboard that is anti-discrimination protection in the United States requires a virtual tally sheet to understand who is protected against which type of discrimination and where. That said, protection against discrimination in the provision of fertility services on the basis of marital status or sexual orientation occupies only a tiny portion of the national landscape.

PROTECTION UNDER FEDERAL LAW

At the federal level, Title VI of the Civil Rights Act of 1964 prohibits physicians and hospitals receiving federal funding from discriminating in the provision of health care on the basis of race, color, or national origin.[42] Glaringly, several categories are excluded from this specific federal civil rights protection, including sex, marital status, and sexual orientation. While portions of other federal laws provide categorically broader protection against discrimination in other areas of daily life,[43] many Americans remain vulnerable to physician bias under our fifty-year-old national civil rights law. Scholars studying the effectiveness of Title VI voice frustration over the law's seeming inability to address well-known misbehavior in the covered categories. One structural problem with the law is the requirement that private individuals who experience disparate treatment must often show intentional discrimination on the part of the health care provider.[44] In describing the history of health care civil rights litigation under Title VI, Dayna Matthew observes that the law has been "singularly ineffective in addressing certain well-known forms of persistent health care inequalities."[45] As any plaintiff's lawyer knows, finding a "smoking gun" in a discrimination case is a near impossibility. In the case of federal protection against discrimination on the basis of social infertility, there is simply no gun at all.

In the years since passage of the federal Civil Rights Act of 1964, Congress has enacted more than a dozen other laws considered within the civil rights rubric. These include laws protecting against discrimination on the basis of age,[46] disability,[47] pregnancy,[48] and need for family and medical leave.[49] While none of the current federal laws expressly include protection against marital status or sexual orientation discrimination, federal agencies have interpreted select laws to touch such forms of discrimination. The Equal Employment Opportunity Commission (EEOC), for example, has interpreted protection against employment discrimination on the basis of sex to include LGBT status.[50] This same federal agency has also interpreted another federal law pertaining to the civil service to prohibit workplace discrimination on the basis of marital status.[51]

While perhaps offering hope for those left vulnerable under federal law to relationship and sexual orientation discrimination, these broader interpretations have not been applied to the withholding of health care services, let alone infertility care services. The limited amount of federal litigation relating to infertility treatment (almost always medically based) arises under Title VII of the Civil Rights Act of 1964, which prohibits employment practices that "discriminate against any individual with respect to his compensation, terms, conditions, or privileges of employment because of such individual's race, color, religion, sex or national origin."[52] Recently, the category "sex" has been interpreted to offer some protection against sexual orientation and marital status discrimination in the employment context, but the scope of this protection is exceedingly narrow and has never migrated to the health care setting.[53]

ART-related litigation under Title VII typically involves claims arising in the employment and health insurance contexts. For example, a language arts teacher at a Catholic junior high sued her employer after she was not renewed following disclosure that she was undergoing IVF. The school reasoned that her doing so violated Catholic Church teachings, which require that conception occur only through married heterosexual intercourse. The teacher's lawsuit alleged sex and disability discrimination, in violation of Title VII and the Americans with Disabilities Act (ADA).[54] Other IVF-related federal cases challenge employers' or health insurance companies' refusal to reimburse for ART-related expenses as a violation of the ADA, Title VII, and the Pregnancy Discrimination Act.[55] No cases mimic the scenario in *North Coast* in which a patient is denied fertility care based on his or her relationship or sexual status.

The limitations of federal law in combating discrimination in accessing ART for social infertility are many. The most applicable statute addressing discrimination in health care is limited to a few discrete categories such that it could not reasonably be interpreted to apply to treatment denials on the basis of marital status or sexual orientation. Moreover, proving up a successful claim under this law may require direct proof of a provider's discriminatory reason for refusing service, something rarely available in a litigation setting. Additionally, the federal laws that could be potentially useful—those protecting against discrimination on the basis of sex—are limited to venues outside the health care setting, including, for example, employment and housing. ART refusals arise in the health arena, not in the context of a prospective patient's job or dwelling situation. For these reasons, a patient turned away for infertility care based on her social status has little hope for recovery in law or equity under federal law. She will have to look instead for a possible state remedy.

PROTECTION UNDER STATE LAW

The void in federal anti-discrimination law has been acknowledged and addressed by a number of state statutes with far more comprehensive protections against discrimination in access to public accommodations, including health care facilities. The structure of protection by states typically follows the pattern discussed by the California Supreme Court in the *North Coast* case. In the Golden State, as well as numerous other states, the legislature has enacted one or more civil rights laws protecting individuals within the state. These laws generally parallel the federal civil rights laws, but can often offer greater protection along a wider spectrum of demographics. For example, the California Unruh Civil Rights Act referenced in Lupita Benitez's case currently provides as follows: "All persons within the jurisdiction of this state are free and equal, and no matter what their sex, race, color, religion, ancestry, national origin, disability, medical condition, genetic information, marital status or sexual orientation are entitled to the full and equal accommodations, advantages, facilities, privileges, or services in all business establishments of every kind whatsoever."[56] Clearly, the protected categories in California exceed the limited protections offered in federal civil rights laws. The California law specifically protects against discrimination "in all business establishments," which has been interpreted to include private medical practices.[57] Other states' civil rights laws also exceed federal protection in several areas, including marital status and sexual orientation in the list of covered classes. Today about half of all state civil rights laws prohibit discrimination in public accommodations—which generally encompasses the delivery of health care services—on the basis of marital status, and another third include sexual orientation as a protected category.[58] More recently, some states have added gender identity to their civil rights laws, meaning that transgender individuals can seek protection against discrimination in places of public accommodation.[59]

The law may be developing at the state legislative level, but activity at the judicial level has been very low. Other than the decision in

North Coast, no state court–published opinion tackles the application of a state's civil rights law to the provision of infertility services for the treatment of social infertility. One way to interpret this case law dearth is to celebrate the effectiveness of the state statutes that do protect against such misconduct. If patients and providers are aware that such statutes are in place, they may be more apt to calibrate their conduct so as not to land on the wrong side of the law. But the data presented earlier in this chapter defy such a sunny interpretation. We know that marital status and sexual orientation discrimination occur in ART practices. Whether this behavior is limited to the states that don't include these categories in their civil rights laws, or whether individuals who are turned away are reluctant to sue for fear of reducing their chances of obtaining care from a different provider, is unknown. What we do know is that formal law has offered little comfort to the socially infertile. To make matters worse, other aspects of American law indirectly prevent or discourage the socially infertile from obtaining ART care.

Indirect Maltreatment of Social Infertility

Formal law directly addressing the rights of socially infertile persons to access ART care is neither extensive nor particularly helpful in clearing barriers to treatment that we know exists in the clinical arena. At the same time, unlike laws in other countries, American law does not expressly prohibit unmarried or LGBT individuals from accessing fertility care. France, for example, bans single women and same-sex couples from accessing AID and IVF. Laws in Italy, Sweden, and Germany prohibit single women from accessing AID, while Switzerland requires couples seeking ART to be married.[60] The absence of restrictive regulation in the United States is not for lack of attempt or interest on the part of lawmakers who continue to introduce bills in their respective legislative bodies that would expressly prohibit physicians from treating patients who are unmarried or homosexual. In addition to these direct assaults on access to social infertility care, laws in many states indirectly discourage nontraditional patients from seeking care. Laws in two areas—health insurance and parentage—serve to isolate single and LGBT patients from their married heterosexual counterparts in terms

of access to fertility care. Like provider treatment denials, laws that indirectly suppress access to ART for the socially infertile are a powerful
reminder of majoritarian views on certain individuals' worthiness for
parenthood.

"MARRIED ONLY" BILLS IN U.S. STATEHOUSES

In October 2005, Indiana senator Patricia Miller (R-Indianapolis) introduced a bill into the legislature that would have required that couples
who seek assistance to become pregnant—such as through IUI; donor
eggs, sperm, and embryos; IVF; or "other medical means"—must be
married to each other.[61] After a brief period of consideration the bill
was dropped, with its author remarking, "The issue has become more
complex than anticipated."[62] Complex, indeed—it turns out there were
several other parts of the bill for Hoosiers to dislike. While unmarried
persons were barred from accessing ART, married persons who did
so would have been required to seek judicial approval before beginning treatment. Failure to obtain court approval would have resulted
in "unauthorized reproduction" under the law.[63] Moreover, unauthorized reproduction was classified as a Class B misdemeanor, subjecting
offenders—including patients and physicians—to criminal penalties.

   Laws making reproduction a crime should concern us all, even if
limited to assisted conception. Such laws stray very little from the legal
regime that deprived so many Americans of their procreative freedom
during the first part of the twentieth century. The significance of this bill
being introduced in Indiana should not be overlooked. Recall that Indiana was the first state in the nation to enact a eugenic sterilization law in
1907. That Indiana law embraced the tenets of the eugenics movement,
providing in the preamble, "Heredity plays a most important part in
the transmission of crime, idiocy and imbecility."[64] The law authorized
surgeons "to perform such operations for the prevention of procreation
as shall be decided safest and most effective."[65] While the 2005 bill didn't
go so far as to permit physicians to surgically remove an unmarried
person's reproductive capacity, its reach into contemporary procreative
liberty was equally intrusive. Moreover, both laws rely on discredited

assumptions about the welfare of future offspring born to the targeted population.

A few months after the Indiana fiasco, lawmakers in Virginia—the state that forcibly sterilized Carrie Buck—made a similar misguided attempt to limit ART to married couples. In January 2006, Virginia House Bill 187 was introduced, providing in relevant part: "No individual licensed by a health regulatory board shall assist with or perform any intervening medical technology, whether in vivo or in vitro, for or on an unmarried woman that completely or partially replaces sexual intercourse as the means of conception, including, but not limited to, artificial insemination by donor, cryopreservation of gametes and embryos, in vitro fertilization, embryo transfer, gamete intrafallopian tube transfer, and low tubal ovum transfer."[66] Read literally, this bill could mean that if a single woman developed cancer and sought to have her eggs or a portion of her ovary cryopreserved for later use, a Virginia doctor would risk loss of a medical license by assisting this patient. Such a doctor would be cryopreserving gametes for an unmarried woman for purposes of (future) conception. Though the patient might be married when she thawed the gametes, certainly the statute could be read to prohibit cryopreservation for single individuals. Conversely, a married woman undergoing fertility preservation via egg retrieval prior to chemotherapy would also be prohibited from using her own frozen gametes for IVF after her recovery if she divorced in the interim.

Fortunately, the Virginia bill failed to garner sufficient support and was dropped by the Committee on Health, Welfare, and Institutions two weeks after it was introduced. This swift rejection could have been in recognition of the abject unfairness and unintended consequences of the bill's language, but it also could be that lawmakers recognized its obvious clash with existing civil rights law. At the time the bill was introduced, the Virginia Human Rights Act protected against discrimination on the basis of marital status in places of public accommodation. In relevant part, the Virginia law provides, "It is the policy of the Commonwealth to . . . safeguard all individuals . . . from unlawful discrimination because of race, color, religion, national origin, sex, pregnancy, childbirth or related medical conditions, age, marital status, or disability, in places of public accommodation . . . ; preserve the public safety, health and general welfare; and further the interests, rights and privileges of individuals within the Commonwealth."[67] Barring physicians from treating unmarried women seems a gross violation of both the marital status and sex provisions (notice the bill applies only to unmarried women—what about unmarried males who are infertile?), let alone the pledge to preserve the public health.

Currently, no state code contains a legislative directive prohibiting ART providers from treating unmarried patients. But the lack of such a direct barrier does not mean that the law is fully supportive of, or even neutral toward, the provision of assisted conception services to single and LGBT patients. Indirect barriers can be as effective in suppressing the reproductive freedom of those whose lives and loves do not conform to marital and heteronormative standards. These indirect barriers are fairly entrenched and long standing, giving advocates for reform little hope that breakthroughs will soon be forthcoming.

HEALTH INSURANCE REGULATION AS A BARRIER
TO SOCIAL INFERTILITY CARE

We learned earlier that fertility care is woefully underinsured in our country. About 85 percent of all ART care is paid out of pocket, with only a small segment of the infertile population having any coverage through their health insurance provider. While the provision of ART coverage is generally a matter of discretion for health insurance companies, laws in fifteen states require that insurers operating in the jurisdiction either cover or offer to cover the cost of infertility diagnosis and treatment for their policyholders. These fertility care mandates do provide greater access to care for some, but many of the laws setting out coverage are so riddled with exemptions and requirements as to be wholly unhelpful to many. Two such provisions render social infertility exempt from coverage in the states where they have been enacted: (1) a requirement that any covered patient be married, and (2) a definition of infertility that limits treatment to those with medically based causes. Lack of reimbursement often translates into lack of treatment-seeking; thus, while

not direct prohibitions on the treatment of social infertility, these legislative provisions stand as significant barriers to accessing care.

Of the fifteen mandate states, at least five require that a patient be
married in order to seek reimbursement from a participating provider.[68]
For example, Rhode Island mandates that insurance policies delivered
in the state "shall provide coverage for medically necessary expenses of
diagnosis and treatment of infertility for women between the ages of
twenty-five (25) and forty-two (42) years."[69] While this coverage may
sound broad, the law defines "infertility" as "the condition of an otherwise presumably healthy *married* individual who is unable to conceive
or sustain a pregnancy during a period of one year" (emphasis added).[70]
Other states limit coverage to a "policyholder or the spouse of the policyholder," suggesting marriage is a qualifying requirement for application of benefits.[71] Further restrictions that rule out coverage of social
infertility are found in provisions that limit treatment to situations in
which "the patient's oocytes are fertilized with the patient's spouse's
sperm."[72] This restriction withholds coverage for the use of gamete donors for either the wife or the husband.

Limiting covered treatment to nondonor IVF bars more than just
unmarrieds from seeking reimbursement. Married same-sex couples
would be excluded, as they don't produce the dual gametes required
for treatment between them; married heterosexual couples in which
the male has a low or absent sperm count, or whose sperm may contain a heritable genetic disorder would be excluded; a woman without
viable eggs would be excluded; and certainly a single woman with a male
partner or donor sperm specimen would be turned away. Scholars have
argued that restricting infertility insurance coverage to married heterosexual couples who use their own gametes is constitutionally suspect
and likely a violation of federal and state anti-discrimination laws.[73]
Perhaps, but there is little to suggest that any of these laws are being
considered for revision. In fact, in 2007 the governor of Rhode Island
vetoed a bill that would have extended infertility insurance coverage to
unmarried women.

The other indirect barrier to social infertility treatment embedded
in health insurance law, besides outright requirements for marriage,

can be found in the statutory definitions of infertility. To the extent that infertility is defined, as it often is, as a failure to conceive after some period of unprotected intercourse, this definition excludes those whose partnering does not include this activity. Typically, state laws that mandate infertility coverage do not expressly reference this sex-based definition, but do so implicitly by limiting coverage when "the patient and the patient's spouse have a history of infertility of at least five continuous years' duration."[74] The only exceptions to this requirement that a married couple's long-term inability to conceive rest in medical, and not social, terms. A married couple need not wait five (or in some cases, two) years to seek covered treatment if their inability to conceive is caused by some somatic infirmity such as endometriosis, exposure in utero to diethylstilbestrol (DES), or blockage of or surgical removal of the woman's fallopian tubes.[75] Again, those with social infertility may or may not experience these medically based causes of infertility, but they remain outside of coverage parameters because of their relational structure.

Statutory barriers to the treatment of social infertility take shape as specific qualifications that a person must meet before becoming eligible for some state-sponsored fertility care benefit. Requirements that a couple must be married or that an individual must prove a medical infirmity that prevents conception through intercourse are structural roadblocks to state-supported ART for unmarrieds, same-sex couples, and transgender persons. While these statutory requirements typically do not extend to the provision of ART services in general, barring the socially infertile from accessing mandated insurance coverage can have the effect of making care unaffordable and thus out of reach.

Changes to these discriminatory schemes are best made in the legislature. At least one state has recognized that existing law defining infertility in medical terms is potentially harmful to those whose inability to conceive naturally is unrelated to their physical health. In 2013, California lawmakers enacted a revision to the state law governing the provision of health insurance coverage for infertility care. The California scheme mandates that health insurance carriers operating in the state offer coverage for infertility, excluding IVF. Thus, ART benefits are not terribly robust because insurers are not required to cover fertility care, and can exclude IVF from any coverage that is offered. Still, the law regulating fertility care came to the attention of a state lawmaker who saw the potential for discrimination in the statute's definition of infertility. According to the California Health and Safety Code, "infertility means either (1) the presence of a demonstrated condition recognized by a licensed physician and surgeon as a cause of infertility, or (2) the inability to conceive a pregnancy or to carry a pregnancy to a live birth after a year or more of regular sexual relations without contraception."[76] Both of these definitions would seem to rule out coverage for a person with a healthy reproductive system who *could* conceive via heterosexual intercourse.

The new law, introduced as Assembly Bill 460 and signed into law by Governor Jerry Brown in October 2013, adds a specific nondiscrimination clause at the end of the existing statute. Now, the infertility coverage law in California also provides, "Coverage for the treatment of infertility shall be offered and provided without discrimination on the basis of age, ancestry, color, disability, domestic partner status, gender, gender line expression, gender identity, genetic information, marital status, national origin, race, religion, sex, or sexual orientation."[77] Instead of amending the definition of infertility, California lawmakers made clear that insurance carriers cannot discriminate against those with social infertility when providing coverage within the state. This approach may be preferable to an attempt to rewrite the definition of infertility to include social infertility. Such a definition might read, for example, "the inability to conceive or carry a pregnancy to live birth due to the insured's marital status, gender identity, or sexual orientation." Perhaps even progressive California lawmakers thought this was a step too far.

FAMILY LAW AND THE PREFERENCE FOR MARRIED PARENTS

A final stop for investigating the ways in which the legal system hinders access to family formation for nontraditional reproducers is the law on parentage in third-party reproduction. Specifically, the legal treatment of intended parents in surrogate parenting arrangements reveals, in some states, the rejection of parental configurations other than a married opposite-sex couple. Let's briefly consider the general legal landscape governing surrogate parentage, and then look at the marriage bias that attaches to the use of surrogates in some instances. Surrogate parenting is an arrangement in which a woman agrees, typically for a fee, to provide gestational services to an individual or couple who intend to rear the resulting child. A traditional surrogate is a woman whose eggs are used in this arrangement, meaning that she is impregnated using artificial insemination with sperm originating with the intended father or a sperm donor. Since the traditional surrogate is both the gestational and genetic mother of the child, she is often deemed the legal mother and accorded the rights and responsibilities of parenthood. For the vast majority of prospective parents who look to surrogacy to form their families, this legal outcome is highly undesirable, and thus traditional surrogacy occupies a very small percentage of the overall surrogacy market.[78]

The far more common use of gestational surrogacy involves the transfer of embryos into a woman's uterus; the embryos are formed either through the intended parents' gametes or with some combination of donated eggs, sperm, or embryos. The legal status of the resulting child is complicated by the fact that the surrogate gives birth but has no genetic tie to the child. As the use of gestational surrogacy increases — now estimated to produce around two thousand infants in the United States each year — nearly half of all states have undertaken to create legal regimes surrounding surrogacy.[79] These regimes generally address two legal questions: (1) Is commercial surrogacy legal in the jurisdiction? and (2) Who are the legal parent(s) of a child born to a surrogate mother? As to the first question, of the twenty-three states and the District of Columbia that have enacted laws on surrogacy, eleven states authorize the practice with varying degrees of restriction.[80] Nine states plus Washington, D.C., ban surrogacy contracts (in some cases traditional surrogacy agreements only), usually by declaring such agreements to be null and void under state law.[81] The remaining states address parentage issues only, impliedly suggesting that the practice is permitted within the jurisdiction.

In states where commercial surrogacy is permitted, the law tends to declare the intended parents as the legal parents of any resulting child. For example, Connecticut addresses surrogacy through its laws on the registry of vital statistics. The law permits the Department of

Public Health to issue a birth certificate naming the intended parents as the child's legal parents, provided the surrogacy agreement is approved by court order.[82] The Connecticut law makes no distinction between intended parents who are married and those who are not. The law also references "the intended parent or parents," permitting single individuals to become parents via gestational surrogacy. Regrettably, this scheme is an outlier in the universe of surrogate parentage laws, the majority of which limit legal recognition to married heterosexual couples.

In the handful of states that do recognize the legal parentage of intended parents to a valid surrogacy agreement, at least three contain an express marriage requirement. In Florida, for example, in order for a surrogacy agreement to be valid, the "commissioning couple" must be legally married.[83] At the time this statute was enacted, marriage equality for same-sex couples was not available in the state, so it is fair to say the legislature did not contemplate whether a married gay couple would be encompassed within the "commissioning couple" rubric. Even though same-sex marriage is now recognized in the state, other parts of the law may continue to bar married male couples from gaining parental recognition through gestational surrogacy. In addition to mandating the intended parents be married, Florida law requires that "the commissioning mother cannot physically gestate a pregnancy to term."[84] This requirement rules out lawful surrogacy by a single man and male couples, both of whom cannot achieve biological parenthood through any means other than surrogacy. Similar marriage and medical requirements thwart gestational surrogacy by single individuals, unmarrieds, and married male couples in Texas (requiring the intended parents be married and the intended mother be unable to carry a pregnancy),[85] and Utah (requiring marriage and that the intended mother be unable to bear a child).[86]

Is requiring that an intended mother be part of the parental equation in order for a surrogacy arrangement to be deemed valid the equivalent of expressly invalidating such agreements where no intended mother is present? On their face, these surrogacy validation laws do not provide that surrogacy attempts by unmarried individuals or married male couples are illegal, but rather that these arrangements would not receive the same protection under the state's family law. This means that any intended parent who operates outside the letter (and probably the spirit) of the law would be vulnerable to a court invalidating the surrogacy arrangement, producing disastrous results. Such was the case with a New Jersey couple whose surrogacy story stands as a cautionary tale for many.

In *A.G.R. v. D.R.H.*, a gay male couple entered into a gestational surrogacy arrangement with the sister of one of the partners.[87] Using donated eggs and the sperm of the other partner, twin girls were born to the surrogate/sister in October 2006. Notably, before any treatment began, the parties entered into a series of contracts making clear that neither the egg donor nor the gestational carrier would have any parental rights with respect to any resulting children. The agreements further provided the two men would both be legal fathers with all accompanying parental rights. Shortly after the babies were born, tensions and hostilities arose between the fathers and the surrogate/sister, culminating in the woman filing a petition seeking parental rights and custody in March 2007. The judge hearing the case held that the surrogacy agreement was invalid under *In re Baby M*, a ruling of the New Jersey Supreme Court in 1988 holding that surrogacy contracts were void as against public policy.[88] This ruling left the twins with two legal parents—the gestational carrier and the biological father—who had no desire to co-parent. The ruling completely excluded the intended father whose sister had gestated the children. The case then proceeded to a custody fight between the two legal parents, in which the court awarded sole legal and physical custody to the biological father.[89]

This case typifies the insecure environment in which the socially infertile must operate in pursuit of their parental desires. Since the majority of states do not expressly recognize the validity of surrogate parenting arrangements (with many deeming them unlawful), the rights of a nongestational or nongenetic intended parent are dependent upon the local bench to interpret the law in a way that accommodates the parties' intent. The recent New Jersey case exposes the downside of that approach. The case the judge relied on, *In re Baby M*, involved a traditional surrogacy arrangement in which the birth mother was also the child's genetic mother. This factor played a key role in the 1988 decision as the surrogate had both a gestational and a genetic link to the child.

In the more recent surrogacy case, the sister was not the girls' genetic mother and thus could have been distinguished from the surrogate in the *Baby M* decision. Instead, the judge applied the prior precedent quite broadly, rejecting any distinction based on the lack of a genetic tie between the surrogate and the children and reiterating that New Jersey public policy finds surrogacy agreements have a "potential for devastation" to women.[90] Arguably, the devastation in this case was visited on all the parties, including the two men who took whatever legal care they could to protect their family's interests.

At this chapter's outset, we noted the role that physical and emotional love play in shaping our reproductive lives. We learned that while physical barriers to procreation can often be overcome by modern reproductive medicine, a host of other roadblocks remain. Provider unwillingness to treat social infertility combines with a weak and under-evolved legal system to permit the continued suppression of nonmajoritarian parenthood. If we learned any lesson from our eugenic forebearers, it should be that the things we fear most today are better addressed by repair rather than rejection. Sterilizing tens of thousands of Americans did nothing to rid our society of crime, disease, poverty, or disability. Instead, it left a legacy of mistrust and regret that persists to this day. Today's fears that parenting outside the heteronormative bubble ought to be discouraged to promote a healthy future are equally misguided. Instead of suppression, we should consider providing the necessary support that every prospective parent needs to undertake the creation of our next generation.

Disability and Procreative Diminishment

Several years ago a woman named Kijuana Chambers sought infertility treatment at a Colorado clinic. Single and lesbian, Ms. Chambers understood her path to parenthood depended upon artificial insemination with donor sperm. After initially providing treatment, clinic doctors abruptly refused to further assist their patient, claiming Ms. Chambers was not fit to care for a baby— not because she was single or lesbian, but because she was blind. In a subsequent lawsuit, attorneys for the clinic defended the physicians' actions as "the right thing to do," adding that the "case is about the moral and ethical responsibility of a physician."[1] Responsibility to whom? The unborn? The patient? The public? According to the National Council on Disability (NCD), treatment refusals and discrimination against individuals with disabilities in the ART setting are widespread.[2] Physical and provider barriers to infertility care are "significant, and sometimes insurmountable," depriving many within the disability community of the ability to exercise their reproductive liberty.[3]

Today's denials for ART treatment based on a prospective parent's disability are worrying analogues to our eugenics past, an era in which misguided judgments about parental fitness culminated in the involuntary sterilization of thousands of Americans. Whereas the eugenicists of a century ago coerced the "feeble-minded" into surrendering their reproductive capacity through forced sterilizations, today's practices act to deprive the differently abled of their capacity to reproduce by withholding the technological means necessary to produce a child. In this chapter, we explore these new eugenics, focusing on the meaning of disability in contemporary society as both an acquired and inherited characteristic. The presence of a disability in a would-be parent and its likely appearance in any resulting offspring shape the conduct of physicians and patients alike. Based on a combination of medical fact, lived experience, and an imagined future, these conducts often clash as each stakeholder pursues a disparate goal. The ART/disability equation is complicated by what we know, what we think we know, and what we may never know.

Disability in the Modern Era

The scope of disability that captured eugenicists' ire in the early twentieth century occupied a broad range of physical, emotional, intellectual, and social characteristics. Recall that compulsory sterilization laws enacted in a majority of American states were aimed at ridding future societies of the "socially inadequate class," broadly defined to include the feebleminded, insane, criminals, epileptic, drug and alcohol addicted, diseased, infectious, deaf, blind, deformed, poor, homeless, and "ne'er-do-well."[4] Based on the (now discredited) belief that all human traits and characteristics were inheritable, eugenics law and policy wielded a combination of authoritarian and incentivizing tactics to encourage the "well born" to reproduce, while discouraging, and even preventing, those considered less suitable from adding to the human race. Eugenic enthusiasm was generated and sustained by the burgeoning field of genetics, which introduced the concept that human characteristics are not entirely random. Looking back, we cringe at the blunt assault this relatively infinitesimal understanding of genetics permitted. Looking forward, we hope that our vastly more sophisticated grasp of the science of heredity will steer us to make wiser decisions about our collective reproductive experience.[5] This more hopeful future lies in a greater understanding of what it means for oneself and one's offspring to be disabled.

What does it mean to be disabled in the modern era? Legally speaking, disability is defined under federal law as having or being regarded as having "a physical or mental impairment that substantially limits one or more major life activities."[6] Embedded in the Americans with Disabilities Act of 1990, this definition has been interpreted to include conditions that are physical (e.g., blindness, deafness, quadriplegia), mental (e.g., psychiatric, learning, developmental), genetic (though limited to active or symptomatic disease processes), and infectious (even if asymptomatic). Moreover, the major life activity rubric includes everyday activities such as walking, eating, and sleeping, as well as few-in-a-lifetime activities such as reproduction. This last activity was deemed to be included within federal disability law by the U.S. Supreme Court in *Bradgon v. Abbott,* a 1998 case holding asymptomatic HIV to constitute a covered disability because of its (then) interference with an infected individual's ability to safely procreate.[7] The high court's designation of reproduction as a major life activity serves as a contemporary reiteration of its broad language in *Skinner v. Oklahoma* (1942) deeming procreation "one of the basic civil rights of man . . . fundamental to the very existence and survival of the race."[8]

Given that the disability spectrum includes sensory, mobility, somatic, psychological, emotional, intellectual, genetic, and infectious impairments, we can begin to appreciate the significant impact that disability plays in the lives of those affected as well as society as a whole. Disability, by the numbers, can be measured in a variety of ways. According to the U.S. Census Bureau, nearly 20 percent of Americans have a disability.[9] Of these 57 million disabled individuals, many are of reproductive age (fifteen to forty-four), and many are parents of young children. Parenting and disability, by the numbers, is explained by the NCD as follows:

> At least 4.1 million parents with reported disabilities in the United States have children under age 18; meaning that at least 6.2 percent of American parents who have children under age 18 have at least one reported disability. The rates are even higher for some subgroups of this population; for instance, 13.9 percent of American Indian/Alaska Native

parents and 8.8 percent of African American parents have
a disability. Further, 6 percent of white, 5.5 percent Latino/
Hispanic, and 3.3 percent of Asian/Pacific Islander parents
have a disability. Of these parents, 2.8 percent have a mobility
disability, 2.3 percent have a cognitive disability, 2.3 percent
have a daily activity limitation, 1.4 percent have a hearing disability, and 1.2 percent have a vision disability.[10]

Odds are the vast majority of disabled parents included in the
above numbers reproduced through natural conception, either before
or after acquiring their disability. After all, a disability can arise at any
point in a person's life from genetic, disease, traumatic, or other processes. For disabled individuals who desire to have a family and who
require medical assistance to do so, accessing treatment can present
many challenges. Physical access to medical equipment—even as basic
as a gynecological examination table—can be difficult for women with
mobility deficits.[11] Adequate financial resources to pay for treatment,
a major barrier in the general population, can be even more problematic for the disabled.[12] Assuming these structural and financial barriers can be overcome, disabled infertiles can come up against the most
unforgiving barrier of all, provider unwillingness. As explained by Ora
Prilletensky, professor, author, and mother with a disability, "In addition to the myth of asexuality and skepticism regarding their ability to
attract partners, women with disabilities have been discouraged from
having children for a variety of other reasons. Concerns that they will
give birth to 'defective' babies and prejudicial assumptions about their
capacity to care for children often underpin the resistance that they may
encounter."[13] Kijuana Chambers's story evidences that this resistance
can emanate from the provider side.
    An ART provider's unwillingness to assist a disabled person to
reproduce can be based in several rationales, nearly all grounded in
concern for a resulting child's welfare. Before looking deeper into the
child welfare rationale for ART treatment denials, let's assume that these
physicians are a microcosm of our larger society that reflects the attitudes and biases of the majority. Disability scholars often remark on
these generalized views toward disability, noting that many regard "the

birth of a child with 'defects' as a tragedy, to be avoided by every means that science and technology can muster."[14] According to Alicia Ouellette, "Those parents who allow a disabled child to come to term report negative consequences for themselves and their children. Despite that these children are beloved members of the family, and children of choice, they are referred to and treated by others as 'mistakes,' 'tragedies,' and 'burdens.'"[15] The experience of living a life with a disability, as reported by Ouellette, is quite different from the imagined tragedy that prevails among the nondisabled: "Life with disability can be, and is, meaningful, productive, and worthwhile. Moreover, disability scholars emphasize the many rich contributions that human variation provides in society. From the work of blind and deaf artists, to the various contributions of people with autism, to the joy brought to an individual family by the presence of a child with disabilities, the contributions are many."[16] While disability rights advocates (and others) try mightily to advance this perspective in the public sphere, negative attitudes and discrimination against the disabled continue to be a factor in modern life.[17] Reproductive medicine specialists, as part of this larger community, are imbued with the skill and knowledge to assist in the reproductive plan of a disabled person but may bring their own values to the bedside. If one cannot imagine living with a disability, then those same fears, concerns, and (mis)perceptions could influence one's willingness to assist in the conception and birth of a child who may inherit the parent's disability or be harmed by presumed inadequacies in child-rearing. These two factors—concern that offspring will inherit the parent's disabling condition and fear for the child's post-birth safety and well-being— serve as the major rationales for ART treatment denials among the disabled. While the heritability rationale seems more grounded in eugenics than the concern for rearing-related child welfare, both rest on shaky empirical ground, as is revealed below.

Conceiving and Permitting Harm

Before exploring the possible rationales for denying ART treatment to disabled individuals, it is vital to note that not all treatment refusals are wrong—legally, medically, or morally. Physicians are duty bound to consider the risks and benefits of any requested treatment, and have no ethical or legal duty to provide services that offer no medical benefit or pose greater harm than benefit to the patient.[18] A physician cannot ignore or dismiss an individual's disability, and must take into account its clinical impact on the delivery of ART-related interventions. In some cases, a particular disability could pose a contraindication to fertility therapy or pregnancy, and thus could reasonably form the basis for an acceptable reason to deny treatment.[19] This "maternal harm" rationale is recognized as a valid basis on which to deny treatment that poses a substantial risk of harm to the mother.[20] The difficulty arises in determining when a treatment denial is clinically justified and when it crosses established medical, legal, and ethical boundaries. On the one hand, denials based on objective and evidence-based certainty that fertility treatment or pregnancy would cause the patient or the resulting child serious harm or death are most likely reasonable and defensible.[21] On the other hand, denials based on prejudice or unsubstantiated predictions about a woman's pregnancy, a child's health, or a parent's ability to provide an adequate level of care would not likely be reasonable or defensible. Most clinical scenarios do not fall into either extreme camp but rest somewhere in between.

Refocusing on the two-part rationale that underpins most disability-related ART denials, we can shorthand these concerns as "conceptive harms" and "rearing harms." The former imagines that in conceiving a child (presumably using the disabled parent's gametes), a genetic or infectious harm will attach itself to the embryo and manifest at some point during the child's life. Conceptive harm can manifest at birth, such as when a child inherits a genetic form of deafness, or in adulthood, such as when a child inherits Huntington's disease, a devastating neurodegenerative genetic disorder that typically becomes symptomatic in mid-adult life. Conceptive harm can also remain latent, or be entirely treatable, throughout the child's life, such as with the transmission of HIV, for which highly effective therapies have been developed.[22] Each of these aforementioned conceptive harms would have served as justification for forced sterilizations during the eugenics movement. But, do they stand up today as a legitimate basis for fertility treatment denial?

Rearing harms imagine inadequate parenting skills that could place the child in serious, even mortal, danger. A blind mother, for example, might not be able to provide necessary attention or discipline; a quadriplegic father might not be able to adequately supervise a young child; a seriously ill parent could die while the child is young. Rearing harms can converge with conceptive harms (as in the case of transmissible genetic anomalies), or they can be entirely freestanding (as in the case of a traumatic injury or nongenetic impairment in the parent). While the clinical severity and likely penetrance of a conceptive harm are highly variable and often unpredictable, calculations about a parent's rearing capacity are even more speculative. What's more, unlike our eugenic forefathers, we have the technology to prevent the transmission of numerous heritable impairments as well as enhance a disabled person's everyday functionality through advanced adaptive equipment and services.[23] The ability to suppress disease transmission and enhance functionality should work to lessen provider fears about assisting disabled prospective parents, but other factors—including disparate patient preferences—can complicate the situation.

INHERITING DISABILITY

On the matter of genetic or infectious heritability, once a person enters the ART world the opportunities for detecting and preventing the transmissibility of a parent's disability abound. Particularly in the realm of known genetic disorders, evolved techniques in preimplantation genetic diagnosis (PGD) enable a prospective parent to view the genetic makeup of their would-be child within days of conception, before the embryo is transferred into a woman's uterus for implantation. PGD involves the extraction of one or more cells from a three- to five-day-old embryo, then examining the cells to detect if the embryo has the correct number of chromosomes or is harboring a disease-associated mutation in one or more of its genes.[24] Using PGD, physicians and geneticists can counsel patients with a large degree of certainty about genetic anomalies present (and absent) in their developing embryos.[25] Today, PGD can be used to detect well over two hundred and fifty genetic conditions.[26]

While PGD can boast a high degree of clinical accuracy, there are drawbacks to its use. First, it is expensive. Since PGD can only be performed on embryos during IVF treatment, both techniques must be employed. Together, a single round of IVF plus PGD will cost around $15,000.[27] These procedures generally are not covered by health insurance and thus must be paid out of pocket by patients. Also, a patient may not want to use PGD, either because of concern about its safety or because she simply does not want to discover if an embryo carries an anomaly or not. Just because a disabled person needs assistance in conception does not necessarily mean she is interested in avoiding the same disability in her future child. For example, as discussed more fully below, some genetically deaf parents relish the possibility of rearing a deaf child within their cherished nonhearing culture. For some providers, this type of patient refusal to avoid passing a heritable disease can undermine their willingness to provide ART services.

The possibility of horizontal transmission (from partner to partner) or vertical transmission (from parent to unborn child) of an infectious disease may also give a physician pause in assisting an infected individual. The most frequent clinical scenario in which this arises is in instances where one or both prospective parents are HIV-infected. Research reveals that treatment denials for HIV infection are the norm, with only around 3 percent of all ART clinics in the United States offering care to these individuals.[28] Physician concern about partner harm or conceptive harm to offspring from HIV-infected individuals seems almost irrational in light of abundant data showing that horizontal transmission can be virtually eliminated and vertical transmission rates hover at less than 2 percent when the mother is treated with antiretroviral therapy.[29] Moreover, more recent techniques can essentially ensure that an HIV-infected male will not infect the gestating female or the child. Years of research investigating sperm washing to remove any viral parts from the male gametes reveal the technique to be highly effective, as detailed in numerous studies showing no horizontal or vertical HIV transmission in thousands of patients studied.[30]

If a disabled prospective parent is willing to accept all reasonable medical interventions to avoid transmission of a disability to his or her offspring, is it still reasonable for an ART provider to refuse service? Since we know that such refusals continue to occur, it is worth thinking about why treatment denials persist. One possible explanation rests in the ever-present world of medicolegal liability. In science, as in life, nothing is an absolute certainty, and errors in the detection of genetic anomalies have occurred. In a few reported cases, patients who underwent PGD sued their physicians for negligence in misdiagnosing the health status of the tested embryos. In *Bergero v. University of Southern California Keck School of Medicine*, for example, parents of a boy born with Fabry's, an X-linked recessive genetic disease, sued the physicians who performed IVF and PGD resulting in their son's birth. The mother had previously been diagnosed as an asymptomatic carrier of the disease. Since the father was not a carrier, the couple sought PGD to detect which embryos were affected by the genetic mutation, and to rule out transferring any impacted male (XY) embryos. The couple agreed to transfer what they were told were unaffected female (XX) embryos, but an affected male was mistakenly transferred.[31] The jury found in favor of the defendant physicians, and this verdict was affirmed on appeal.

From the provider perspective, the nonliability outcome in *Bergero* may have provided some solace to the defendant physicians, but their multiyear legal battle stands as a cautionary tale to those who dwell in the PGD arena. Whether caused by technical or human error, mistakes in the delivery of preimplantation genetic information can be devastating and long lasting. It is understandable that an ART provider would express some concern over engaging in a treatment plan that could subject him or her to significant legal liability. That said, the error rate in PGD is exceedingly low, and physicians (and other professionals) are well aware of their generalized susceptibility to meritorious as well as frivolous tort claims. From the patient perspective, having the PGD option can be enormously relieving, but should a mistake occur, patients are forewarned that legal relief may not be forthcoming.

Though not foolproof, current genetic and infection detection technologies can substantially reduce the chances that a person afflicted with a detectable disability will transmit this same health status to his or her biological offspring. With rare exception (discussed below), patients willingly and happily engage these technologies to the best of their financial ability. As such, treatment denials out of concern for conceptive harm would seem to fall under the weight of these myriad avoidance techniques. The persistence of ART refusals is more probably grouped under the second major rationale, concern for the child's post-birth rearing.

PREDICTING PARENTAL FITNESS

Disability scholars and advocates express grave concern that fertility doctors discriminate against disabled prospective patients by employing screening techniques that identify and reject individuals on the basis of their perceived inability to care for children. Survey research conducted at U.S. fertility clinics reveals that many private practices do employ screening techniques to determine a prospective patient's suitability for treatment. In Chapter 5, we reviewed the results of one such survey, discovering that parental fitness is of great concern to some providers. When ART providers were asked whether it was "acceptable . . . to consider a parent's fitness before helping them conceive a child," a full 70 percent agreed or strongly agreed with this position.[32] Nearly the same percentage ratcheted this consideration to a duty, agreeing that fertility care providers have "the responsibility to consider a parent's fitness before helping them conceive."[33] Exactly how is parental fitness determined, when, and by whom?

The notion that perceived parental fitness should be a barrier to ART treatment has played out in clinical gatekeeping that, according to Richard Storrow, accounts for hundreds of treatment denials each year.[34] Yet, while clinical gatekeeping is a reality in ART care, it has rarely been the subject of a published judicial opinion, making it somewhat difficult to study in any systematic way.[35] Calling it an "under-examined" area of clinical practice, Storrow provides some empiric guideposts to better understand clinical gatekeeping in ART. Using blood tests, psychological evaluations, and genetic screening to determine whom they will allow to proceed with treatment, fertility clinics turn away about 4 percent of applicants each year.[36] Three percent (three-quarters of the total) are turned away due to medical concerns ranging from futility of treatment to the high risk of transmitting a serious genetic disorder to a resulting offspring. One percent of applicants are refused treatment due to psychosocial concerns.[37] From these figures, it is impossible to discern what percentage of applicants is rejected for legitimate versus discriminatory reasons.

The range of disabilities that could affect parental fitness includes each category described earlier in this chapter, encompassing sensory, mobility, and intellectual deficits. Anecdotal evidence suggests that providers decline to treat patients in each of these categories, but patients with intellectual deficits are the most likely to be turned away for treatment. In another concerning nod to the earlier eugenics period, recent data suggest that ART providers are far more likely to refuse treatment to an individual or couple with limited intellectual capacity, defined as "cannot do much more than basic reading and math."[38] Thirteen percent of respondents said they were "very or extremely likely to turn away" a couple with limited intellectual capacity, compared with 3 percent who would decline to treat a couple who became blind from an accident. This deprivation of procreative opportunity eerily recalls Justice Oliver Wendell Holmes Jr.'s infamous pronouncement that "three generations of imbeciles are enough" in upholding the Virginia eugenical sterilization law that robbed Carrie Buck and many others of the use of their own reproductive organs. While denying ART services does not rise to the level of brutality and bodily invasion occupied by forced sterilizations, both are deprivative in their impact on the subject's reproductive activities.

Just as Justice Holmes was wrong in his assessment of Carrie Buck's lineage (records reveal three generations of intellectually normal women),[39] it is possible that current ART providers could mispredict the rearing capacities of their disabled patients, whatever the source of their disabilities. After all, reproductive medicine specialists are not formally trained to assess a potential parent's child-rearing abilities; any assessment, particularly an assessment backed by no specific expertise, would be purely speculative. Moreover, research conducted on the lives of disabled parents shows them to be effective, loving, and fit parents.[40] Acknowledging that one person's experience does not a generalization make, let's return to the story of Kijuana Chambers, the blind woman denied fertility care because her doctors said it was "the right thing to do."[41] After being turned away by one clinic, Ms. Chambers sought and received treatment at another facility, eventually giving birth to a baby girl in 2001. There are no public accounts of any harm that has befallen this child.

It may be that those without a disability cannot imagine life with a disability, and thus cannot further imagine the added challenges of parenthood under those circumstances. Even so, those with disabilities have the same parental aspirations as their able-bodied counterparts. True enough, certain disabilities can pose challenges over and above those experienced by nondisabled parents, but in the main these challenges would not render a person per se unfit to parent. An a priori judgment that a person with a disability will be an unfit parent defies experience and research to the contrary.[42] Moreover, concerns about child welfare at the hands of disabled parents could theoretically require physicians to take into account the possibility that a nondisabled person can be afflicted by a disease or accident at some point in the future, even during pregnancy. Certainly we can't imagine requiring a pregnant woman who is rendered blind in an accident to have an abortion; nor should we accept that a blind infertile woman without objective manifestations of parental unfitness be deprived the opportunity to reproduce with medical assistance.

Parental Choice: Selecting Against and for Disability

The willingness of a provider to assist a disabled person in achieving biological parenthood is an essential but not all-encompassing aspect of a disabled person's ART journey. Once a provider is enlisted, a model of shared decision making should ideally take hold, allowing physician and patient to converse about the course of treatment. Current thinking supports an approach of nondirectiveness, in which the physician sets out the range of options without inserting a personal or paternalistic view as to the patient's choice.[43] The panoply of services available to ART patients can raise unique concerns when the gamete provider harbors a genetic anomaly that is transmissible to a resulting child. Normative reasoning suggests any such prospective parent would take all available measures to ensure the birth of a child free from such genetic constraints. But experience suggests otherwise.

Looking first at the fertile population, these individuals may know through family history or learn through genetic counseling that they face a certain degree of risk of passing on a genetic harm to their naturally conceived offspring. Some may choose to forgo childbearing; some may conceive naturally and undergo prenatal genetic testing and abortion; some may employ IVF and PGD to select only healthy embryos; and some may accept the stated risk and forge ahead with unscreened childbirth.[44] Each of these aforementioned choices is available to those who can procreate on their own. No regulatory or medical regime interacts with fertile individuals' rights to procreate, even when so doing poses a 50 percent likelihood of birthing a child with a devastating autosomal dominant genetic disorder such as Huntington's disease or neurofibromatosis.

Disabled individuals who need medical assistance to reproduce enjoy some, but not all, of the choices available to naturally conceiving prospective parents. Particularly when a disability is genetically based, parental choices are more scrutinized once they are exercised in the ART context. As discussed previously, PGD allows parents and providers to view the genetic makeup of their embryos, informing the decision about whether to transfer or discard any individual specimen. Normatively, one might expect that a disabled person would elect, in every instance, to implant only "healthy" embryos, but research teaches us this is not the case. Armed with this powerful information, gametic parents have selected both against and in favor of transferring embryos diagnosed with genetic anomalies. The rationales that support this decision making are complex and much discussed in the academic and popular literature.

SELECTING AGAINST DISABILITY

Advances in the detection and thwarting of inheritable disabilities would seem a boon to modern society. Before the invention of PGD, parents could only be apprised of the statistical odds of transferring a generations-long genetic anomaly to their offspring; any decision to procreate or forgo biological parenthood was rife with difficult life-affecting trade-offs. Since genetic testing of embryos was introduced in the early 1990s, parental choices have shifted from risk assessment to sifting through highly predictive information about their embryos' genetic health. This sophisticated level of genetic information poses ethical and clinical dilemmas. Today, PGD can detect the presence of well over 250 genetic disorders in the developing embryo. The list of detectible diseases includes fatal and crippling illnesses such as Tay-Sachs disease, Huntington's disease, and amyotrophic lateral sclerosis; devastating blood disorders such as hemophilia and Fanconi anemia; adult-onset cancers such as inherited breast and ovarian cancer; sensory impairments such as inherited deafness and optic atrophy; and mobility disorders such as achondroplasia (dwarfism) and certain types of muscular dystrophy.[45]

Given the choice, what parent—and for that matter what society— would not want to work toward the birth of a healthy child? Herein lies the eugenic logic of PGD. Parents who opt to investigate the genetic makeup of their developing embryos implicitly agree that they will participate in the selection (and the corresponding deselection) of embryos based on their revealed genetic health. Are parents who, with assistance from their reproductive medicine specialists, discard embryos that are genetically flawed really any different from the eugenic enthusiasts of the early 1900s who built a network of coercive institutions aimed at ridding society of the unfit? A few obvious distinctions come to mind, but are they enough to ward off the eugenics taint that PGD sometimes attracts?[46]

First, the decision to use PGD is a personal and voluntary one, in contrast to the state-mandated directive to submit to an unwanted surgical procedure. While detractors argue that the opportunity to detect embryonic anomalies will soon convert into an obligation to do so via tort law, medical practice standards, and ethical maxims that favor child welfare over parental autonomy, no current clinical data suggest PGD has become a coerced procedure.[47] Second, parents take up PGD as part of their reproductive autonomy, whereas eugenics practices infringed on the reproductive rights of those deemed unworthy of contributing to the human race. The counterargument here is that while adult reproductive rights may receive disparate treatment under eugenic versus ART scenarios, the children fared exactly the same—they were never born. Whether procreative suppression to prevent the birth of potential

offspring with certain anticipated characteristics occurs before conception or before implantation is of no importance when the inquiry is,
Did the regimen prevent the birth of disabled offspring?

Third, the use of PGD is part of a bundle of parental opportunities
to act in a child's best interest, which might mean birthing one child over
another. In this regard, parents are empowered to make decisions about
the benefits and harms they are willing to experience in pursuit of their
reproductive aspirations. This construction of parental rights stands in
contrast with eugenic philosophy, which elevated societal good over individual harms. While positive eugenics did encourage birth of certain
offspring, the movement's main thrust was in preventing creation of
those predicted to place a strain on society. Embryo discard may have
the purpose of relieving anticipated strain within the family by preventing the birth of a disabled child, but it also works to create a healthier
child than random natural conception might yield. In this way, parents
who use PGD might be regarded as fulfilling their duty to maximize the
well-being of their future children from the earliest moments.[48] Adhering to duty to one's family versus duty to the state stands as a vital distinction between the use of PGD and compulsory sterilization.

Whatever similarities and distinctions exist between selecting
against disability today and a hundred years ago, we live in an era of
greater medical knowledge about the causes and treatments for (certain)
disabilities, greater access to treatment options for (many) persons with
disabilities, greater adaptive services and equipment to enhance the lives
of (some) disabled individuals, and greater (yet limited) legal protection
against discrimination on the basis of disability. Progressing toward a
society in which the disabled are fully and equally integrated, respected,
and valued remains an aspiration rather than a reality, prompting some
to worry that selecting against disability via PGD inhibits realization of
this more optimal society. The argument against the unrestrained use
of preimplantation selection on the basis of embryonic health is sometimes referred to as the "disability critique" of PGD.

As explained by Alicia Ouellette, the critique against the use of
reproductive technologies to prevent the birth of babies with disabling
traits is composed of four arguments:

First, the purposeful use of technology to prevent the birth of a disabled child expresses discriminatory negative attitudes about disabling traits and those who carry them. Second, disability-based selection signals intolerance of human variation, which causes harm to parental relationships with children. Third, selection against disability through pre-implantation screening and selective abortion is based on, and perpetuates, misinformation about the lived experiences of children with disabilities and their families. Finally, selection reduces individuals with disabilities to a single trait, diminishing and eliminating their value as full human beings.[49]

The disability critique highlights the ways in which individual decisions about the worth of a future child impact society as a whole. Those living with a disability or those unfortunate enough to be born with a disabling condition, the critique warns, will be regarded as subpar, second-class citizens of the human species because the norm is to avoid the production of such members. As one disability advocate laments, "The message . . . is the greatest insult: some of us are 'too flawed' in our very DNA to exist; we are unworthy of being born."[50] Society is also worse off for its rejection of human variation, its resistance to embrace the value that disabled people bring to the world and its unwillingness to work toward improving the lives of the differently abled.

Counterarguments to the disability critique focus on two neglected factors—the individual nature of parental decision making and the duty to act in the best interest of one's children. Just as disability advocates argue that one trait should not define the whole person, can the acts of individual parents stand as a broad pronouncement about the status of disability in our society? Our celebrated history of protecting reproductive liberty counsels against state interference with the highly meaningful procreative choice embedded in PGD. Further, if parents are prohibited from adjusting the health status of their to-be-born offspring in the name of disability acceptance, how far would this prohibition extend? Carried to a more extreme level, this approach might caution parents to shun medical therapies that treat or improve the health of their disabled children. If a parent has the right (and in many cases the duty) to seek medical intervention that improves an existing child's quality of life, should exercise of that right in pursuit of a particular child's healthy birth be deemed pejoratively eugenic? If this question seems morally freighted, imagine the complexities when a parent seeks to select *for* a disabling condition.

SELECTING FOR DISABILITY

Earlier in this chapter we documented the reticence of ART providers to assist disabled patients who are likely to give birth to offspring with inheritable disorders, or whose parenting skills are perceived to endanger a resulting child's well-being. In seeking fertility care, we assumed that these prospective parents were desirous of children who would not inherit or develop the same disabling conditions, and that these reproducers would be willing to use technology to ensure their child's genetic and somatic health. What if an otherwise fertile disabled person approached a fertility specialist to orchestrate the birth of a child with the parent's same disability? Here, truth may be stranger than fiction.

In 1996, longtime partners Sharon Duchesneau and Candy Mc-Cullough sought the services of a sperm bank in order to have a child that resembled them—deaf. The sperm bank told the couple that congenital deafness is precisely the sort of condition that would eliminate a prospective donor from their ranks, thus they had no "deaf sperm." Determined to maximize the chances that their child would be deaf, Sharon and Candy turned to a deaf friend who agreed to serve as a donor. Six years later, the couple were parents to a daughter and a son, both deaf.[51] Even though Sharon and Candy did not use PGD to select for deaf children, their story did stir emotions about the so-called intentional diminishment of offspring using ART. One particularly harsh criticism was published as a follow-up letter to the newspaper story detailing the women's parental journey: "That three people (I include the sperm donor) could deliberately deprive another person of a natural faculty is monstrous and cruel and reveals their basic resentment toward people who can hear. There are laws that give access to medical care for children of parents who would deny it on religious grounds. There should be similar protections for children subject to the abuse of being genetically programmed to replicate the disabilities of misguided parents."[52]

These harsh words are spoken in response to a perception that parents have intentionally harmed their children by actively seeking out a genetically based diminishment. The deaf women strongly object to the classification of deafness as a life deficit, arguing that it is a cultural identity, not a medical disability. They maintain they will be better parents to a deaf child than to a hearing one because they will be better able to talk to the child, to understand the child's emotions. Even accepting deafness as an identity rather than a disability, the women's critics would still argue that the limits of reproductive liberty do not permit a parent to intentionally limit a child's potential.[53] One scholar has identified this parental desire to impose a certain genetic makeup upon one's offspring as depriving the child of "a right to an open future."[54] Sharon and Candy's children's future was orchestrated to occupy the deaf world, albeit a world their mothers believed would provide them the best opportunity for a happy and healthy life. Others have gone so far as to argue such parental behavior warrants either civil or criminal liability.[55]

What role should providers play in a patient's quest to make a genetic choice in favor of disability? Should it matter to the physician if the requesting patient is infertile and thus making a selection as a byproduct of necessary IVF treatment, compared with a fertile individual who seeks out PGD for the sole purpose of selecting for a child with a disability? We know very little about the patient populations who seek out embryos with known genetic anomalies other than that they do exist in some small measure. We also know the two most common traits that affected patients seek are inherited forms of deafness and dwarfism. In addition to the public tale of Sharon and Candy's desire to raise deaf children, other deaf couples have sought out PGD for this same purpose. A British couple who visited their local fertility clinic to ensure the birth of a deaf child defended their actions in the press by explaining, "Being deaf is not about being disabled. It's about being part of a linguistic minority."[56] Likewise, prospective parents of short stature caused by achondroplasia have approached fertility specialists to ensure the birth of a little person, expressing a desire for a child who is "just like them."[57]

Anecdotally, some physicians express an unwillingness to treat patients in pursuit of intentional diminishment. One physician in the Washington, D.C., area who has denied requests to use PGD for selecting deafness and dwarfism said in an interview, "In general, one of the prime dictates of parenting is to make a better world for our children. Dwarfism and deafness are not the norm."[58] Another Chicago ART provider agreed, commenting on the appropriate use of genetic screening technologies, "If we make a diagnostic tool, the purpose is to avoid disease."[59] At the same time, survey research indicates that a few ART practices are willing to assist patients to select in favor of a disabling condition. In 2008, researchers at the Genetics and Public Policy Center asked ART clinics about their practices and perspectives on genetic testing of embryos. When asked if the responding clinic performed PGD to "select for a disability," 3 percent of clinics answered in the affirmative.[60] The authors did not define the term "disability" but in their report associated this response with using PGD "simply to satisfy the preferences of the future parents."[61]

Placing modern practices into a historic context, it is clear that early American eugenicists would not have approved the use of medical intervention to ensure the birth of a disabled child. In fact, we might describe the entire eugenics movement as a fight against intentional diminishment, given the prevailing certainty at the time that all parental deficits would be inherited by their offspring. Surgically stopping unfit and feebleminded parents from procreating, to the early eugenicist's mind and medical worldview, was the same as declining to assist a disabled parent in pursuit of a similarly situated child. At the same time, eugenicists would have approved, even mandated, that disabled parents take up selection technologies to avoid birthing like children. Today, both practices proceed legally unfettered in the United States, modulated only by providers' willingness to assist inquiring patients. What does this clinical reality say about our eugenics legacy or our relationship with eugenics in the modern ART world?

We can say with equal fervor that we both reject and embrace eugenic tenets based on our contemporary genetic selection behavior. On the one hand, we permit parents to intentionally risk (via natural conception) and orchestrate (via assisted conception) the birth of children with disabilities. In this way, unlike our eugenicist ancestors, we display our neutrality toward or acceptance of disability as part of our societal fabric. Individual parental evaluation of a child's worth is elevated over collective societal views that are often uninformed and discriminatory. On the other hand, the vast majority of prospective parents, with the aid and approval of their assisting physicians, choose to avoid the birth of disabled children by selecting against embryos that bear any genetic deficits. Though we no longer outwardly advertise our disdain for the less able-bodied, as was so prevalent in the early 1900s, our actions may speak just as loudly.

ART-based manipulation of reproduction based on the likelihood that a child will inherit an unwanted familial trait is the closest analogue we know to our eugenics past. Disability advocates, understandably haunted by these now repudiated practices, warn that "disability-based selection and disability-based denials of access to fertility treatment are part of the same culture of pernicious discrimination in medicine."[62] If there are any lessons to be learned from this dark period in our history, one is that reproductive decision making is best left to the individual rather than the state (or its proxies). The imposition of community-based values in procreation was not a good fit for American society, in part because of its flawed scientific foundation and in part because we were destined to favor an individual liberty model. Justice Douglas's broad-minded midcentury pronouncement that procreation was a "basic civil right . . . of man . . . fundamental to the very existence and survival of the race," marked the beginning of the decline of the American eugenics movement and paved the way for parents to control their reproductive destinies.[63] Today, it is essential for a broad spectrum of parents to be able to partner with reproductive medicine specialists in their quest for procreative opportunities. In all but the rare cases of serious and certain harm to mother or child, these reproductive partnerships should proceed without conflict or intervention.

The Harms of Procreative Deprivation

I n December 1982, historian and law professor Paul Lombardo had an encounter with a historical figure that would change his academic future and reshape decades-old perceptions of the American eugenics movement. In a nursing home near Charlottesville, Lombardo interviewed Carrie Buck, subject of the infamous Supreme Court decision in 1927 upholding the Virginia eugenic sterilization law. In *Buck v. Bell*, Justice Oliver Wendell Holmes Jr. lauded the public health benefits of compulsory sterilization, confidently asserting, "It is better for all the world, if . . . society can prevent those who are manifestly unfit from continuing their kind."[1] Holmes then added the stunning blow, "Three generations of imbeciles are enough."[2] As records discovered by Lombardo would later show, Carrie, her mother, and her daughter were of normal intelligence, the victims of a conscious campaign to implement the aspirations of several powerful eugenic enthusiasts.[3] Meeting Carrie Buck, Lombardo remarked that her "frailty reflected the trials of a long hard life."[4] Newspaper accounts revealed the depth of Carrie's enduring pain as well as that of her sister Doris, who was also forcibly sterilized, the latter lamenting, "I wanted babies bad."[5] Other victims of forced sterilization have spoken of the pain and anguish wrought by the state's butchery, living out their lives with deep regret over their lost parenthood.[6]

Recent efforts to address the harms done to tens of thousands of Americans over half a century have taken shape as formal apologies and payments to surviving victims.[7] This contemporary hand-wringing is an important acknowledgment that state-sponsored reproductive deprivation is among the most profound offenses a citizen can suffer. Our journey so far has queried whether barriers to ART in the form of high costs, suppressed access for racial and ethnic minorities, and treatment refusals to those who are disabled or experience social infertility resemble the thinking and tactics embraced during the eugenics movement. If so, are the harms from deprivation of assisted conception services of equal impact to those wrought by unconsensual, unwanted, and procreative-robbing surgeries? Whatever the comparison, each person deprived of an opportunity to parent by law, policy, or provider suffers gravely in ways that go beyond the first-line harm of forced childlessness. In this chapter, we explore the myriad harms produced when an infertile individual or couple is denied access to effective fertility treatment. These harms befall patients, providers, children, and society in various ways, strengthening the case that disparities in access to ART warrant attention and reform.[8]

Harm to ART Patients

As human beings, in the main we have a natural inclination to reproduce and to value the products of our reproductive efforts. Ask virtually any parent about the relative value of his or her life experiences, and you will most often hear, "The most significant and meaningful thing I have done in my life is parent my child(ren)." Because of the central importance of parenthood to the human experience, denial of the opportunity to procreate—through refractory infertility, lack of resources, provider unwillingness, or government restrictions on ART—strikes at the core of how we see ourselves and our place in the world. As articulated by John Robertson, "Reproductive experiences . . . are central to personal conceptions of meaning and identity. To deny procreative choice is to deny or impose a crucial self-defining experience, thus denying persons respect and dignity at the most basic level."[9]

The experience of being denied access to lawful means of reproductive assistance is equally devastating, knowing that biological parenthood is at hand but feeling the wrench of denial of those services based on personal characteristics largely outside of one's control. The harms to prospective ART patients caused by such denials affect human well-being in a variety of ways, ranging from measurable financial burdens to more ethereal, but no less haunting, constitutional infringements and dignitary harms. Since prospective patients are on the front line of treatment denials, the harms are felt most acutely by those denied the fundamental right to reproduce.

FORCED CHILDLESSNESS

Individuals who confront reduced or restricted access to ART may resign themselves to a life without children, suppressing or managing their feelings of disappointment, shame, and worthlessness that often accompany unresolved infertility.[10] The prospect of forced childlessness from reduced or denied ART treatment can provoke a range of responses in the affected population, depending upon the basis for the curtailed access. In some instances, the reaction may be to seek alternative routes to parenthood; in others, infertiles may withdraw entirely from a health care system that has utterly failed to meet their reproductive needs.

Ample research surrounds the psychology of infertility, but little empirical data exist to explain the physical and mental health status of individuals who confront insurmountable barriers to ART access. Secondary sources for investigating the impact of forced childlessness include studies measuring involuntary childlessness following unsuccessful fertility treatments. In a Swedish study, researchers found that couples who underwent failed IVF had a lower quality of life than couples with children.[11] Overall, the women reported childlessness as feeling like bereavement, while men said they often felt frustrated by not knowing the cause of the infertility. The study's author explained that the enrolled patients who were unable to have children "perceived their infertility as central to their lives, and above all that quality of life amongst men without children was more negatively affected than had been previously reported in studies of involuntary childlessness."[12]

A Danish study reinforces the ill health effects of unsuccessful fertility treatment, finding that women and men who underwent IVF cycles and never conceived had shorter life spans than couples who did conceive through IVF.[13]

Whether forced childlessness produces greater harm than involuntary childlessness has not been formally studied, but anecdotal evidence suggests the impact is severe and long lasting. The personal accounts of those denied access to ART share a common theme of humiliation and anguish. Recall the words of Lupita Benitez, who was denied ART treatment because her partner was a woman. In describing "the indignity of being turned away," she reflects, "It does do a great deal of damage to a person when you tell them they aren't worthy of having a child or having a family."[14] Upon being turned away for treatment, the blind Kijuana Chambers described her reaction to a reporter. "The doctor treated me like I wanted a new doll for Christmas. I had spent two years thinking about this before I made the decision to have a child."[15] Andy Inkster, a transgender man who was refused treatment at a Massachusetts ART clinic, recalls being told he was "too masculine" to have a baby and that he would have to undergo a mental health evaluation to determine his "emotional ability to handle pregnancy and parenting," something other patients are not asked to endure.[16]

Lupita, Kijuana, and Andy shared at least two commonalities: they each brought a legal action against their ART denier, and each went on to have a child with the aid of another medical provider. Fortunately, each had the resources and the emotional stamina to pursue further treatment, but this will not be the case for every person denied access to assisted conception. Age, lack of resources, absence of a clinic within a reasonable distance, or sheer exasperation can pose an insurmountable obstacle to further pursuing biological parenthood. Other than accepting forced childlessness, are there other options for aspiring parents facing such obstacles? A common suggestion to those unable to procreate on their own is to look to the possibility of adoption. Two questions arise in the context of ART-spurred adoption—is it possible, and is it desired?

First let us examine the question of whether those denied fertility treatment can substitute adoption to achieve their dreams of parenthood.

The answer is less than certain. As described by Ellen Waldman, there are at least two routes to adoption in the United States, public agency adoption and private/independent adoption, with cost representing one of the main differences between the two.[17] Public agency adoption places children who come into the care of the state, often via parental abandonment or abuse and neglect. Agency adoption can be relatively low cost (compared with the cost of IVF), and thus can offer parenthood to couples who are financially unable to access ART. The drawback, however, is that the demand for healthy infants far exceeds the supply, forcing eligible couples to endure long waits for a much-wanted infant. Moreover, state agencies often limit placement of infants to opposite-sex married couples, thus shutting out single people and same-sex couples from this adoption process.[18]

Adoption through a private agency or through independent means is legal in most states, and usually involves only a lawyer or physician as an intermediary between the pregnant woman (or parent of an existing child) and the adopter(s). However, all private agencies have their own requirements regarding age, marital status, and income that may exclude, for example, couples of lower socioeconomic status, older single women, or same-sex couples. Additionally, private adoptions can be as expensive as IVF, ranging in cost from $10,000 to $25,000, a prohibitory expense that may have placed a prospective parent outside of the ART realm in the first place. Finally, laws in several states prohibit same-sex couples from adopting children, thus imposing a secondary barrier to parenthood for this select group of socially infertile persons.[19]

Even if adoption were a viable option for those denied access to ART, would this route be desirable? Interesting research by I. Glenn Cohen and Daniel Chen looked at the relationship between ART and adoption, specifically investigating whether state mandates for increased coverage of IVF had an impact on domestic or international adoption in the jurisdiction. The pair collected data to test the often heard critique of ART that it crowds out or diminishes adoption, suggesting the latter is a substitute for the former. In fact, the results showed that increases in IVF insurance coverage do increase ART utilization, but that subsidizing this form of assisted conception does not diminish adoptions in the same jurisdiction.[20] The authors concluded that adoption is not an equal substitute for biological parenthood; many turned away for fertility treatment may not even consider this alternative family formation option.

As a practical matter, adoption offers only a limited and often undesirable reprieve from ART denials, primarily for married heterosexual couples whose income is sufficiently high to meet wealth requirements, but not high enough to afford the staggering cost of infertility treatment. Both practice and law reveal that adoption is not widely available to many of the individuals and couples who are shut out of the ART arena for reasons of race, ethnicity, marital status, and sexual orientation. Considering the ineligibility of older single women, same-sex couples, and racial and ethnic minorities of lower socioeconomic status, coupled with the scarcity of adoptable children and lack of desire to engage in the adoption process, adoption is hardly a recipe for combating the devastating harm of forced childlessness engendered by barriers to ART.

UNDUE BURDENS ON PROCREATION

Denial of access to assisted conception works as a deprivation of desired medical care and, because of the special nature of the services, arguably as a constitutional infringement as well. Reproduction as a protected constitutional right enjoys a rich history, told mainly through U.S. Supreme Court precedents. From the perspective of the right to engage in reproductive activity, the story begins with the Court's 1942 decision in *Skinner v. Oklahoma*. The Court in *Skinner* overturned the Oklahoma Habitual Criminal Sterilization Act, a eugenics-era law authorizing state officials to sexually sterilize repeat felons for crimes involving "moral turpitude."[21] Writing for a unanimous court, Justice William O. Douglas described the case as "touch[ing] a sensitive and important area of human rights . . . the right to have offspring."[22] In repudiating the law and helping bring an end to the eugenics era, Douglas declared: "Procreation involves one of the basic civil rights of man . . . fundamental to the very existence and survival of the race."[23]

The *Skinner* legacy remains much debated in terms of its contemporary impact, but the fact is the case remains the only high court precedent to consider the right to procreate as an affirmative act. Every other case to come before the Court in the realm of reproduction has involved the right to avoid procreation, through the use of either contraceptives or abortion. Taken as a whole, John Robertson describes this body of case law as giving rise to "procreative liberty," the right to be left alone by the state in pursuit of reproductive choices.[24] Thus, the meaning and viability of procreative liberty, like any constitutional right, derives from a cadre of cases raising challenges to governmental actions that arguably affect a protected right. In the modern era, comprehensive judicial discussion of the fundamental right to procreative liberty is embedded in *Planned Parenthood of Southeastern Pennsylvania v. Casey,* the Court's abortion decision from 1992.[25]

In *Casey,* the Court began by confirming that the constitutional protection of a woman's decision to terminate her pregnancy derives from the Due Process Clause of the Fourteenth Amendment.[26] The language extolling that no state shall "deprive any person of life, liberty, or property, without due process of law" gives rise to the procreative liberty at stake in the abortion context. This liberty, the Court explained, is not absolute but must be balanced against the state's legitimate interest in the life of the unborn. Thus, the Court formulated a legal standard for evaluating state regulation of elective abortion, weighing the woman's liberty interest against the government's interest in potential life. State abortion regulation, the Court declared, will be invalid if it poses an "undue burden" on the right of a woman to decide whether to terminate a pregnancy. An undue burden exists "if its purpose or effect is to place a substantial obstacle in the path of a woman seeking an abortion before the fetus attains viability."[27]

The undue burden test remains the centerpiece of the Court's abortion jurisprudence, though the high court has taken precious little opportunity to elucidate exactly when state action constitutes an undue burden on a reproductive liberty. In the years since *Casey,* the Supreme Court has cited the 1992 case over two dozen times, but only two of these decisions involved direct regulation of abortion.[28] With no express limitation, the concept of undue burden and procreative liberty need not be confined to the abortion context.[29] The same procreative liberty supporting the right to choose to end one's pregnancy arguably applies equally to actions intended to initiate conception and childbirth. If this logical inference is sound, then state action that interferes with the decision *to* procreate should also be evaluated under the undue burden analysis. Imagine, for example, that the undue burden test was the reigning analysis in 1942 when the *Skinner* court evaluated the Oklahoma law authorizing forced sterilizations. We can be confident that Justice Douglas would have found the law to pose an undue burden on the right to procreate. We should query whether contemporary laws that indirectly regulate access to reproductive technologies can likewise withstand constitutional challenge.

The barriers to ART discussed throughout this book take the form of enacted law and private conduct. Since, very generally speaking, only state action can rise to the level of constitutional infringement, for purposes of applying the undue burden test to ART denials we will limit our inquiry to relevant enacted law. While lawmakers have attempted to enact statutes that would directly prohibit certain individuals from accessing infertility care (recall the "married only" bills introduced in Indiana and Virginia discussed earlier), to date no state or federal law is so blatant in its language or stated purpose. Instead, a substantial number of laws pose indirect barriers to access, mostly by limiting state-sponsored benefits of ART to married couples. A prime example of these laws are the state-based insurance regulations that require carriers to provide coverage for infertility care, but permit insurance companies to limit benefits to married couples. As we saw, at least five of the so-called mandate states require that a patient be married in order to seek reimbursement from a participating provider.[30] Does this indirect limitation on access to ART pose an undue burden on unmarried individuals who need reproductive medical assistance? A strong argument can certainly be so made.

The notion of singling out unmarried individuals for disparate treatment in the realm of reproduction was long ago shunned by the Supreme Court. In a 1972 case striking down a state law prohibiting, inter alia, the distribution of contraceptives to single people, Justice William Brennan penned the much-quoted admonition, "If the right of privacy means anything, it is the right of the individual, married or single, to be free from unwarranted governmental intrusion into matters so fundamentally affecting a person as the decision whether to bear or be-get a child."[31] A law that prevents an infertile single woman from access-ing safe and effective assistance in reproduction is a clear affront to her "right to privacy," a right that today is framed in terms of the procre-ative liberty interest. Depriving a single person access to reproductive assistance that is readily available to married individuals seems unlikely to serve any state interest, let alone a compelling state interest needed to justify infringement on the fundamental right to procreate.[32]

State laws that deprive unmarried individuals of access to ART seem ripe for invalidation under the Constitution on the grounds of deprivation of liberty, but what about discriminatory policies that are the product of private conduct? These offenses may not inflict consti-tutional harm because of their failure to trigger state action, but they can still be seen as imposing undue burdens on a person's right to seek medical assistance in reproduction.[33] Private conduct that limits an in-dividual's right to access assistance in reproduction may not work a for-mal constitutional affront, but its burdens affect a person's economic, geographic, and health status.

ECONOMIC BURDENS

Denial of ART services by one or more providers does not always mean the end of a person's reproductive journey. As noted above, the three individuals whose stories of ART denial were made public went on to have successful infertility treatment. Each is now a parent to at least one biologically related child. In the case of unmarried lesbian Lupita Beni-tez, who was turned away by the only ART provider in her employer-sponsored health insurance plan, she and her partner Joanne Clark sub-sequently sought treatment from an "out-of-plan" physician. The pair incurred substantially greater cost than continuing treatment with the provider listed on her health insurance plan would have posed.[34] In ad-dition to denying treatment and forcing Lupita outside the health plan, the covered provider—North Coast Women's Care Medical Group—refused to reimburse its patient for the added expense she incurred by its refusal. Despite these setbacks, Lupita was fortunate in at least two ways; she had the resources to fund her treatment, and she resided in an area with a relatively large number of ART providers.[35]

The economic burden on "disqualified" patients who rely on health insurance coverage for all their medical needs, including their reproductive needs, cannot be ignored. It is certainly possible that medically and socially infertile individuals choose their jobs, or even their domiciles, on the basis of a proffered health care plan. A person who selects a job, or a health plan, in reliance on its availability for covered fertility services suffers unduly from being forced to seek and individually bankroll ART treatment elsewhere. Since a clinic's deprivative policies are generally not formalized or published, there is simply no notice to treatment-seekers that they will be disqualified from receiving service, either when they select a health plan or when they visit a covered clinic for an initial consultation.[36] As noted in the preface of this book, not only did the clinic in the *Benitez* case not formally post its policy stating its providers' religious objections to treating certain patients, but Lupita and Joanne reported that the clinic did post a nondiscrimination policy that included the categories of marital status and sexual orientation. Lack of notice and hidden selectivity force rejected patients to search out alternate providers, possibly incurring additional expenses for travel or time away from work, adding to their already unanticipated economic burden. Traveling to obtain fertility care is another burden worthy of independent examination.

FERTILITY TOURISM

A somewhat overlooked but costly burden that befalls individuals who are denied ART treatment based on their personal characteristics is the involuntary foray into "fertility tourism," the act of traveling outside of one's domicile to access fertility services. More formally designated "cross-border reproductive care" (CBRC), the phenomenon of individuals and couples leaving home to access fertility care is a global issue raising a host of legal, practical, and ethical concerns.[37] The two primary driving forces behind fertility travel are a need to reduce the cost of care and an effort to circumvent legal restrictions in a departure jurisdiction.

While CBRC is mostly studied as an international practice, with citizens of one country traveling to another country for cheaper or more accessible care, fertility travel can occur within a single country. Interstate and intrastate fertility travel in the United States does take place for both reasons that motivate international cross-border travel—better cost and more favorable legal treatment. The cost of treatment can vary from locale to locale, motivating those who are paying out of pocket to seek the most affordable treatment. In terms of legal rationales, our state-by-state treatment of family law, including parental rights associated with the use of gamete donors and gestational carriers, prompts many ART users to consider seeking treatment in a state other than their own.

The main barriers to ART discussed throughout the book can be addressed in some measure by CBRC. Being denied or having difficulty accessing fertility treatment because of cost, race, ethnicity, marital status, sexual orientation, or disability may be relieved by seeking treatment outside of one's domicile. In some cases, the desire to escape one barrier produces another barrier in its place. For example, Andy Inkster, the transgender male turned away by a clinic in Springfield, Massachusetts, was eventually able to receive treatment at a Boston-area facility, some two hours away from his home.[38] Overcoming the barrier of sexual identity discrimination meant adding to his already heavy cost and inconvenience burden associated with fertility treatment.

Imagine a prospective parent who lives in an area where the only ART clinic has (or all have) adopted a "no singles" policy. This patient will be forced to travel, possibly great distances, to receive care. The economic burden of this forced travel is obvious, but there are psychological and emotional costs as well. Leaving one's home, one's job, one's partner, one's family, to pursue a quest that itself poses physical and mental challenges disproportionately burdens, in this example, unmarried individuals compared with their married counterparts. Regrettably, some commentators have downplayed this burden of localized reproductive deprivation, remarking that rejected patients can "simply go elsewhere."[39] Such callousness wholly discounts the realities of ART treatment in this country. The spatial disparities of fertility clinics in the United States mean that as many as six states are under- or poorly served (including Alaska, Montana, Wyoming, and West Virginia), requiring patients to travel great distances from their homes to access care.[40] Moreover, this travel burden may be heaped on top of the economic burden incurred from having to pay for "out-of-plan" services, since a health plan is unlikely to cover an out-of-state or out-of-network ART clinic. Unlike most tourists, fertility tourists take no pleasure in their jaunts from home.

HEALTH IMPACTS

The affront of being turned away from medical treatment on the basis of personal characteristics can affect a person's likelihood and willingness to seek other health care in the future. The relationship between the American health care system and certain racial and ethnic minority populations, particularly African Americans, remains strained based on years of mistreatment and abuse. Seeking treatment for infertility care is lower among black women than white and Hispanic women, due in part to historic health injustices that continue to taint and disincentivize the traditionally underserved from seeking medical care.[41] Several recent studies suggest this same repression of medical treatment-seeking is prevalent in the LGBT community. One research project investigating health disparities among gay, lesbian, and transgender patients revealed that nearly 15 percent of older adults surveyed reported that they were fearful about accessing health care services outside of the LGBT community, and roughly 13 percent reported being denied health care services or provided with inferior care as a result of their sexual orientation or gender identity.[42]

The impact of ART treatment denials can extend beyond the quest for further fertility care to treatment-seeking for preventive and essential health services. A 2011 study by the National Center for Transgender Equality and the National Gay and Lesbian Task Force found that 28 percent of those surveyed said they had postponed medical care because of prior instances of provider discrimination.[43] This same deferral, and at times complete refusal, to seek medical care out of fear of further discrimination has been studied in the lesbian population. According to a study conducted by a Stanford University researcher, lesbian patients experience widespread sexual orientation bias by health care providers, shutting down critical communication between patient and physician and driving gay women away from the medical system. As a result, this population experiences greater incidence of illness because these women limit "their utilization of standard screening modalities, potentially resulting in higher morbidity and mortality from cancers and heart disease."[44] A sister researcher at the University of California–Los Angeles concurs, finding that "research has repeatedly documented that lesbians report frequent negative encounters in health care settings, including inappropriate interventions, hostility from providers, and violation of confidentiality."[45]

ART treatment denials on the basis of personal characteristics are uniquely and profoundly damaging to patients. Medically qualified individuals are denied a particular type of treatment strictly because of their social or demographic status. In clinical practice, doctors do withhold certain types of treatment on the basis of a patient's social status in non-ART settings, but these treatment denials are based on legitimate concerns about poor medical outcomes. For example, intravenous drug users are often denied organ transplantation on the grounds that they will be unable to adhere to the strict postoperative regimen of anti-rejection medications. Denying a person the opportunity for biological parenthood based on social status has no equivalency to medically driven treatment refusals. Such discriminatory rejection only magnifies the emotional and psychological trauma already associated with infertility. Feelings of worthlessness, withdrawal, alienation, and self-doubt may mount in the face of a direct attack on a person's worthiness to contribute another member of the human race. After such an affront, it is no surprise that members of targeted populations would retreat from the medical system altogether, risking their health and ultimately their lives. As poignantly put by one lesbian woman after she and her partner were denied IVF, "I don't feel I will be able to trust anyone in the health-care profession again after this."[46]

DIGNITARY HARMS

Embedded in our nation's tradition of protecting individual civil rights is the recognition that denial of equal access to public goods on the basis of immutable characteristics is an affront to personal dignity. This sentiment was codified in Title II of the Civil Rights Act of 1964, which provides in relevant part: "All persons shall be entitled to the full and equal enjoyment of the goods, services, facilities, privileges, advantages, and accommodations of any place of public accommodation, as defined in this section, without discrimination or segregation on the ground of race, color, religion, or national origin."[47] Almost immediately after passage of the Civil Rights Act, in *Heart of Atlanta v. U.S.*, the Supreme Court affirmed both the wisdom and constitutionality of Title II as a legitimate legislative effort to "vindicate the 'deprivation of personal dignity that surely accompanies denials of equal access to public establishments.' "[48] The Court observed that laws prohibiting discrimination in public accommodations "eliminate [the] evil" of businesses serving only those "as they see fit," which demeans both the individual and society as a whole.[49]

From a litigation strategy perspective, one might want to explore whether ART clinics are "public accommodations" under the Civil Rights Act (they probably are not),[50] or other federal laws (they probably are),[51] such that treatment denials are actionable federal civil rights offenses (this is likely only if the claim arises on the grounds of race, color, religion, or national origin).[52] But from a policy perspective, the more salient inquiry is whether intentional withholding of ART services on the basis of personal characteristics works a deprivation of personal dignity. A strong case can be made in the affirmative.

The provision of ART services is at its heart a medical activity in which physicians control and patients seek the technical means to procreate. Central to the provision of reproductive medical services is the patient's right to decide whether to accept or reject a proposed treatment, after due consideration of the risks and benefits attendant to a given modality. Both common law and bioethics principles have long acknowledged the preeminence of patient autonomy and respect for persons in the arena of medical decision making. Nothing suggests these values would not extend to decision making surrounding assisted conception. Such values, bioethicists argue, also support recognizing the dignitary rights of patients, rights that arise in the health care setting independent of physical injury and even emotional distress.[53] Dignitary rights arise from a patient's common-law right of self-determination in medical decision making, a century-old right first described by Judge Benjamin Cardozo in *Schloendorff v. Society of New York Hospital.*[54] As explained by Richard Saver, "This common law right safeguards not only patients' physical health but also arguably advances their intrinsic worth as independent moral agents."[55]

Borrowing from Saver's language, the act of procreating can certainly be described as an activity that advances a person's intrinsic worth as an independent moral agent. Deciding whether and when to create another life, a life that (typically) takes on the procreator's genetic traits and social history, is deeply tied to an individual's sense of self and place in the world. Those who are fertile may exercise their positive right to reproduce as independent moral agents, free from interference by state or private actors (other than intimate partners whose procreative prospects may also be at stake). Infertile people, on the other hand, are not generally free to make independent procreative decisions, as their choices must be vetted by those who hold the means to assisted conception. The fortuity of infertility places an awesome power in the hands of ART providers that would otherwise rest solely with the individual. Abuse or misuse of that power works not just a deprivation of parenthood, but a deprivation of the human dignity that is at the root of procreative decision making.[56]

Dignitary harms are particularly acute when treatment denials are based on personal characteristics, rather than personal circumstances. The barriers to ART discussed herein fall into these two categories. Race, ethnicity, marital status, disability, sexual orientation, and gender identity are examples of personal characteristics, whereas wealth and employment status are better categorized as personal circumstances. Whereas structural economic reforms are best suited to address personal circumstance barriers (such as greater access to insurance coverage), formal anti-discrimination law is our system's best defense against personal characteristic discrimination. Both federal and state civil rights laws recognize the invidious nature of characteristic-based discrimination, prohibiting discriminatory conduct that is motivated by fear, hatred, or stereotyping of individuals who bear the protected qualities. In many instances, as we saw, state civil rights laws offer broader protection to individuals than are available under federal law, including protections against discrimination on the basis of marital status and sexual orientation.

Even if dignitary harms arising from ART denials gain recognition as legally cognizable claims, questions remain about the appropriate mechanism for redress and the impact on physician autonomy. Both of these uncertainties can be resolved by codifying existing antidiscrimination policy statements by physician organizations within the framework of enacted state civil rights laws. For example, the American Medical Association Code of Medical Ethics provides a comprehensive statement of nondiscrimination in the provision of medical services by licensed physicians: "Physicians who offer their services to the public may not decline to accept patients because of race, color, religion, national origin, sexual orientation, gender identity or any other basis that would constitute invidious discrimination."[57]

With the exception of express inclusion of marital status discrimination, this statement encircles the bases on which ART providers might refuse to provide care to a medically qualified "ready, willing, and able" patient.[58] Codifying this prohibition and applying it to ART refusals on the basis of specific enumerated personal characteristics could go a long way toward remedying the dignitary harms suffered when essential reproductive services are denied. An ART-specific statute might read: "A physician and surgeon or other health care provider offering fertility treatment to the public shall not decline to accept, or incite others to decline to accept, any patient because of race, color, religion, national origin, sexual orientation, gender identity, marital status or any other basis that would constitute unlawful discrimination." Moreover, incorporating a calculus for damages further addresses the serious harm to dignity that results when reproductive opportunities are arbitrarily withheld. Borrowing from existing state laws, violations of an ART-specific antidiscrimination law could be punishable by monetary damages. Similar to California's civil rights law, a remedy could be set out as follows:

> Whoever denies, aids or incites a denial, or makes any discrimination or distinction contrary to [the applicable antidiscrimination law] is liable for each and every offense for

the actual damages, and any amount that may be determined by a jury, or a court sitting without a jury, up to a maximum of three times the amount of actual damage but in no case less than [$12,000 — representing the average cost of an ART cycle], and any attorney's fees that may be determined by the court in addition thereto, suffered by any person denied the rights provided in [the applicable antidiscrimination law].[59]

Providing monetary damages that are loosely linked to the cost of the sought-after services seems a fair solution and a fair penalty for unlawful discrimination. Other solutions might include imposing a duty on physicians to refer patients to a willing provider, or imposing monetary damages equal to the out-of-pocket losses incurred by patients who are forced to seek ART care outside their health insurance network, or outside the area where they live. But the imposition of treble "actual damages, and any amount that may be determined by a" trier of fact, bests other options by expressing the seriousness of the harm inflicted. Providers who discriminate will incur losses that exceed the cost of "buying off" the patient by sending her to another physician (and paying the differential costs). Moreover, creating a secondary market of nondiscriminating ART providers only emphasizes and institutionalizes the second-class status of those who experience barriers to ART. Separate but equal is not a value the ART community, or any community, should strive to achieve.

Harm to ART Providers

By nature and profession, physicians are generally motivated to offer medical assistance to people in need. Turning away a medically and financially qualified prospective patient from sought-after treatment is contrary to the vast majority of doctors' sensibilities, as well as basic tenets of the profession. The American Medical Association sets out as a foundational principle of medical ethics that "[a] physician shall support access to medical care for all people."[60] With such a strong inclination to provide treatment at the core of medical practice, the act of turning a patient away extracts a certain cost to individual physicians and to the profession as a whole. ART providers do suffer harm as a result of treatment denials, though these harms may not appear as direct and self-evident as those experienced by affected patients. The harms visited upon physicians can be analyzed along a scale of voluntariness that corresponds to the nature and source of the barrier imposed. Barriers imposed upon a physician-patient relationship (most commonly by the state) are herein referred to as external barriers; barriers that are voluntarily adopted—that is, self-imposed—by individual and group providers will be referred to as internal barriers.

Examples of external barriers include prohibitions on providing service imposed by law or other authoritative third-party actors. Recall the state lawmakers who introduced bills that would make it unlawful for ART physicians to provide treatment to unmarried women. If these laws were enacted, violation of them would place physicians in jeopardy of professional disciplinary action, essentially forcing them to withhold desired and medically appropriate treatment. Other external barriers include laws and regulations governing health insurance that dictate a patient's eligibility for coverage. While these insurance parameters to not necessarily prohibit a physician from offering treatment to a patient (who is able to afford the out-of-pocket expenses), these limitations do inhibit a physician's ability to provide care to all who need or desire assisted conception services. External barriers are involuntary as they are imposed upon providers without solicitation of their agreement or consent.

Internal barriers are impediments to ART treatment voluntarily put in place by providers themselves. Clinic policies that dictate specific exclusions or individual providers who refuse to accept patients based on proxies for race and ethnicity (such as source of income), marital status, family background, disability, or sexual orientation are examples of internal barriers. Interestingly and arguably contradictory to its principle of equal access to all, the AMA principles of medical ethics also support a physician's right to refuse to accept a patient as an expression of professional autonomy.[61] The freedom "to choose whom to service," as described in the AMA Principle of Medical Ethics, is, in some cases, essential to maintain a high quality of medical practice and professionalism. In other instances, service refusals impose tremendous harm on patients and providers alike. In the following sections we explore the provider harms produced by both external and internal barriers to ART access.

EXTERNAL BARRIERS: ECONOMIC AND REPUTATIONAL HARMS

Laws and policy decisions that restrict or reduce patient access to ART affect the economic well-being of ART providers. When providers are effectively barred from assisting certain patients by measures such as the "married only" bills or insurance regulations that limit treatment based on patient demographics, these physicians are deprived of income and professional satisfaction from these prospective patients. As a percentage of the overall ART patient population, the market of single individuals and same-sex couples desiring assistance in conception is ample and growing, such that a physician's inability to tap into that patient segment could be financially and professionally devastating. Additionally, policy decisions among health insurance providers to limit or withhold coverage for ART are also likely to negatively affect a provider's economic health. At a minimum, casting fertility services into a "fee for service" mode—in which patients pay out of pocket for medical services—limits the number and breadth of patients a physician encounters.

Measuring economic harms to a provider's bottom line seems straightforward enough, though it depends largely on the ability to identify the lost market and calculate the corresponding lost revenues. We do know that treatment-seeking among medically infertile women in the United States hovers at around 50 percent, meaning that only half of all American women who are classified as infertile ever seek medical assistance for the condition.[62] Further, when treatment-seeking is scored along racial and ethnic lines, the number of minority patients who seek treatment declines significantly.[63] While a number of factors affect treatment-seeking in general and among minority populations in particular, affordability is certainly the biggest barrier for most patients. Research on the relationship between treatment-seeking and insurance coverage confirms that ART utilization increases when coverage is provided.[64] Focusing just on the potential patients who are formally excluded by insurance barriers within their jurisdictions—that is, by mandates that cover only married individuals—logic dictates that the loss of this market share translates into measurable economic harm to providers in that state.

External barriers can also pose reputational harms to physicians. Admittedly, harms to a provider's reputation as a result of external barriers are far more speculative, but nevertheless worthy of exploration. Initially, it may seem that a law or policy prohibiting a physician from servicing members of a group would not induce blame on the provider, but rather on the body propounding such a restriction. As demonstrated by at least one historic example discussed below, physician cooperation with enacted directives that violate societal norms can generate ill will against the regulated actors. Why, those outside the ART community might wonder, didn't the physicians object to the imposition of the mandate as a sign of support for their patients? Why, a shunned patient might ask, would providers allow such restrictions unless they viewed them as permission to act in a desired discriminatory fashion?

Prospective or even current patients who perceive their physicians' willingness to submit to exclusionary policies as a sign of endorsement may find themselves among the growing group of fertility tourists. Outrage, distress, or even solidarity with their shunned counterparts could prove harmful to a physician's reputation, perhaps even decimating his or her patient population. Such was the concern among physicians in Sweden who faced a government-mandated change in the administration of ART services. When Swedish lawmakers abolished donor anonymity for sperm donors in 1985, a significant number of fertility specialists expressed their unwillingness to support the new legislation.[65] These physicians understood that donors opposed the law, and would be unlikely to participate in open-identity donation. In addition, the Swedish physicians also perceived that their patients would prefer a system of donor anonymity, leaving the decision of disclosure up to each individual parent rather than the state.[66] Thus, instead of working within a system they considered seriously flawed, these physicians stopped recruiting sperm donors altogether and referred their patients abroad.

While the Swedish physicians may have been motivated by economic factors (a downturn in the AID market), their actions are also fairly viewed as an attempt to shore up their professional integrity among vital stakeholders in their ART world. Showing respect for a patient's desire for autonomy in her procreative and parental decision making by providing her alternatives to existing, restrictive services can go a long way toward protecting a provider's reputation for independence and compassion.

INTERNAL BARRIERS: THE ROLE OF PHYSICIAN AUTONOMY

Physician motivation for refusing to provide medical treatment to interested parties derives from the principle of physician autonomy. The concept that a physician is free to determine whether or not to enter into a doctor-patient relationship with a prospective patient is embedded in medical ethics and health law. As noted earlier, the American Medical Association recognizes physician autonomy in the selection of patients as a basic principle of medical ethics.[67] Legal recognition of physician autonomy is also a key component of American health law. Barry Furrow and his colleagues, who authored a major textbook in health law, describe the principle of physician autonomy in the context of the doctor-patient relationship as follows: "The traditional legal principle governing the physician-patient relationship is that it is a voluntary and personal relationship which the physician may choose to enter or not for a variety of reasons. Legal obligations on the part of providers to furnish care operate as exceptions to this general rule."[68] The exceptions to which Furrow and his colleagues refer are the statutorily enumerated categories of impermissible discrimination contained in federal and state civil rights laws. Under federal law, these categories include race, color, religion, national origin,[69] and disability.[70] State laws similarly prohibit discrimination of the bases enumerated in federal law, but some states extend the group of protected classifications to include other categories, including marital status, sexual orientation, and gender identity.[71]

Despite these explicit prohibitions against health care discrimination on the basis of personal characteristics, values-inspired ART treatment refusals do persist. Recall that the physicians refusing to treat the partnered but unmarried lesbian patient in San Diego asserted what can be considered a subset of physician autonomy—a religious objection to facilitating single and LGBT parenthood. Specifically, the objecting physicians argued they were constitutionally insulated from adhering to the state's anti-discrimination law because the First Amendment protected exercise of their sincerely held religious beliefs.[72] The California Supreme Court rejected this argument, holding that valid and neutral state laws of general applicability preempt assertions of religious freedom in derogation of civil rights statutes. Whether other states would strike this same balance favoring civil rights protections over religious freedom is uncertain.[73] At the federal level, the preeminence of religious freedom over compliance with health care mandates won a victory in the U.S. Supreme Court in 2014. In *Burwell v. Hobby Lobby*, the Court permitted closely held corporations asserting religious objections to be exempt from a portion of the Affordable Care Act mandating that employers provide contraceptive coverage for female workers.[74] Undoubtedly, the robust debate over the role of individual religious freedom in the health care setting will continue well into the future.[75]

In addition to religious beliefs and practices, the inputs that compose and drive physician autonomy arise from moral, cultural, educational, familial, and other experiences and principles. These inputs influence physician conduct in every area of practice, yet two areas stand out as particularly nettlesome in the clash between physician autonomy and a patient's right to treatment—reproductive health care and end-of-life treatment. As to the former, assertions of physician autonomy over the reproductive decision making of another accompany the delivery of ART and abortion services. Whereas physician autonomy in the delivery of ART services is somewhat underdeveloped legally, the law is highly structured in the abortion arena. Legislation in almost every state, known as "conscience clauses," permits physicians and other health care workers to refuse to participate in abortion services if performing those services conflicts with their individual conscience.[76] These legislative safe harbors are designed to honor a physician's professional conscience by providing immunity from institutional, civil, or criminal liability that might otherwise arise from a doctor's refusal to provide medical care.[77]

The value and supremacy of physician autonomy in the abortion context is heavily debated. It has been argued that "these abortion refusal statutes demonstrate . . . that our society is sensitive to the fact that doctors are not mere technicians who, because of their special training, must use their skills whenever asked. Instead, society accords physicians a right to moral autonomy in selected clinical settings."[78] This moral autonomy, according to the American Congress of Obstetricians and Gynecologists (ACOG), is not absolute. In a published opinion on conscientious refusals in reproductive medicine, ACOG expresses respect for physician conscience but ultimately instructs that "in an emergency in which referral is not possible or might negatively affect a patient's physical or mental health, providers have an obligation to provide medically indicated and requested care regardless of the provider's personal moral objections."[79] Given the potential conflict between legal and professional duties, a physician trained to perform abortion may confront a difficult choice in the face of an emergency termination request.

Clashes between physician values and patient choice also dot clinical care at the end of life. The issue is often discussed as the problem of medical futility—the provision of care to critically ill patients who are highly unlikely to receive any medical benefit from the requested treatment. These disputes at the bedside pit family members demanding intensive care for loved ones against physicians whose medical judgment dictates that treatment should be withheld or withdrawn because it will provide no benefit to the patient.[80] In such clashes, forcing physicians to provide medically ineffective care is an assault on their professional integrity and a violation of their professional autonomy. Several solutions have been proffered, including state laws that permit health care providers to refuse to provide medically futile care as well as institutionally based policies that permit providers to transfer these patients to another willing provider.[81] Is this latter solution of elective transfer to another provider also a viable solution for physicians who wish to refuse to provide ART treatment to certain populations? No, it is not.

Transfer rights in the medical futility context allow doctors to show empathy toward a family's anguish while exercising their medical judgment about a patient's clinical condition. Transfer rights in the case of selective ART refusals would allow doctors to express their personal animus toward a patient's social characteristics. Cases of treatment refusal involving medical futility or abortion share the commonality that what is being refused is based on the nature of the procedure, not the nature of the patient. If doctors were to refuse to provide ventilator support, for example, only to black patients, or Jewish patients, or Asian patients, while providing such support to other patients with identical medical profiles, this conduct would be wholly impermissible. Likewise, if obstetricians refused to perform abortions only on white patients, but agreed to abort all other races, the race-based discrimination would be obvious and actionable.

ART treatment denials are never wholesale refusals to provide a specific procedure; they are selective refusals to provide treatment to specific individuals. In fact, ART providers are solicited by prospective parents of all stripes because of their skill in performing AID, IVF, IUI, PGD, and the like. Physicians who routinely provide these services in their practices should not be able to withhold specific treatments on the basis of a patient's personal characteristics if the treatments would be provided to other patients with similar medical profiles. Such a policy does not prevent physicians from exercising their medical judgment. For example, telling a single woman or a woman with a lesbian partner that IUI is not available, while providing this treatment to a medically similar married woman, is not an expression of the physician's medical judgment. Rather, in that case, selective distribution of ART services is a powerful indictment of single and lesbian women as unworthy reproductive actors. Physicians should not use patients as a means to express their views about the social context of parenthood.

At first blush, the idea that reducing physician autonomy to deny ART services works as an overall benefit to physicians may sound counterintuitive. But a strong argument can be made that physicians suffer harm when they individually or collectively impose barriers to treatment by private acts of discrimination against individuals who are as medically and socially capable of bearing children as their fertile counterparts. Patient defection and loss of confidence—either among the rejected patients or even among those who support the latter group's right to reproduce—can be devastating to a physician's practice. Without opportunities to deny treatment on the basis of personal characteristics unrelated to patient well-being, physicians can operate in an environment of medical objectivity and administrative certainty. For physicians who remain refractory to providing ART services to certain populations based on personal characteristics, they cannot reasonably expect to be permitted to use their state-issued medical license for purposes of discrimination. For the vast majority of physicians who recognize the value and import of access to ART for virtually all, the rewards in patient trust and regard substantially outweigh any perceived reduction in autonomy. After all, without patient support, physicians would suffer a total deprivation of livelihood.

Harm to ART Children

Barriers to ART access profoundly affect family growth, depriving those who have never procreated the opportunity for biological parenthood and limiting the growth of families whose progenitors experience secondary infertility after the birth of one or more children. Primary or secondary infertility can be medically or socially based, and can result in forced childlessness or curtailment of family expansion. Thus, ART denials can potentially impact two categories of offspring—the never born and the born.

THE NEVER BORN

Children who are never born because their potential parents are denied access to assisted conception services occupy a more theoretical than actual place in our catalogue of harms, but their inclusion is worthy of brief mention. As an initial inquiry, we might wonder, can a person who is never born be harmed from lack of existence? Sounding in philosophical disquisition, resolution of whether a person can be harmed by nonbirth depends upon the value placed on human existence. If one views human life, no matter its quality or quantity, as an absolute good, then its deprivation could be said to work a harm to those denied the opportunity to come into existence. But if one views human life as a balance of benefits and burdens, then skirting existence would not necessarily work a harm in every case to the never born.[82]

Assuming widespread agreement with the proposition that depriving a child the opportunity to be born should be considered a harm to that never-born person, what can be done to address that harm? Harm compensation, as a practical matter, is typically addressed by the law. The law's relationship with such existential matters as nonbirth is one of skittishness and reluctance. In fact, the law almost never deals with the harm of nonexistence but rather inverts the calculus to address whether being born is ever worse than never being born. Classified as claims for wrongful life, assertions of harm caused by life itself arise when a child is born with disorders or anomalies that cause great pain and suffering. In wrongful life actions, parents argue that a physician acted negligently in failing to inform them prior to or during a pregnancy that their child would be born with a disabling condition. Had they known, the parents assert, they would have chosen not to conceive or aborted an existing fetus.[83] In general, American law does not recognize wrongful life as a legally cognizable claim. Courts, claiming they are ill equipped to decide, as a legal matter, "whether it is better never to have been born at all than to have been born with even gross deficiencies," punt this mystery by denying recovery for claims related to harms for human existence.[84]

The utility of the wrongful life analysis to calculating the harm to never-born ART offspring is slim but extant. In wrongful life, as well as other tort cases alleging injury as a result of a particular child's birth, some harm has befallen a child or a parent as a result of that birth. The law's reluctance to measure that harm by comparing it to nonexistence can be interpreted as legal support for the net benefit of existence over nonexistence. In ART denials, existence itself is thwarted, and thus the result of these actions can be seen as posing a net harm. Looking at the puzzle from a clinical perspective, in wrongful life cases a child is born diminished in some way. Physicians who turn away potential parents do so in some instances because they believe a resulting child would suffer harm, from either an inherited disability or wholly inadequate parenting. Empirically, we know that predictions about the quality of a future child's life are often wrong; those who are classically denied access to ART who go on to reproduce overwhelmingly enjoy normal and stable relationships with healthy children. Thus, the claim that ART denials work a net benefit because they spare the resulting children a diminished life cannot be sustained. Overall, assisting in the conception of much wanted children who suffer no greater harm than other similarly conceived children works a benefit such that its deprivation can be classified as a harm to the never born.

THE BORN

Individuals who seek ART are not necessarily childless. They may have conceived naturally one or more times, but later experience secondary infertility. Secondary infertility, defined as the inability to conceive or carry a pregnancy to term after successfully and naturally conceiving one or more children, is fairly common. According to the National Center for Health Statistics, about half of all instances of infertility in women are classified as secondary infertility. Between 2006 and 2010, of the 6.71 million women who experienced infertility, 3.63 million involved cases of secondary infertility.[85] Persistent infertility can also follow the birth of a child from ART. A parent may have procreated using ART, but now faces a barrier to accessing assisted conception to expand his or her existing family. In either case, barriers to ART affect existing children in ways that can be harmful to their well-being.

For a child or children whose parents are experiencing infertility following natural or assisted conception, the pain and frustration of failing to conceive may come to infect the family dynamic. There is little, if any research, exploring the psychological impact of a parent's infertility on his or her existing children, but narrative evidence of such distress abounds. Websites offer parents undergoing fertility treatments the chance to share their unique position of having a child and struggling to have another. One mother writes of her four-year-old daughter's awareness that her parents are trying to have another baby, praying nightly to bring her a sibling. Another describes how her young son watches as she injects herself with daily doses of hormones, asking if it hurts.[86] Still another woman undergoing IVF reports that she didn't share too much information with her young daughter "so she didn't get amped and heartbroken when things didn't work out."[87] Experts warn parents not to include young children in their ongoing fertility struggles, explaining, "Children do not have the cognitive capabilities that adults do."[88] Even if not formally measured, life experience tells us that a parent's stress is often visited upon a child.

The psychological stress on the family may be even greater if the parents' inability to expand the family is attributable to one or more barriers to ART access. Parents who lack insurance coverage for assisted conception and cannot afford to pay for these medical services out of pocket may stretch the family's resources to fund treatment. If the treatment fails, or even if it succeeds, the parents may face tremendous debt that detracts from their ability to care properly for their existing children. In addition to economic barriers, couples with secondary infertility may encounter ART barriers due to their race or ethnicity. As discussed, an African or Arab American couple, for example, may shun treatment for fear of confronting a provider's stereotypic attitudes toward their desired multiple reproduction. In the event that these attitudes surface, whether real or perceived, they are likely to become known to the existing children, threatening dignitary harm to a second generation.

For children who were conceived using ART whose parents desire another child, subsequent barriers to assisted conception can impact the self-worth and identity of these first-born children. For example, a child born via AID may feel the absence of a father in her life, and long for a connection with a sibling who understands the unique circumstances of her birth.[89] It is becoming increasingly common, if not routine, for donor-conceived children to search out each other, helped along by the Internet, in order to make a connection with a genetically related individual.[90] Closing the door to family expansion via ART means that existing ART children will not enjoy the companionship of siblings who share the distinct nature of their conception.[91] While it is certainly true that singleton children in families thrive in this world, sibling-less ART children whose parents face insurmountable barriers to family expansion may interpret their singleness as a wrong that is being addressed by repressing further similar births.

Children whose parents face ART barriers may be part of a newly blended family configuration. For example, a woman who was previously married, or who had a child as a single woman via AID, may now be part of a same-sex relationship. If the new couple wishes to expand their family but is unable to do so because they encounter marital status or sexual orientation discrimination, their existing children may view this treatment denial as an expression of society's negative view toward their nontraditional family. The child comes to symbolize the unworthiness of the family unit. Conversely, bringing desired children into a newly blended family may be a sign of strength in the developing relationship, a sign that could reassure existing children about the stability of their own place in the family unit and the world around them.

Whether children are in traditional or nontraditional settings, one cannot discount the impact that infertility could have on their lives. A parent's frustration at the inability to further reproduce, whether attributable to medical or social causes, may easily bleed into the parent-child relationship, igniting a host of feelings within the child ranging from empathy, to helplessness, to fear, to self-doubt. Treatment denials based on subjective perceptions of parental worth can morph into societal expressions about the worth of existing children, expressions that these children are likely to perceive and internalize. If for no other reason than avoiding harm to existing children, treatable infertility should not be used as an opportunity for social engineering.

Harms to Society

Can a harm inflicted on a single individual or couple translate into a harm to society? Put more specifically in the context of our topic, is denial of reproductive assistance to individuals a societal harm worthy of redress by comprehensive measures that reach beyond the life of the affected persons? For reasons steeped in the past, significant in the present, and vital to the future, this book's trope urges analysis, recognition, and reform of individual harms precisely because they inflict a greater harm on us as a society. Constructing or refusing to dismantle barriers to human reproduction causes harm to society in at least two ways. First, as our theme asserts, imposing reproductive regimes that deny procreative rights to certain members of a society is dangerously reminiscent of our eugenics past. The network of laws, policies, and social pressures that robbed tens of thousands of their reproductive capacity left a legacy of pain and mistrust that continues to permeate wide swaths of today's society. If we learn nothing else from the eugenics movement, it should be the importance of avoiding the same grand reproductive-related mistakes in the name of societal betterment.

The second way in which society is harmed by ART barriers is through the imposition of disapproval and disdain that the act of reproductive deprivation expresses. Formal and informal mechanisms that restrict access to ART on the basis of personal characteristics, as opposed to objective medical criteria, express societal attitudes that unfairly stigmatize the barred population. Public expressions of stigma are harmful to both the individuals being stigmatized as well as the communities from which they hail. Whether by coercion or deprivation, removing reproductive decision-making capacity from the individual has broad, negative consequences for society as a whole.

THE EXPRESSIVIST ARGUMENT

All conduct, according to some legal theorists, expresses values and attitudes of the actor. Whether the actor is an individual, a group, or the state, the expression of negative or inappropriate attitudes toward an individual causes harm to that person. This "expressive harm" is addressed by the expressive theory—a theory that strives to direct actors "to act in ways that express appropriate attitudes toward various substantive values."[92] As applied to law, expressive theorists measure conduct by governments according to the message that state-backed actions convey.[93] One legal scholar explains that expressive theories of law "converge on the idea that wrongful governmental expressive acts matter because of the stigma they involve; the theories argue that government should neither make nor enforce laws that express attitudes that unfairly stigmatize people."[94] Expressive theory works to decipher the message sent by government-sanctioned action by studying the reaction it generates in individuals, groups, and the state.[95]

Applying this theory to issues of access to assisted conception, attitudes toward those who face medical or social infertility are expressed in at least two ways—by enacted law and by provider conduct. Enacted law directly regulating ART access is relatively sparse, but it can be gleaned from state laws limiting the availability and legal security of family formation through assisted conception. The overwhelming number of states that fail to mandate coverage for infertility treatment, coupled with the handful of states that do mandate such coverage but limit its reach to married heterosexual individuals, is an expression of the state's devaluation of certain individuals' reproductive desires. Arguably, both enacted and neglected laws on insurance coverage for ART express a negative attitude toward its utilization by those who are single or LGBT, as well as those who cannot afford to pay for these expensive services out of pocket. States whose laws legitimize the family status of ART-conceived children only when their parents are married and heterosexual likewise express a negative attitude toward families outside preferred heteronormative configurations.

Physician conduct expressing negative views toward certain patients may be less apparent in the public sphere, but these stigmatizing attitudes are discernable upon careful inspection. We know from survey research, published court opinions, and isolated cases reported in the media that ART providers have refused to provide service to medically eligible patients on the basis of their marital status, sexual orientation, gender identity, disability, race, and source of income. Taken together, enacted law and provider conduct that limit or reduce access to ART cause expressive harm to prospective patients, to others who share the despised characteristics of the shunned patients, and to the children of both of these groups of adults.

Expressive harm can be measured by the unwarranted stigma it causes its victims.[96] Stigma, according to Alan Strudler, "is harm, even if not tangible or monetary harm, and harm, particularly wrongful harm, should not be taken lightly."[97] Patients who seek but are denied ART services suffer stigma by being cast out of the core group of human beings that exercise their natural inclination to reproduce. As discussed earlier, infertility itself is stigmatized (particularly within certain minority populations), and the stigma is surely exacerbated when patients are turned away from treatment. Denying treatment expresses a view that the patient is herself unworthy of parenthood, and therefore unworthy of membership in the human race. If one believes that one's individual worth can only be validated by the production of offspring—whose mere existence confirm that their progenitor has value—then denying the right to biological parenthood imposes an irreparable stigma.

Even people who themselves are not denied access to ART may be stigmatized by the expressive harms suffered by rejected patients.

For example, a lesbian couple with no desire to procreate may learn of the disappointment suffered by other gay couples in their quest to have a child. Even though the voluntarily childless couple will suffer no measurable consequence from the treatment denial, they may be profoundly affected by the attitude expressed toward their peers. Understandably, the lesbian couple may internalize their friends' experience as a message about their own worth as human beings. The couple may worry that if gay people are denied access to parenthood, the most basic of human activities, then what is to stop society from denying them all forms of human rights? Living with this worry can be both stigmatizing and stultifying. If the negative attitudes of providers are seen as representative of societal attitudes in general, such worrying is both justified and necessary.

The expressivist argument that treatment deprivation harms all who share the disfavored trait seems weighty and valid in the context of assisted conception: denying procreation to those who are not wealthy, not white, not married, not heterosexual, and not able-bodied signals that parenthood outside majoritarian constructs is a problem to be solved, not understood and accommodated, because of the threat it supposedly poses to society as a whole. The offspring of nontraditional parents are viewed as a diminishment of a certain persistent myth in contemporary society—the myth that only well-off, white, straight, nondisabled, married couples can bring joy into the life of a child. Purposefully withholding the means to reproduce sends a message to would-be parents, to existing children of nontraditional parents, and to society at large that nonnormative parenthood lacks value in today's world. Allowing such antiquated and outright inaccurate expressions of parental fitness seems to serve no current legitimate societal purpose. As history proves, what is seen as a legitimate basis for stigma at one moment in time reveals itself to be totally unfounded a short while later. Revisiting our eugenics past holds many of the secrets to ensuring the well-being of our ART future.

The New Eugenics

On April 10, 2013, Robert Edwards, a British physiologist and co-creator of human IVF, died at the age of eighty-seven. He long survived his collaborator, Patrick Steptoe, whose passing in 1988 deprived him of the opportunity to share in the Nobel Prize in Physiology or Medicine bestowed upon Edwards in 2010. News of Edwards's death inspired tributes and reflections from around the globe, most lauding his development of a technique responsible for the birth of over five million children worldwide.[1] Hidden among the swell of praise for Edwards and his "passionate belief in humanity" emerged a little discussed fact about the father of modern reproductive medicine: Robert Edwards was an avid and longtime eugenicist. According to documents reported on after his death, Edwards was a member in good standing of the Eugenics Society in Britain for much of his career, even holding leadership positions on several occasions.[2] Impliedly acknowledging the link between emerging reproductive technologies and eugenics as a coercive practice in service of human betterment, in 1999 Edwards reflected, "Soon it will be a sin of parents to have a child that carries the heavy burden of genetic disease. We are entering a world where we have to consider the quality of our children."[3] The revelation of Edwards's views added verdure to long-simmering fears about the eugenic impact of ART.

Even before the 1978 birth of Louise Brown, the world's first IVF-conceived baby, the pallor of eugenics hung over the very idea that man could intervene in the natural conceptive process.[4] Medical journals published at the time Steptoe and Edwards were developing IVF featured dire warnings by critics that any attempt to create human beings in the laboratory constituted "unethical medical experimentation" that should be "subject to absolute moral prohibition."[5] In the early days of IVF, the eugenic critique took shape as broad-based concerns about co-opting control over human reproduction. After all, at that time the eugenics legacy of the American movement and its horrendous role in Nazi atrocities centered on the perils of imbuing the medical profession with authority over the reproductive lives of the disempowered. Reflecting on the allocation of power in human reproduction, Edwards averred that developing IVF "was about more than infertility. . . . I wanted to find out exactly who was in charge, whether it was god himself or whether it was scientists in the laboratory. He quickly concluded, "It was us."[6]

Beginning in the 1990s with the development of embryonic genetic screening technologies, the association between ART and eugenics has morphed into warnings about the resurrection of manipulating individual births to effect human betterment. Instead of the state overseeing this grand project, critics charge that parents who take up techniques such as preimplantation genetic diagnosis to select the fittest embryo for transfer are reigniting an era in which those who are predicted to express illness, weakness, or other flaws are deprived the opportunity to be born. Dubbed neoeugenics, the voluntary, individual decisions by prospective parents stand in for the coercive, collective directives by the state to support reproduction in certain instances and suppress it in others.[7] This chapter sets out the argument that use of ART to select—and perhaps someday enhance—early embryos constitutes a "new eugenics." The merits of this contention, it is argued, are weak and ultimately distract from the true eugenic nature of modern reproductive technologies. It is not the decision of individual parents to foster the well-being of their future children that recalls our eugenics past but rather the inability of a significant number of would-be parents to access the means necessary to achieve parenthood. Barriers to ART serve to manipulate procreation at a population level in a manner that is far more evocative of the degrading practices that characterized our early fascination with good births. To address and perhaps reverse this regression to our eugenics past, a set of recommendations is proffered at chapter's end.

Neoeugenics and the Use of Embryo Screening Technologies

Developments in the field of embryonic genetics are proceeding at a rapid pace, enabling scientists to view the entirety of a future child's genome within days of conception. The advent of PGD using whole genome sequencing gives prospective parents an in-depth glimpse at the genetic makeup of their child to be, making decisions about embryo transfer or discard—at the very least—highly informed.[8] Current technologies permit the detection of over 250 genetic conditions, ranging from benign characteristics such as sex to lethal and painful disorders such as Tay-Sachs disease and cystic fibrosis.[9] Looking into the future, some predict that genetic technologies will expand beyond detection to enhancement, enabling reproducers to select the nonmedical traits of their offspring including intelligence, eye color, height, hair thickness, freckling, memory, and baldness.[10] Embryos that don't possess the full complement of desired characteristics may, perhaps, be tweaked to ensure complete parental satisfaction. The prospect of this depth of procreative manipulation is truly mind boggling, but awareness of the futuristic possibilities brings the potential spectrum of embryonic genetics into clearer focus.

Concerns about the eugenic essence of embryo selection can be categorized into three distinct arguments, each garnering support from leading and influential thinkers in the field of medical ethics. For the sake of discussion, the arguments will be identified as grounded in: (1) the moral status of the embryo, (2) reproductive liberty, and (3) the duty to maximize the well-being of offspring. Each argument finds strength in a different value, ranging from the absolute sanctity of human embryonic life, to the import of individual reproductive autonomy, to the promotion of health over sickness. Yet each argument also provokes discussion about the eugenic aspects of modern reproductive technologies.

EMBRYO DISCARD AS A FORM OF EUGENICS

Absolutist arguments about the sanctity of human life at all biological stages reject embryo discard for any reason. While not initially tinged in eugenics, the argument progresses once gene-based selection technologies are introduced. The broad argument asserts that the use of PGD necessarily contemplates and often involves the discard of developing embryos, and thus is a morally reprehensible act in and of itself. Layering selection for the purpose of discarding disabled persons-to-be adds a degree of inhumanity that rests at the core of eugenic practices. The most ardent, consistent, and long-standing advocate for this position is the Catholic Church, which is unabashed in its opposition to all forms of assisted conception.[11] The church teaches that all embryos "ought to always be born from an act of love and should already be treated as a person."[12] The basis for PGD, the creation of extracorporeal embryos using IVF, is a per se violation of the Catholic requirement that embryonic life result only from heterosexual intercourse. In addition to this generalized opposition to the creation of IVF embryos, the church has expressed its specific disapproval of PGD.

In December 2008, the church released a paper addressing the development of "new biomedical technologies" in its *Instruction on Dignitas Personae on Certain Bioethical Questions.*[13] The paper specifically addresses PGD, declaring that it "constitutes an act of abortion" because it "is directed toward the qualitative selection and consequent destruction of embryos."[14] Going further, the church highlights what it considers to be the inescapable eugenic aim and purpose of PGD, categorizing the technique as an: "expression of a eugenic mentality that 'accepts selective abortion in order to prevent the birth of children affected by various types of anomalies. Such an attitude is shameful and utterly reprehensible, since it presumes to measure the value of a human life only within the parameters of "normality" and physical well-being, thus opening the way to legitimizing infanticide and euthanasia as well.'"[15] Thus, while the church (along with similar thinkers) condemns the act of embryo discard for any reason, its condemnation is elevated in the face of discard based on the detection of genetic anomalies. Preventing the transfer and birth of children destined to display disease or disability simply shifts eugenic reproductive suppression from the act of parental sterilization to the discard of preimplantation embryos. For the church, the fact that this procreative avoidance decision making also shifts from the state to the individual is of little import. Both actors interfere with God's plan to bring life into the world, thwarting birth in the name of human betterment.

REPRODUCTIVE LIBERTY AS LIBERAL EUGENICS

The second argument that embryo selection technologies revisit eugenic principles acknowledges the surface similarities between PGD and the selective breeding techniques of the early American movement, but distinguishes the practices on the basis of voluntariness and individual choice. The ideology most closely associated with this argument is known as liberal eugenics, which advocates for the unrestrained use of reproductive technologies for the purpose of enhancing human characteristics and capacities as an exercise of individual parental preference.[16] In theory, liberal eugenics permits prospective parents to utilize technologies to avoid the birth of offspring with genetic or congenital anomalies (a contemporary clinical reality), as well as to enhance their future children's traits by genetic manipulation (a futuristic scenario). The supporting foundation for liberal eugenics is the assertion that an individual's reproductive liberty includes the right to control her reproductive life by gathering information and using technologies that she deems relevant and important to her procreative decision making.[17] Accompanying this protection of reproductive liberty is a values assumption that parents will act in the best interest of their future children.

Liberal eugenics is unabashed in its support of parental choice to avoid the birth of children with health or other deficits, yet it disavows direct comparison with the early American movement and its strong negative valence.[18] In support of its merit and distinction, advocates for the worthiness of liberal eugenics typically advance three significant differences from its namesake predecessor. First, today's use of ART to promote the birth of healthy offspring (positive eugenics) and correspondingly avoid the birth of children with diseases or deficits (negative eugenics) is entirely individualistic and voluntary. The absence of state coercion in the parent's reproductive decision making converts the act from one required by authoritarianism to one permitted by liberalism. Second, liberal eugenics embraces a parent's decision to avoid the use of detection technologies or to implant an embryo known to have genetic defects. In this way, liberal eugenics is more pluralistic in practice and spirit than classic eugenics. Finally, the tremendous growth in our fund of knowledge about genetics and its role in reproduction separates us from the dark days when heredity was thought to account for all human characteristics and expression. Since we know vastly more about the relationship between genes and health, we are in a better position to navigate the selection process that ART affords.[19]

Critics of unrestricted and unregulated access to PGD tend to place less value on reproductive autonomy and worry more that parents will use this freedom to reinstitute a culture of intolerance and rejection of those outside the norm. Michael Malinowski strenuously warns: "Unless we choose to block our ears and look away, the United States' haunting eugenics legacy beckons us to remember the consequences of allowing the appeal of genetic improvement and controlling evolution to reach well beyond the limitations of science and to skew the practice of medicine and related law and policy. . . . The present largely consumer-driven law and policy environment for assisted reproduction . . . threaten[s] . . . to bring us dangerously close to past mistakes."[20] Embedded in overall concerns about the use of reproductive technologies to avoid the birth of children with disease-producing genetic abnormalities sits a deeper worry that parents will increasingly select against milder and more treatable conditions as well as benign traits that have no impact on a child's health. As the genetic basis of an increasing array of human characteristics is discovered, parental choice will broaden in the number and type of traits their future children will possess. Liberal eugenics may approve the discard of embryos diagnosed to carry lethal or significant life-affecting genetic disorders, but would it also condone a parent who rejects an embryo destined to be color-blind—a detectable autosomal dominant genetic trait?

On this transition from selection against disease to "social selection," Sonia Suter observes, "The more we use technology to select against lesser conditions and traits, the more perfectionist we may become as a culture, and the more demanding we may become with respect to what is acceptable, normal, or healthy."[21] Liberal eugenicists who value the exercise over the consequence of autonomy may oversee a transition from a culture of reproductive choice to one of reproductive requirement, much in line with our eugenic ancestors. As envisioned by Suter, "If we begin to medicalize what we now consider normal traits, enhancement and trait-selection will become more 'legitimate' because they will be understood as part of medical treatment, driving people toward using these technologies."[22] Put another way by the American Medical Association, "The aggregate result of individual choices creates societal and cultural norms which substantially influence or limit the scope of autonomous decision making in regard to the use of genetic technologies."[23] This idea that widespread use of PGD will give rise to a duty to take up genetic technologies in the name of child betterment occupies the third argument that links ART with classical eugenics.

THE MORAL DUTY TO EXERCISE PROCREATIVE BENEFICENCE

The third argument linking the use of ART in general and PGD in particular to eugenics advances the moral duty of parents to maximize the well-being of their children at the earliest stage, even before implantation if the opportunity presents. Australian philosopher and bioethicist Julian Savulescu coined this duty "procreative beneficence," under which he argues that a "couple (or single reproducers) should select the child, of the possible children they could have, who is expected to have the best life, or at least as good a life as the others, based on the relevant, available information."[24] Savulescu applies this parental duty broadly to selection based on disease and non-disease genes, even if such behavior maintains or increases social inequality. The focus under the principle of procreative beneficence is the life of the individual person-to-be, not on any immediate or short-term macro or societal effect. The notion that parents have a duty (that is, should be compelled) to select the "fittest" child is reflective of the tenets of both negative and positive eugenics. On the one hand, parents are enlisted to avoid the birth of less fit offspring so that a future society may prosper (negative eugenics), while being encouraged to select the fittest embryo for transfer (positive eugenics).

Procreative beneficence differs from liberal eugenics in the degree of coerciveness associated with parental choice. Whereas liberal eugenics takes the view that parents should have autonomy to utilize available technologies to determine what is in the best interest of their future children, they should not be required to access or incorporate genetic information into their decision making. In contrast, procreative beneficence imposes a duty on prospective parents to utilize existing technologies and to act on discovered information in a way that maximizes the health and well-being of a future child. Two subset ideologies within procreative beneficence display its alignment with the early twentieth-century eugenics movement. Commentators who favor the imposition of an affirmative duty to maximize offspring health would limit this duty to actions that avoid or prevent known harms. This position is elucidated by philosophers Allen Buchanan, Dan Brock, Norman Daniels, and Daniel Wikler in their book *From Chance to Choice: Genetics and Justice*. After debating the merits of existing genetic screening technologies and possible future enhancement possibilities, the quartet conclude "that both justice and our obligations to prevent harm make genetic interventions to prevent disabilities not only permissible but also obligatory."[25]

The second subgroup within procreative beneficence advocates that prospective parents have a positive moral duty to use genetic technologies to enhance the well-being of their offspring, enabling them to live longer, run faster, think clearer, and so on. British bioethicist John Harris makes the case for this position, arguing in his much-discussed book *Enhancing Evolution: The Ethical Case for Making People Better,* "It is not only feasible to use genetic technology to make people more healthy, intelligent and longer-lived, it's our moral duty to do so."[26] In a future world in which myriad enhancements are available, Harris and others see parents being required to birth a child with certain favored characteristics (and correspondingly being prohibited from birthing a child with disfavored characteristics). The parallels of this public policy to the early American eugenics practices are obvious and, to many, highly concerning.[27]

The New Eugenics: The Case
for Recognition and Reform

Defining the new eugenics along lines that match the use of reproductive technologies with the birth of fitter, more able-bodied, and intelligent children has understandable appeal for its reflection of similarly aimed classic eugenic law and policies. For those who worry over the use of ART as a neoeugenic tool, it matters little whether the affiliation arises from a foundation of the sanctity of the early embryo, reproductive liberty, or procreative beneficence. But this view of ART as the new eugenics is, if accurate at all, so limited in scope as to perilously overlook the true eugenic nature of today's emerging procreative technologies. As argued throughout, the true eugenic effect of ART is not in its use but in its deprivation. Numbers alone bear this out. Of the roughly ten million Americans who suffer from medical infertility, and the uncounted cohort who experience social infertility, only a small fraction even seek treatment, and a minuscule percentage avail themselves of genetic selection technologies. In 2013, of the 190,773 ART cycles performed in the United States, only 6 percent (roughly 11,400) involved PGD.[28] Further, studies show that within overall PGD usage, less than 10 percent of all embryonic genetic testing involves a search for nonmedical characteristics.[29]

The fractional use of ART in relation to its potential to benefit millions of individuals is explained by a host of factors, including its affordability, disparate availability to racial and ethnic minorities, discretionary withholding to single and LGBT patients, and diminished provision to people with disabilities. This collective procreative deprivation is far broader and more impactful than even the most dire predictions about our genetically manipulated future. The new eugenics are plaguing the less wealthy, less white, less able-bodied, less traditional, and less politically powerful in much the same way that decades of restrictive immigration policies, years of discriminatory marriage laws, and a half-century of forced sterilization afflicted these same groups—by depriving them the opportunity to reproduce in unison with more favored populations. The new eugenics as selective breeding in an era of reproductive technologies is enmeshed in the various barriers to ART discussed herein, barriers that need not stand today, tomorrow, or in perpetuity. Once we recognize the nefarious nature of these eugenic barriers, we can begin to address each in ways that are both practical and aspirational.

To address the new eugenics, I recommend the following reforms. As with any set of recommendations, some ideas are not new and already have garnered widespread support in the field; others are modified from reforms adopted in other arenas, and still others are—to the best of my knowledge—novel. Consideration, at the least, and adoption, in an ideal world, of one or more of these suggested reforms will do much to advance greater and more equal access to ART.

RECOMMENDATION 1: BROADEN FISCAL SUPPORT AND INSURANCE COVERAGE FOR INFERTILITY CARE AT THE NATIONAL AND STATE LEVELS

Cost is the steepest and most pervasive barrier to ART access. Even small incremental changes that increase affordability can have widespread impact, opening ART doors to many who now regard assisted conception to be out of reach. At least two avenues for fiscal reform can be considered—insurance coverage and tax relief. The former is more likely to be achieved at the state level, while the latter depends upon action by federal law makers. The ART insurance labyrinth continues to play out at the state level in the wake of dashed hopes that the Affordable Care Act of 2010 would address the pressing need for fertility coverage at the national level. As of this writing, it seems unlikely that insurance coverage for IVF will flow from future tweaks to the ACA or any legislation originating in Congress. Thus, advocacy transpires at the state level, where patient groups continue to press for initial or expanded coverage mandates. With thirty-five states embracing no mandate for fertility care coverage, bringing even a few states "on board" at several-year intervals would ease the generalized burden that high costs impose. Research on the impact of state insurance mandates for infertility coverage consistently shows that treatment-seeking increases when insurance is provided.[30] Moreover, the cost of mandating IVF coverage has been shown to be reasonable, adding only a few dollars to annual premiums,[31] as well as demonstrating a public health benefit, reducing the incidence of multiple births in covered jurisdictions.[32] The cost savings alone from reducing maternal and infant health problems associated with multiple births could lower or neutralize any fiscal impacts that mandates impose on insurance companies and policyholders.

Fiscal relief at the federal level could take shape as tax relief for those who pay out of pocket for fertility care. In 2011, such a proposal was introduced in Congress as the Family Act, a bill that would create a tax credit for moneys paid for IVF and fertility preservation treatment.[33] The 2013 version of the bill would have permitted patients to claim a credit for up to one-half of their treatment expenses, up to a maximum of $12,000, the average cost of a single IVF cycle. The credit is means-tested, available only to patients earning less than $189,000 annually. The primary sponsor for the bill, the national infertility advocacy group RESOLVE, says that an actuarial study concluded utilization of IVF would increase by 30 percent in the United States if the bill were passed.[34] Even if this estimate is overly optimistic, surely such a credit could lessen the budgetary impact of treatment enough to expand access to some who would otherwise go untreated. Despite the bill's appeal as a family-friendly, middle-class-oriented reform, it has failed to gain passage. Concurrent advocacy for more robust insurance coverage and meaningful tax relief is a frontline issue in the battle to dismantle ART barriers.

RECOMMENDATION 2: DEVELOP AND PROMULGATE
PROGRAMS AND INNOVATIONS FOR REDUCED-COST
TREATMENT STRATEGIES WITH POSITIVE OR
NEUTRAL FISCAL IMPACTS ON ART CLINICS

Expanding mandated insurance coverage will aid but in no way solve the fertility care cost problem in our country, given the broad exclusions for self-funded and small-scale employers who occupy a large percentage of the market and the high co-pays that even the most generous plans require.[35] Greater accessibility must also run through reducing the net costs to patients, an outcome dependent upon voluntary shifts in the market and innovations that lower the price of reproductive medicine services. The average cost of a single IVF cycle, pegged at $12,400, has changed little over the past decade. Any legislative efforts aimed at directly reducing IVF costs would be impermissibly anti-competitive, while even "soft" attempts to persuade ART physicians to lower their fees would strike many as targeted and unfair. Moreover, coercive measures to reduce patient costs could disincentivize physician participation in the field, making treatment more scarce and potentially of lower quality. Instead, voluntary offerings to lower or adjust fees, often according to patient income, have been advanced and are showing promise.

In our private health care market, in which ART operates, it is uncommon for fee-for-service pricing to be means-tested to accommodate a patient's ability to pay. This is not to say that physicians (or their billing services) do not routinely make ad hoc adjustments to assist patients on an individual basis, but systematic fee structures based on patient income do not appear to be widespread in ART medicine. A good number of fertility clinics, however, do advertise low or reduced-cost IVF. In some cases, clinics offer lower fees for patients without insurance coverage,[36] or financial aid in the form of grants for those who may not quality for a traditional loan.[37] One clinic offers a reduced fee—from $10,000 to $7,800—for members of the military, teachers, firefighters, and police. This discount, the clinic advertises, is in recognition of the "sacrificial careers" these individuals have undertaken.[38] Another growing trend to reduce IVF costs looks to a lower level of service in which the standard of care medications and procedures are cut back. Styled "mini-IVF" or "micro-IVF," costs are cut in half by reducing or eliminating the use of high-priced injectable medications that stimulate the woman's ovaries, resulting in lower drug costs, fewer office visits, less frequent ultrasound procedures, and fewer blood draws. These pharmaceutical and clinical reductions culminate in overall lower costs for an IVF cycle. Preliminary data on the efficacy of mini-IVF are promising, with at least one study showing patients in certain age ranges had higher pregnancy rates using reduced medications compared with conventional IVF.[39] ART clinics that offer reduced fees or mini-IVF may calculate that the resulting reduction in revenue per cycle is neutralized or converted into an overall gain by increases in the patient pool.

In addition to cost-saving reconfigurations of standard IVF treatment, researchers are exploring new innovations that could dramatically reduce the cost of ART worldwide. In 2013, Belgian researchers tested a shoebox-sized IVF laboratory built from inexpensive glass tubes that uses baking soda and citric acid to create the carbon dioxide needed for fertilization to occur.[40] Pregnancy rates using this laboratory reportedly matched those from a standard laboratory, but costs were reduced significantly. Another recent cost-saving innovation involves placement of hours-old embryos into a small plastic cylinder that is then inserted inside the woman's vagina for several days. The cylinder replaces the expensive laboratory incubators now used to nurture the early embryos.[41] The idea, ultimately, behind these types of bare-bones setups is to make IVF accessible in every corner of the globe at very low cost, say $300 per attempt. Advances aimed at bringing IVF to resource-poor areas of the world can also benefit patients of modest means in developed countries. In the United States, adoption of the "mini-lab," the "in vitro incubator," or other cost-saving innovations will depend upon their safety and efficacy, but should they prove clinically meritorious they may greatly increase access to ART. The ART market, like most markets, welcomes betterment through fair competition and innovation.

RECOMMENDATION 3: EXPAND THE CHARITABLE ARM OF THE FERTILITY INDUSTRY TO PROVIDE NO- AND LOW-COST TREATMENT TO UNDERSERVED POPULATIONS

IVF costs have three main components: (1) professional fees for physicians, nurses, lab personnel, and administrators, (2) laboratory and equipment costs, and (3) drug costs for the array of pharmaceuticals used in a standard IVF cycle. Recommendation 2 addresses possible avenues to reducing hardware-related costs, shifting attention to service and drug costs. To improve ART access, both the medical profession and the pharmaceutical industry could be called upon to expand what seems an underdeveloped charitable arm of the fertility industry. Visibility of robust nonprofit organizations devoted to fertility assistance is low, but a few fledgling projects do dot the landscape. For example, the International Council on Infertility Information Dissemination, Inc. (INCIID), describes itself as "the world's leading infertility consumer advocate and provider of information and support related to fertility, family-building and pregnancy loss."[42] Despite this rather grandiose bio, the group raised less than $100,000 in 2012 and reported negative net assets to the Internal Revenue Service.[43] Moreover, INCIID's impact is small; in its first year of operation granting IVF cycles to low-resource applicants (through medical services donated by ART physicians),[44] the organization received 120 applications and awarded 45 IVF cycles that ultimately yielded one live birth.[45] A few other IVF-granting nonprofits exist, but also appear to provide assistance to a very small number of patients.[46]

Charitable assistance for fertility preservation in the wake of a cancer diagnosis enjoys a somewhat higher profile because of its initial affiliation with the nonprofit organization Livestrong founded by Lance Armstrong in 1997. The Sharing Hope Program, launched in 2001 with support from the Lance Armstrong Foundation, offers financial assistance and ART services to cancer patients seeking fertility preservation services. Sharing Hope is supported through donated fertility medications; discounted sperm, egg, and embryo banking services; and donated professional services from physicians across the country.[47] The nonprofit was founded, in part, as a response to the lack of insurance coverage for fertility preservation services. In some cases, cancer patients' insurance actually covered infertility treatment, but they did not qualify for reimbursement, which was dependent upon "the failure to conceive from unprotected intercourse." Prior to cancer treatment, patients do not meet this clinical definition. Without preserving eggs or sperm before undergoing chemotherapy, options for procreation upon recovery are more limited and more expensive. Donations in money and services from all three essential sectors of the ART market—physicians, laboratory service providers, and drug manufacturers—have coalesced to form a comprehensive charitable operation that may be worthy of imitation.

Perhaps the emotional appeal of aiding cancer victims far outstrips the plight of otherwise healthy individuals who are unable to reproduce on their own. But both cohorts share the plight of unrequited parenthood, a life deficit capable of provoking widespread empathy. This recommendation urges the ART community to develop a broader charitable arm that provides services to those who cannot otherwise access fertility treatment. Such an effort could mimic aspects of Sharing Hope, with physicians, laboratories, and drug companies asked to donate products and services that are then made available to eligible patients. The administrative costs of such an endeavor would be substantial and could be supported by targeted fund-raising in the ART world. For example, ASRM (the largest U.S.-based organization of reproductive medicine professionals) could create a foundation dedicated to providing ART assistance on a charitable basis. Similar efforts have been undertaken by legal professional groups, such as state bar associations, to provide no- or low-cost services to under-resourced populations.[48] Once in place, the ASRM foundation could seek voluntary donations from its members via the annual membership invoice, while also educating the three key ART provider groups about opportunities for pro bono service to the patient community. Harnessing the strength of this long-established and well-regarded organization for charitable purposes would send a powerful message about the value of ART access for all.

RECOMMENDATION 4: DEVELOP STRATEGIES TO EXPAND AVAILABILITY OF ART SERVICES IN UNDERSERVED AREAS

The vast majority of ART clinics in the United States are located in highly populated cities, and within those cities, in pockets that are home to the wealthiest and least diverse segments of the surrounding metropolis. Geographic stratification of fertility care means that historically underserved patient populations will often find it challenging to access ART, even if cost does not present an overwhelming barrier. The metropolitan focus of ART clinics also means that wide swaths of our country house few, and in some cases no, facilities, making treatment a logistical impossibility for those unable to temporarily relocate or surrender hours per day in transit.[49] The rigorous treatment schedule associated with IVF entails sometimes daily visits to the clinic for blood draws, ultrasounds, and other needed interventions.[50] Improving access by locating or relocating ART clinics to underserved areas requires an investment of financial capital and human resources that may be unavailable or wholly impractical. After all, the highly competitive nature of ART practice suggests that strategic decisions about clinic placement already take into account projected return on investment; large parts of our nation are medically underserved for a variety of reasons, including business economics that counsel against infrastructure investment. ART clinics are particularly vulnerable to these economic factors, considering the high-cost equipment and surgical space required for a quality operation.

To address geographic stratification, ART providers could consider incorporating two trends in health care aimed at increasing access to distinct patient populations. First, the growth of satellite and affiliated medical offices across the country is changing the landscape of health care delivery from a hospital-centered tradition to more community-based options. Placement of medical services more proximate to patient access means more clinics located in retail parks, near malls, and other "off-campus" locales where potential health care consumers otherwise tend to congregate.[51] Some of these changes are attributable to reforms set out in the Affordable Care Act, while others merely capitalize on the higher level of convenience that patients increasingly demand. ART clinics could bring their services closer to underserved patients by, for example, affiliating with community-based medical providers that could perform some of the routine testing associated with IVF. Blood draws, injections, and even ultrasounds could be performed at a satellite locale that spares the patient long travel times required to visit the primary clinic. Of course, these services would still require oversight by a qualified infertility specialist, who could be made available by a second trend in health care delivery.

The shifting medical office has also been accompanied by a shifting medical provider, at least measured by the potential reach of diagnostic, consultative, and treatment services. The uptick in telemedicine, virtual monitoring, and technology-enabled home health care has eliminated the need for in-person interactions in some instances.[52] At present, the advent of telesurgery (surgery performed distant from the patient using medical robotics and multimedia communication) for egg retrieval and IVF is futuristic, but we can imagine such a breakthrough given the rapid pace of technological advancement in medicine. For now, remote ART treatment might include visualization of ultrasounds performed at a distant location, or immediate reporting of blood draws to the "home" provider. Even minor adjustments to the IVF clinic regimen that make the difference in a patient's ability to access treatment are worthy of consideration.

RECOMMENDATION 5: ADVANCE AND IMPROVE CULTURAL COMPETENCY TRAINING AND AWARENESS FOR ALL ART PROVIDERS THROUGHOUT THEIR PROFESSIONAL LIFE CYCLES

On the theory that familiarity breeds empathy and understanding, this recommendation strives to create a closer connection between the historic and lived experiences of traditionally underrepresented infertility patients and the knowledge, attitudes, and skills of ART providers in addressing those nonmedical features. The import of sensitizing health care providers to recognize and respond to their patients' varied cultural backgrounds has been a formal component of physician training for well over a decade, at both the medical school and continuing medical education levels.[53] This notion of cultural competency has been variously defined, with one offering as follows: "The knowledge of the cultural backgrounds of one's patients, including their native language and preferred methods of communication, system of values and beliefs, religious affiliations and customs that can belong to a person of a specific racial, religious or ethnic group."[54] Today, nearly 90 percent of all medical schools offer some form of cultural competency education as part of their training program;[55] practicing physicians are exposed to cultural competency training through continuing medical education programming, which in some states is required to include clinically relevant cultural information.[56] The success of such efforts is debated, with some research showing that cultural competency improves physician-patient communication and collaboration, increases patient satisfaction, improves clinical outcomes, and reduces health disparities.[57] Other data suggest that current methods of imparting cultural competency have no impact on clinical practice, leaving practitioners unprepared to provide appropriate cross-cultural care.[58]

Cultural competency in reproductive medicine poses unique challenges that may not be adequately addressed by a generalized approach to raising cross-cultural awareness. One challenge arises from the patient population that seeks or could benefit from fertility care. This population is diverse in more ways than are typically included in cultural competency training efforts. Much of the emphasis in cultural competency focuses on race and ethnicity, though there is increasing effort to broaden the covered categories to include sexual orientation and gender.[59] Still, the cultural barriers that suppress and disrupt ART treatment-seeking include but exceed race, ethnicity, and sexual orientation. Features of socioeconomic status, income source, marital status, gender identity, disability, and social history can prompt providers to refuse treatment, certain that in so doing they are forestalling some envisioned harm. As argued throughout this book, in most instances these predictions of harm are not supported in law, medicine, or sociology. Thus, cultural competency training in ART should be tailored to address the vast array of diverse individuals whose journey to parenthood must run through a fertility clinic.

A second challenge for cultural competency training in ART notes the seeming lack of attention paid to this topic among active practitioners in the field. A survey of the academic literature in reproductive medicine yielded almost no published writings on the topic. A literature search in the National Institutes of Health's PubMed database for the terms "cultural competency + IVF" turned up no items, and a similar search in the ART specialty journal *Fertility & Sterility* displayed only two relevant articles, both focusing on access to treatment in racial and ethnic minority populations.[60] Further, perusing the detailed forty-page program booklet for the 2014 ASRM annual meeting revealed only one presentation with the words "cultural, racial, and ethnic differences" in the description.[61] The field can do a better job of embracing cultural competency as a value in the provision of fertility care.

Informing and sensitizing ART providers to the meaning and relevance of patients' cultural backgrounds should consider a team approach, including all branches of the clinic organization. Since patients frequently interact with nurses, administrators, mental health professionals, and lab personnel as well as physicians, it makes sense to engage the entire team in cultural competency training. In the case of health care professionals, such training can be (and often is) incorporated into undergraduate and graduate training, as well as continuing education often required to maintain professional licensure. Further competency can be achieved through collaboration with advocacy and service groups affiliated with the diverse communities that have experienced historic barriers to ART. Dialogue, education, and shared research efforts between reproductive medicine professionals and culturally underrepresented groups can promote a closer connection between patient experience and provider understanding.

RECOMMENDATION 6: ENCOURAGE AND ASSIST ART
CLINICS IN ADOPTING AND MAKING AVAILABLE BROAD-
BASED WRITTEN PATIENT NONDISCRIMINATION POLICIES

A theme reiterated throughout these pages is that ART providers are generally free to agree or decline to treat patients seeking infertility treatment, constrained only by federal and state anti-discrimination laws that lack broad-based reach into demographic features that can form the basis for discriminatory treatment denials. In addition to law, physicians are sometimes guided by individual clinic policies that spell out the providers' philosophy and practice on the matter of access to service. This recommendation flows from research showing that fewer than half of all ART clinics have formal written policies addressing patient selection,[62] and those that do often fail to include the full range of categories that would provide a comprehensive assurance of nondiscrimination. For example, one clinic seemingly takes pride in its nondiscrimination policy by prominently displaying it on the front page of its website. The policy reads in full, "We maintain our commitment of nondiscrimination based on age, marital status and sexual orientation."[63] What about race, ethnicity, socioeconomic status, disability, and sexual identity? Perhaps the clinic believed that state and federal law addressed non-included patient demographics (race, ethnicity, disability), but gaps remain (wealth status, sexual identity). Moreover, clinics are often called upon to make access decisions that transcend these formal categories. Questions about physician willingness to provide treatment that poses a potential risk of harm to the patient (that is, where pregnancy is health- or life-threatening) or the resulting offspring (born to child abusers, drug addicts, and so on) arise yet are rarely formally addressed in advance.

Sparse promulgation of formal written clinic policies can be attributed to at least two factors. First, it has been shown that in some multi-physician ART practices, significant disagreement exists among the physicians about various policy stances, inhibiting the production of consensus policies.[64] As with many organizations that experience internal disagreements, some ART practices have managed to adopt consensus policies that apply clinic-wide. One interesting study reports that in practices where physicians held a range of personal views on the appropriateness of treating certain patients, the clinic policy reflected the more permissive perspective. Clinic policies, in general, were less restrictive than the opinions held by individual physicians within the practice.[65] The study authors speculated as to the reasons for this result, offering explanations like respect for patient autonomy, fear of litigation, economic pressure to offer a broader range of services, and internal adjustments that match certain patients with willing providers within the practice. This latter approach requires a pre-planned process that makes clear how patient candidates will be vetted and assigned, tasks a clear written policy can accomplish.

A second explanation for the low level of formal clinic policies on access to treatment may be the difficulty of drafting such documents. Physician groups may feel ill-equipped to create and commit to policies that tread on outside disciplines, including law and mental health care. Referral to legal counsel or other experts may be expensive and time-consuming, further suppressing the priority of this group activity. A solution may rest in assembling a national committee of experts to draft model policies that could be made available for adoption at individual clinics. Such model policies could be written broadly to include all potential areas for discrimination, and could include suggested processes for gathering, assessing, and acting on patient information. Moreover, model policies can be drafted in a menu-type format to provide for state-by-state variation and individual clinic preference. Such a committee was formed by a joint effort of ASRM and its affiliated professional society, the Society for Assisted Reproductive Technology (SART), to draft model patient consent forms for use in ART practice. In 2011, the ASRM/SART multidisciplinary committee began to hold regular conference calls to develop model consent forms for various aspects of ART treatment, including first-party IVF, egg donation, and disposition of cryopreserved embryos.[66] Several years of collaborative work by this multidisciplinary group produced over half a dozen model forms, many of which have enjoyed adoption by clinics throughout the country.[67]

Similarly tasking a group of experts to draft model clinic policies on access to treatment could promote greater adoption of clear written statements that alert prospective patients to individual clinic practices. My hope is that providers would favor broad-based nondiscrimination language that promotes the least restrictive access to treatment, but clinics would certainly be at liberty to adjust their policies to meet legally sanctioned personal preferences. The availability of model policies would provide a starting place for clinic members—physicians, nurses, mental health professionals, lab specialists, business administrators—to begin a dialogue about how to reconcile their views in service of those seeking infertility treatment. Experience and observation teach us that discriminatory views can be subconscious or misunderstood in terms of their impact on others. Clinic personnel discussions that touch on these issues may be initially difficult but ultimately highly useful in moving the practice toward publication of an agreed-upon clinic policy. Promoting internal discussion and external disclosure of treatment parameters are vital steps toward removing barriers to ART access that now take refuge in arbitrary, reactive, and ad hoc provider decision making.

The Road Ahead

Invoking the word "eugenics" in any conversation, let alone a conversation about modern reproduction, entails risks and rewards. The risk is that the word is predictably provocative, evoking memories of a regrettable and shameful display of inhumanity toward humankind. At the same time, the word is exquisitely descriptive, leaving no informed participant to wonder about the grand significance of the topic at hand. Linking the ever burgeoning field of assisted reproductive technologies to eugenics means risking a reaction that is instinctively negative, positioning the audience to quickly dismiss counterarguments as inexcusably apologetic. My hope is that this book has navigated away from that path, finding support for the notion that eugenics as applied to ART has valuable lessons for the fair and equal access to the tools of assisted conception. To say that today's barriers to ART are eugenic in nature is not to call for a dismantling of the ways in which reproductive medicine assists in family formation, but rather to highlight the opportunities to improve access for all who could benefit.

This book is an anthem for the democratization of ART. Exposing the many ways in which reproductive assistance is withheld, denied, deprived, diminished, and revoked is to also reveal the widespread need and desire for its adoption. The mismatch between the current use and current need for ART motivates these passages that critique the law and policy that permit access barriers to persist. The actionable recommendations set out herein can help shift the course of ART access to a more democratic future. Even if no such reforms are taken up, I remain hopeful that external factors will coalesce to incrementally widen access to reproductive technologies. Global and national changes that, in some instances, are seemingly unrelated to ART will usher in an era of greater availability and access to reproductive assistance.

Cost barriers will fall as innovation rises. The focus on greater worldwide access to ART, particularly in the developing world, has incentivized development of cheaper and more adaptable conception-aiding technologies. The perfection of safe and effective low-cost IVF may be the result of efforts to bring ART to the four corners of the earth, but surely it will find its way to all corners of the United States. The possibility that introduction of more bare-bones IVF methods will initially stratify ART use along socioeconomic lines exists—with wealthier patients adhering to tried and true methods and less well off infertiles adopting riskier protocols—but eventually some tipping point will yield an overall superior and lower cost technique. Barriers based on race and ethnicity are likely to be addressed by the shifting demographics of our nation. The coming of our majority-minority population, now predicted by 2043,[68] will surely improve access to health care, including assisted reproductive care, for these new majority consumers and voters. Finally, the marriage equality revolution that has swept the nation can only improve access for the socially infertile. Incorporation of more and novel family structures into the fabric of our culture will broaden the need and correspondingly the availability of reproductive assistance.

Let us seize the momentum toward a more democratic distribution of the incredible technology that brings life and love in ways unthinkable only decades ago. Let the specter of the eugenics movement caution us against depriving others of the same choices we demand in the pursuit of parenthood. Let us embrace the possibility that we can make the next generation healthier and better in birth without sacrificing our sustaining commitment to individual liberty and betterment for all.

Notes

ONE The Reproductive Revolution

1. Gen. 30:1 (King James Version).

2. *Id.* at 30:3–5. Jacob's paternal grandfather, Abram, was likewise entreated by his infertile wife Sarai to "go in unto my maid; it may be that I may obtain children by her." *Id.* at 16:2. Jacob's reaction to his wife's infertility may ring timeless for couples who experience a similar medical reality. Upon hearing his wife's plea for issue, "Jacob's anger was kindled against Rachel: and he said, Am I in God's stead, who hath withheld from thee the fruit of the womb?" *Id.* at 30:2. Stress, anger, frustration, and blame remain common modern-day reactions to an infertility diagnosis. *See, e.g.,* B.D. Peterson, C.R. Newton, K.H. Rosen, & G.E. Skaggs, *Gender Differences in How Men and Women Who Are Referred for IVF Cope with Infertility Stress,* 21(9) Hum. Reprod. 2443 (2006); S. Fassino, A. Piero, S. Boggio, V. Piccioni, & L. Garzaro, *Anxiety, Depression and Anger Suppression in Infertile Couples: A Controlled Study,* 17(11) Hum. Reprod. 2986 (2002).

3. Contemporary references to current infertility treatments as modern or medical marvels abound. In an interview about her new book about the money side of assisted conception, *The Baby Business* (2006), then Harvard Business School professor (and as of July 1, 2008, president of Barnard College) Deborah Spar opined that "fertility treatments are yet another medical marvel." Rich Barlow, *In Baby Business, What Are the Rules?,* Bos. Globe, Mar. 15, 2008, at 2B.

4. *See* Elizabeth Scott, *Surrogacy and the Politics of Commodification,* 72 Law & Contemp. Probs. 109 (2009) (discussing the moral panic generated in the wake of early surrogate parenting arrangements in the late 1980s).

5. *See* Paul A. Lombardo, Three Generations, No Imbeciles: Eugenics, the Supreme Court and *Buck v. Bell* (2008). Lombardo's book on the American eugenics movement is a stunningly intelligent, comprehensive, and insightful work that garnered

widespread literary praise and earned its author the 2009 Georgia Author of the Year Award. Much of this book's discussion of eugenics policies and practices traces back to Lombardo's fieldwork as a historian vested in uncovering the core documents that portend and explain the rise and fall of eugenics in American life.

6. Skinner v. Oklahoma, 316 U.S. 535 (1942). For a thorough description and analysis of the events and implications surrounding the *Skinner* case, *see* Victoria F. Nourse, In Reckless Hands: *Skinner v. Oklahoma* and the Near-Triumph of American Eugenics (2008).

7. Nourse, *supra* note 6, at 541. *See also* Lombardo, *supra* note 5, at 219–35.

8. Nourse, *supra* note 6, at 536. In his 2003 biography of Justice Douglas, Bruce Allen Murphy analyzes the import of the *Skinner* decision, concluding that it marked a jurisprudential turning point in constitutional law. The language discussing procreation as a basic liberty and the consequences of its state-sponsored deprivation, Murphy writes, "would one day be credited as a cornerstone for the 'fundamental rights' line of cases, by which any legislation dealing with these areas would be subjected to a higher level of judicial scrutiny than the prevailing standard, which afforded great deference toward legislatures." Bruce Allen Murphy, Wild Bill: The Legend and Life of William O. Douglas 203 (2003).

9. Murphy, *supra* note 8, at 541.

10. A.G.R. v. D.R.H. and S.H. (N.J. Super. Ct. Ch. Div., Dec. 23, 2009) (married male couple contracts with genetic father's sister to act as gestational carrier; after twins are born, trial court awards sister/surrogate parental rights, finding the intent of the parties "of no significance"). In December 2011, Superior Court Judge Francis Schultz modified the previous order, awarding the biological father "sole legal custody" and granting the sister/surrogate substantial parenting time with the children.

11. *See* Jacques Billeaud, *"Pregnant Man" Thomas Beatie's Divorce Stalled,* Huffington Post, *available at* http://www.huffingtonpost.com/2013/01/02/pregnant-man -thomas-beati_n_2397360.html (last visited Mar. 5, 2013) (describing Thomas and Nancy's marriage in Hawaii and subsequent decision to divorce after moving to Arizona. In a state that bans same-sex marriage, a Maricopa County family law judge struggled to recognize the marriage as valid, finding no legal authority defining a man as someone who can give birth).

12. *See* John Bowe, *The Octomom and Her Babies Prepare for Prime Time,* N.Y. Times, Nov. 12, 2009, *available at* http://www.nytimes.com/2009/11/15/magazine/15octomom-t .html (last visited Mar. 12, 2010).

13. The fundamental right to procreate established in *Skinner* has been reaffirmed by the Court on numerous occasions, typically as a starting point for discussing other conduct of an intimate and personal nature. *See, e.g.,* Washington v. Glucksberg, 521 U.S. 702 (1997) (challenge to state-assisted suicide laws that deprive terminally ill patients the right to physician aid in dying); Cruzan v. Director, Missouri Department of Health, 497 U.S. 261 (1990) (upholding right of competent adults to refuse life-sustaining medical treatment); Michael H. v. Gerald D., 491 U.S. 110 (1989) (discussing right of biological father to establish paternity and right to visitation of child born to married woman living with her husband); Bowers v. Hardwick, 478 U.S. 186 (1986) (upholding constitu-

tionality of Georgia sodomy statute as applied to homosexual conduct, later overturned in Lawrence v. Texas, 123 S. Ct. 2472 [2003]).

14. *See, e.g.,* Griswold v. Connecticut, 381 U.S. 485 (1965) (striking down state law criminalizing use of contraceptives); Eisenstadt v. Baird, 405 U.S. 438 (1972) (striking down state law criminalizing distribution of contraceptives to unmarried persons); Roe v. Wade, 410 U.S. 113 (1973) (striking down state law making it a crime to procure an abortion); Planned Parenthood of Southeastern Pennsylvania v. Casey, 505 U.S. 833 (1992) (upholding several regulatory provisions and striking down a spousal notification provision of a state abortion law); Stenberg v. Carhart, 530 U.S. 914 (2000) (striking down state law banning partial birth abortion); Gonzales v. Carhart, 127 S. Ct. 1610 (2007) (upholding federal Partial-Birth Abortion Ban Act of 2003).

15. *See, e.g.,* John A. Robertson, Children of Choice: Freedom and the New Reproductive Technologies (1994) (arguing the right to procreate via ART is constitutionally equal to right attached to natural conception and childbirth); Radhika Rao, *Constitutional Misconceptions,* 93 Mich. L. Rev. 1473 (1995) (rejecting the presumptive primacy of procreative liberty as applied to ART, noting that other constitutional rights may be at issue when donors or surrogates are used and their rights need to be taken into relative account); Ann MacLean Massie, *Regulating Choice: A Constitutional Law Response to Professor John A. Robertson's Children of Choice,* 52 Wash. & Lee L. Rev. 135 (1995) (expressing concern that constitutionally equalizing coital and noncoital means of reproduction might suppress the interests of resulting offspring); Sonia M. Suter, *The "Repugnance" Lens of Gonzales v. Carhart and Other Theories of Reproductive Rights: Evaluating Advanced Reproductive Technologies,* 76 Geo. Wash. L. Rev. 1514 (2008) (finding a right to ART potentially supported by theories based on procreative liberty and autonomy, equality, and family privacy).

16. The world's first "test tube" baby, Louise Brown, was born outside London on July 25, 1978. *See* Peter Gwynne, *All About That Baby,* Newsweek, Aug. 7, 1978, at 66.

17. It is estimated that five million IVF infants were born worldwide as of 2012, and 350,000 such babies are now born each year. *See Five Million IVF Babies Born to Date, Study Says,* BioNews, July 2, 2012, *available at* http://www.bionews.org.uk/page_155201 .asp (citing a 2012 report by the International Committee for Monitoring Assisted Reproductive Technologies estimating the use of 1.5 million ART cycles a year, producing 350,000 babies worldwide).

18. For a fuller description of the history of assisted conception, upon which this section is based, *see* Judith Daar, Reproductive Technologies and the Law 26–38 (2d ed. 2013).

19. P. Morice, P. Josset, C. Chapron, & J.B. Dubuisson, *History of Infertility,* 1(5) Hum. Reprod. Update 497 (1995).

20. *Id.* at 501.

21. *See* Infertility: A Comprehensive Text 310 (Machelle M. Seibel ed.) (1997).

22. *See* A.D. Hard, *Artificial Impregnation,* 27 Med. World 163 (1909).

23. *See* R. Bunge & J. Sherman, *Fertilizing Capacity of Frozen Human Spermatazoa,* 172 Nature 767 (1953).

24. *See* Albert R. Jonsen, *Reproduction and Rationality,* 4 Cambridge Q. Health-care Ethics 263 (1995). The relationship between artificial insemination by donor and adultery was also supported by courts asked to review the legal parentage of an AID child. *See, e.g.,* Doornbos v. Doornbos, No. 54 S. 14981 (Super. Ct., Cook Co., Dec. 13, 1954), *aff'd* 12 Ill. App. 2d 473, 139 N.E.2d 844 (1956) (artificial insemination by third-party donor, with or without consent of husband, constitutes adultery by mother; child is not a legitimate child of the marriage). For a historian's insight into the introduction of AID in America, *see* Kara W. Swanson, *Adultery by Doctor: Artificial Insemination, 1890–1945,* 87 Chicago-Kent L. Rev. 591 (2012).

25. In 1955, the Ohio Senate contemplated a resolution that would have made AID punishable as adultery, subject to a fine of $500 or up to five years' imprisonment. The resolution ultimately failed. *See* E. Donald Shapiro & Benedene Sonnenblick, *The Widow and the Sperm: The Law of Post Mortem Insemination,* 1 J.L. & Health 229, 237 (1986). *See* Gursky v. Gursky, 39 Misc. 2d 1083, 242 N.Y.S.2d 406 (1963) (in divorce action, husband denied parentage of daughter conceived via AID); People v. Sorenson, 68 Cal. 2d 280, 437 P.2d 495, 66 Cal. Rptr. 7 (1968) (in a prosecution for failure to provide for minor child, man whose wife conceived and gave birth using AID denies legal relationship and responsibility for child). *See* Inst. for Sci., Law & Tech. Working Group, *ART into Science: Regulation of Fertility Techniques,* 281 Science 651 (1998) (reporting sixty thousand AID births annually).

26. M. Chang, *Fertilization of Rabbit Ova In Vitro,* 184 Nature 406 (1959).

27. Paul Ramsey, *Shall We "Reproduce"?,* 220 JAMA 1346 (1972).

28. *See* Gwynne, *supra* note 16.

29. Increasingly, an IVF embryo is developed in the laboratory for five days to the blastocyst stage before it is transferred into the woman's uterus. A blastocyst contains approximately seventy to one hundred cells (compared with the four to eight cells of a Day 3 embryo). Studies show greater success using Day 5 blastocyst transfers as compared with Day 3 embryo transfers, thus moving the needle toward blastocyst transfer as a standard of care in IVF. *See* Nicolas H. Zech et al., *Prospective Evaluation of the Optimal Time for Selecting Single Embryo for Transfer: Day 3 versus Day 5,* 88 Fertility & Sterility 244 (2007) (showing overall significantly higher success rates after Day 5 transfers).

30. According to the National Council for Adoption, there were 22,291 domestic infant adoptions in the United States in 2002, a decline of 5.3 percent from 1996. *See* Nat'l Council for Adoption, Adoption Factbook IV (2007), *available at* https://www .adoptioncouncil.org/resources/dom_stats.html (last visited June 16, 2009). According to an annual report published by the Centers for Disease Control and Prevention (CDC), in 2013 (the most recent year for which figures are available as of this writing) there were 67,996 children born in the United States who were conceived using some form of assisted reproductive technology (ART), as defined by the CDC to include only those techniques in which both the egg and the sperm are handled. As technology currently stands, this definition includes IVF (in which eggs and sperm are combined outside the body to form embryos, which are later transferred into the uterus) and two rarely utilized techniques—gamete intrafallopian transfer (in which eggs and sperm are

transferred into the fallopian tube) and zygote intrafallopian transfer (in which the early embryo is transferred into the fallopian tube). *See* Ctrs. for Disease Control & Prevention, U.S. Dep't of Health & Hum. Servs., 2013 Assisted Reproductive Technology: National Summary Report 3, 61–63 (2015), *available at* http://www.cdc.gov/art/pdf/2013 -report/national-summary/art_2013_national_summary_report.pdf (last visited May 5, 2016) [hereinafter 2013 ART National Report]. In addition to IVF births, it is estimated that sixty thousand children are born annually via AID, a technique in which only the sperm is handled (and thus births by AID are not included in the annual CDC ART Report). *See supra* note 27. Births via IVF and AID bring the total number of children born through assisted conception to roughly 127,000; the total birth rate for 2013 was nearly four million. *See* Ctrs. for Disease Control & Prevention, U.S. Dep't of Health & Hum. Servs., *Births: Final Data for 2013,* 64(1) Nat'l Vital Stat. Reps., Jan. 15, 2015, at 1, *available at* http://www.cdc.gov/nchs/data/nvsr/nvsr64/nvsr64_01.pdf (last visited May 5, 2016) (reporting 3,932,181 live births in the United States in 2013, down by less than 1 percent from 2012). Thus, total ART births in the United States in 2013 accounted for more than 3 percent of all live births.

31. Data from outside the United States are likewise collected and published by various entities, most notably the European Society of Human Reproduction and Embryology (ESHRE), which, among other tasks, develops and maintains data registries of ART use across Europe. For more about ESHRE's IVF monitoring, visit http://www .eshre.eu/01/default.aspx?pageid=281 (last visited June 3, 2013).

32. *See* Ctrs. for Disease Control & Prevention, U.S. Dep't of Health & Hum. Servs., 2013 Assisted Reproductive Technology: Fertility Clinic Success Rates Report 3 (2015), *available at* http://www.cdc.gov/art/ART2013/PDF/ART_2013_Clinic_Report -Full.pdf (last visited May 6, 2016) [hereinafter 2013 ART Clinic Report].

33. The CDC definition clarifies that ART does "NOT include treatments in which only sperm are handled (i.e., intrauterine insemination) or procedures in which a woman takes drugs only to stimulate egg production without the intention of having eggs retrieved." *Id.* (emphasis in original).

34. 42 U.S.C. 263a-1 (1992).

35. *Id.* at § 263a-5.

36. *See supra* note 27.

37. *See* Dena S. Davis, *The Puzzle of IVF,* 6 Hous. J. Health Law & Pol'y 275 (2006) (asserting that the typical patient in need of IVF is older, married, white, educated, and well-off).

38. *See* Mikki Morrisette, *Redefining Family: Single Women and Lesbian Couples Who Choose Parenthood Are Transforming the Donor Insemination Industry,* Minn. Women's Press, *available at* http://www.womenspress.com/main.asp?SectionID=1&Sub SectionID=1&ArticleID=2391&TM=57580.26 (last visited June 19, 2009).

39. The American Society for Reproductive Medicine defines infertility as the inability "to achieve pregnancy after a year of unprotected intercourse." *See* http://www .asrm.org/Patients/faqs.html#Q3: (last visited June 27, 2013). The World Health Organization recommends twenty-four months as the preferred definition of the condition,

lowering the number of false positive diagnoses in any population study. *See* P. Rowe, F. Comhaire, T. Hargreave, & H. Mellows, WHO Manual for the Standard Investigation and Diagnosis of the Infertile Couple (1993).

40. These views are expressed by RESOLVE, a national support and advocacy organization for the infertile founded in 1974. RESOLVE has argued in a variety of fora, including state legislatures, that infertility is and therefore should be addressed as a medical condition. *See* www.resolve.org.

41. *See* Elizabeth A. Pendo, *The Politics of Infertility: Recognizing Coverage Exclusions as Discrimination*, 11 Conn. Ins. L.J. 293, 336 (2004–5).

42. *See, e.g.*, Conn. Gen. Stat. Ann. § 38a-536 (mandating certain health insurance coverage for "the medically necessary expenses of the diagnosis and treatment of infertility"); Saks v. Franklin Covey, 316 F.3d 337 (2d Cir. 2003) (court agreed that infertility is a medical condition, but employers' failure to provide coverage for IVF to female employee did not violate federal law).

43. *See* 2013 ART National Report, *supra* note 33, at 24.

44. Presumably a gestational carrier or a lesbian undergoing IVF using her partner's eggs would be counted by the clinic as a "routine" ART patient. Since patient demographic data (other than age and diagnosis) are not reported, there is no way to distinguish between use for medical reasons and use for social reasons.

45. *See* 2013 ART National Report, *supra* note 33, at 49 (showing data on ART trends from 2004 to 2013).

46. An ART cycle consists of several steps over an interval of approximately two weeks, designed to prepare the woman to produce eggs for fertilization and transfer back to the uterus. Typically, an ART cycle begins when a woman starts drug therapy to stimulate her ovaries to produce multiple eggs. *See* 2013 ART National Report, *supra* note 33, at 61.

47. *See* Elizabeth Hurvey Stephen & Anjani Chandra, *Declining Estimates of Infertility in the United States: 1982–2002*, 86 Fertility & Sterility 516 (2006).

48. *See* Anjani Chandra et al., Infertility and Impaired Fecundity in the United States, 1982–2010: Data from the National Survey of Family Growth, National Health Statistics Reports, No. 67 (Aug. 14, 2013), at 1.

49. *See* Ctrs. for Disease Control & Prevention, U.S. Dep't of Health & Hum. Servs., 1996 Assisted Reproductive Technology Success Rates: National Summary and Fertility Clinic Reports 1 (1998), *available at* http://www.cdc.gov/art/artreports.htm #1996; http://www.cdc.gov/ART/ART2006/index.htm. (last visited Aug. 5, 2009) [hereinafter 1996 ART National Report].

50. *See* Ctrs. for Disease Control & Prevention, U.S. Dep't of Health & Hum. Servs., 2006 Assisted Reproductive Technology Success Rates: National Summary and Fertility Clinic Reports 3 (2008), *available at* http://www.cdc.gov/art/PDF/508PDF/2006ART .pdf (last visited Feb. 6, 2015) [hereinafter 2006 ART Report].

51. *Id.* at 1.

52. *Id.* at 3.

53. For example, in 2006 the percentage of women who had an infertility-related medical appointment and ultimately underwent IVF was approximately 11.5 percent

(138,198 cycles in 1.2 million women), compared with 9.6 percent in 2002 (115,392 cycles). These rough estimates assume the identical treatment-seeking population, a figure not specifically reported by the CDC 2006 ART Report, *supra* note 53, at 61, Figure 49.

54. Zach Johnson, *Kim Kardashian Addresses IVF Rumors on* Today, June 25, 2015, *available at* http://www.eonline.com/news/670406/kim-kardashian-addresses-ivf -rumors-on-today-reveals-she-s-gained-15-pounds-since-getting-pregnant (last visited Oct. 6, 2015).

55. Marisa Laudadio, *Celine Dion's Struggle for a Second Baby,* People, Feb. 10, 2010, *available at* http://www.people.com/people/article/0,,20343148,00.html (last vis-ited Mar. 8, 2010). The singer eventually gave birth to twin boys in October 2010, con-ceived from her sixth IVF cycle. *See Mother's Day 2013: Star Mums over 40,* People, Apr. 5, 2013, *available at* http://www.people.com/people/package/gallery/0,,20363110_20574208 _21127749,00.html (last visited July 5, 2013).

56. Will Keck, *Celeb Watch: Marcia Cross Is Far from Desperate Housewife,* USA Today, Jan. 13, 2008, *available at* http://www.usatoday.com/life/people/celebwatch/2008 –01-13-marcia-cross_N.htm (last visited July 14, 2009).

57. *Brooke Shields Has a Girl,* People, Apr. 18, 2006, *available at* http://www.people .com/people/article/0,,1174449,00.html (last visited July 14, 2009).

58. *Cox to Wait for Baby Number Two,* S.F. Chron., June 6, 2007, *available at* http://www.sfgate.com/cgi-bin/blogs/dailydish/detail?blogid=7&entry_id=17345 (last visited July 14, 2009).

59. Cindy Margolis & Kathy Kanable, Having a Baby . . . When the Old-Fashioned Way Isn't Working (2008).

60. *See, e.g.,* http://www.nobabyonboard.com/moviestv.html (last visited July 14, 2009); http://www.gomestic.com/Family/Celebrities-Who-Survived-Infertility.106914 (last visited July 14, 2009); http://parenting.ivillage.com/slideshow/parenting/celebrity _surrogacy_see_how_their_families_grow/ (last visited July 14, 2009).

61. *See Baby of the One: Elton John Expecting Second Child from Surrogate Mother,* RT, Nov. 11, 2012, *available at* http://rt.com/art-and-culture/elton-john-second-baby -458/ (last visited Feb. 6, 2015).

62. For more in-depth reporting on the world of celebrity surrogacy, *see,* no kidding, TheFrisky.com (specifically, *10 Celebs Who Are Part of the Surrogate Baby Boom, available at* http://www.thefrisky.com/post/246–10-celebs-who-are-part-of-the -surrogate-baby-boom).

63. *See* Alex Kuczynski, *Her Body, My Baby,* N.Y. Times Mag., Nov. 30, 2008, at 42.

64. *See* Lorraine Ali & Raina Kelly, *The Curious Lives of Surrogates,* Newsweek, Apr. 7, 2008, *available at* http://www.newsweek.com/id/129594 (last visited July 15, 2009).

65. M. Kate Bundorf, Natale Chun, Gopi Shah Goda, & Daniel P. Kessler, *Do Markets Respond to Quality Information? The Case of Fertility Clinics* (Nat'l Bureau of Economic Research, Working Paper No. 13888, Mar. 2008), *available at* http://www .nber.org/papers/w13888.pdf (last visited Mar. 8, 2010).

66. 2006 ART Report, *supra* note 52, at 57. The 40 percent live birth rate figure is the product of two data points—53.7 percent of all fresh embryo transfers produce a live birth, while 32.1 percent of frozen embryo transfers have the same result. *Id.* at 89.

67. *Id.* at Appendix C (listing all reporting and nonreporting clinics by state). An IVF clinic has since opened in Montana, where one reproductive endocrinologist serves patients in the state as well as Wyoming and western North Dakota. *See* Billings Clinic, http://www.billingsclinic.com/services-specialties/womens/reproductive-medicine/ (last visited Feb. 9, 2015).

68. *Id.* Compare the 2006 state-by-state results with those from 1996, reported in Ctrs. for Disease Control & Prevention, U.S. Dep't of Health & Hum. Servs., *Use of Assisted Reproductive Technology—United States, 1996 and 1998,* 51(5) Morbidity & Mortality Wkly. Rep. 97–101 (Feb. 8, 2002).

69. Sylvia Ann Hewlett, *Fast-Track Women and the Quest for Children,* 2 Sexuality, Reprod. & Menopause 15–18 (2004) (summarizing and discussing her 2002 book).

70. In 2000, 30 percent of all ART transfer procedures that used fresh embryos from the patient's eggs were performed on women age thirty-eight and older, compared with 31 percent in 2006. *See* Ctrs. for Disease Control & Prevention, U.S. Dep't of Health & Hum. Servs., *Use of Assisted Reproductive Technology—United States, 2000,* 52 Morbidity & Mortality Wkly. Rep. 1 (Aug. 29, 2003). Ctrs. for Disease Control & Prevention, U.S. Dep't of Health & Hum. Servs., *Use of Assisted Reproductive Technology—United States, 2006,* 58 Morbidity & Mortality Wkly. Rep. 6 (June 12, 2009).

71. *See* Richard T. Scott, *Diminished Ovarian Reserve and Access to Care,* 81 Fertility & Sterility 1489–92 (2004).

72. American Society for Reproductive Medicine, Age and Infertility: A Guide for Patients 3 (2003).

73. 1996 ART National Report, *supra* note 52, at 10.

74. 2006 ART National Report, *supra* note 53, at 31.

75. *See* Gina Kolata, *Fertility Inc.: Clinics Race to Lure Clients,* N.Y. Times, Jan. 1, 2002, at D1.

76. *See* http://fertilitymarketing.com (last visited Mar. 10, 2010).

77. For gateway access to many U.S. fertility clinic websites, *see* http://www.ihr.com/infertility/provider (last visited Mar. 10, 2010). For an empirical analysis of the distribution of minority images on ART clinic websites, *see* Jim Hawkins, *Selling ART: An Empirical Assessment of Advertising on Fertility Clinics' Websites,* Ind. L.J. 1147 (2013).

78. Int'l Comm. Monitoring Assisted Reprod. Tech., prepared by J. de Mouzon, P. Lancaster, K.G. Nygren, E. Sullivan, F. Zegers-Hochschild, R. Mansour, O. Ishihara, & D. Adamson, *World Collaborative Report on Assisted Reproductive Technology,* 24(9) Hum. Reprod. 2310 (2009). As an aside, notice the seven-year lag time between the actual IVF cycles and the published report, compared with a two-year lag in the United States (no doubt reflecting the time-consuming task of collecting medical data across the globe).

79. Crystal Phend, *Rapid Increase Seen in Assisted Reproduction,* Medpage Today (May 28, 2009), *available at* http://www.medpagetoday.com/OBGYN/Infertility/14405 (last visited Mar. 11, 2010). The 25 percent increase in worldwide ART use compares with a 17 percent increase in the United States during that same time period. The CDC reported a total of 99,629 cycles in 2000 and 115,392 cycles in 2002. *See* Ctrs. for Disease

Control & Prevention, U.S. Dep't of Health & Hum. Servs., *Use of Assisted Reproductive Technology—United States, 2000,* 52 Morbidity & Mortality Wkly. Rep. 1–16 (Aug. 29, 2003), and Ctrs. for Disease Control & Prevention, U.S. Dep't of Health & Hum. Servs., *Use of Assisted Reproductive Technology—United States, 2002,* 54 Morbidity & Mortality Wkly. Rep. 1–24 (June 3, 2005). In this same two-year span, the number of babies born worldwide as a result climbed 12 percent, for a total of a quarter million IVF newborns in 2002.

80. *See* Ctrs. for Disease Control & Prevention, U.S. Dep't of Health & Hum. Servs., *Use of Assisted Reproductive Technology—United States, 2002,* 54 Morbidity & Mortality Wkly. Rep. 1–24 (June 3, 2005).

81. For a discussion of ICMART's outreach and data assembly techniques, see their website at http://www.icmartivf.org/ (last visited Mar. 11, 2010).

82. *World's Number of IVF and ICSI Babies Has Now Reached a Calculated Total of 5 Million,* Science Daily, July 2, 2012, *available at* http://www.sciencedaily.com/releases/2012/07/120702134746.htm (last visited July 23, 2013); Int'l Comm. Monitoring Assisted Reprod. Tech., prepared by E.A. Sullivan, F. Zegers-Hochschild, R. Mansour, O. Ishihara, J. de Mouzon, K.G. Nygren, & G.D. Adamson, *International Committee for Monitoring Assisted Reproductive Technologies (ICMART) World Report: Assisted Reproductive Technology 2004,* 28(5) Hum. Reprod. 1375 (2013).

83. *See* Fernando Zegers-Hochschild et al., *International Committee for Monitoring Assisted Reproductive Technologies: World Report on Assisted Reproductive Technology, 2005,* 101 Fertility & Sterility 366 (2014).

84. *See* Siobhan Chan, *Low-Tech, Accessible IVF Could Cost Just 200,* BioNews (July 9, 2013), *available at* http://www.bionews.org.uk/page_320822.asp?dinfo=5g0yGJ zm1NKkIeqXeS1UigGD&PPID=323417 (last visited July 24, 2013); *see also* R. Nachtigall, *International Disparities in Access to Infertility Services,* 85(4) Fertility & Sterility 871–75 (2006) (estimating 80 million infertile people worldwide).

85. *See, e.g.,* Camille Davidson, *Octomom and Multi-Fetal Pregnancies: Why Federal Legislation Should Require Insurers to Cover In Vitro Fertilization,* 17 Wm. & Mary J. Women & L. 135 (2010) (noting voluntary impoverishment by those in need of IVF).

86. The cost of a single IVF cycle can vary depending upon the patient's diagnosis and medical history. Costs become even more variable when third-party donors and gestational carriers enter the treatment mix. That said, data does exist comparing the cost of a basic ART cycle across jurisdictions. One comprehensive survey measured IVF costs in 2009. The United States topped the list as the most expensive site, with IVF averaging $10,000 per cycle. Hong Kong tied the United States at $10,000, followed by the Dominican Republic ($8,300), Sweden ($8,000), the United Kingdom ($7,500), Ukraine ($6,500), and Singapore ($6,300). The least expensive treatment was found in India ($690), followed by Korea ($1,600), Hungary ($2,200), China ($2,400), and the Czech Republic ($2,500). *See IVF Costs, available at* http://www.ivfcost.net/ (last visited Dec. 6, 2011). Basic economics informs that a patient living in the United States could fly to India, seek treatment, and enjoy a two-week vacation for less than she would spend walking down the street to her local fertility clinic. ART price differentials have become so

significant that a cottage industry of patient solicitation has emerged. A Google search of the term "IVF holiday" in February 2015 yields 2,010,000 results.

Any discussion of ART costs should include the fiscal impact the price of treatment has on an individual patient. In countries in which fertility care is a covered benefit under a national health plan, cost impacts are far less than in countries in which no coverage or reimbursement is available. As one researcher remarked, "Depending on a country's national health policy, the cost to the consumer can vary from zero to 100% of the total cost." Nachtigall, *supra* note 87. In Israel, for example, the national health service fully funds unlimited IVF cycles up to two live births, making Israelis the highest per capita users of IVF in the world. *See* D. Kraft, *Where Families Are Prized, Help Is Free,* N.Y. Times, July 18, 2011, at A5. In the United States, in contrast, only fifteen states require health insurance carriers to offer fertility coverage, and upward of 85 percent of IVF costs are borne by individual patients. The insurance puzzle for infertility care is discussed more fully in Chapter 3.

87. *See* Ethics Comm., Am. Soc'y for Reprod. Med., *Cross-Border Reproductive Care: A Committee Opinion,* 100 Fertility & Sterility 645 (2013).

88. Surveys indicate that 5 percent of all IVF treatment cycles done in the European Union are performed on so-called fertility tourists—citizens traveling from another country to access care. Travel to the United States is also a relatively robust portion of the American ART market, with approximately 4 percent of all ART cycles devoted to non-U.S. residents. *See* F. Shenfield, J. de Mouson, G. Pennings, et al., *The ESHRE Task Force on Cross Border Reproductive Care: Cross Border Reproductive Care in Six European Countries,* 25(6) Hum. Reprod. 361–1368 (2010); N. Hudson, L. Culley, E. Blyth, W. Norton, F. Rapport, & A. Pacey, *Cross-Border Reproductive Care: A Review of the Literature,* 22 Reprod. BioMed Online 673–85 (2011).

89. *See, e.g.,* Guido Pennings, *Ethical Issues of Infertility Treatment in Developing Countries,* 1 ESHRE Monographs 15 (2008).

90. *See generally* Miriam Zoll, Cracked Open: Liberty, Fertility and the Pursuit of High Tech Babies (2013).

91. *See* Ctrs. for Disease Control & Prevention, U.S. Dep't of Health & Hum. Servs., 2013 Assisted Reproductive Technology Fertility Clinic Success Rates Report 5 (2015), *available at* http://www.cdc.gov/art/pdf/2013-report/art-2013-fertility-clinic-report.pdf (last visited Oct. 8, 2015) (reporting 163,209 ART cycles performed for reproductive purposes (excluding cycles for egg banking only), yielding 54,323 deliveries of live-born infants).

TWO Our Eugenics Past

1. Paul A. Lombardo, Three Generations, No Imbeciles (2008), at xiv.

2. *See* Stephen Wilkinson & Eve Garrard, Eugenics and the Ethics of Selective Reproduction 5–8 (2013).

3. *See, e.g.,* Leon R. Kass, *Babies by Means of In Vitro Fertilization: Unethical Experiments on the Unborn?,* 285 New Eng. J. Med. 1174 (1971) (decrying the advent of IVF in the human population, arguing, "Because the new procedures for in vitro fertilization

and laboratory culture of human embryos probably carry a serious risk of damage to any child so generated, there appears to be no ethical way to proceed"); Paul Ramsey, *Shall We Reproduce?* 220 J. Am. Med. Ass'n 1346 (1972) (concluding that "technical reproduction" should never be used to supplant human procreation and that IVF "constitutes unethical medical experimentation on possible future human beings, and therefore is subject to absolute moral prohibition").

4. Early commentaries on the ethics of surrogate parenting include Carmel Shalev, Birth Power: The Case for Surrogacy (1989); Richard Posner, *The Ethics and Economics of Enforcing Contracts of Surrogate Mothers,* 5 J. Contemp. Health L. & Pol'y 21 (1989); and Margaret Jane Radin, *Market-Inalienability,* 100 Harv. L. Rev. 1849 (1987).

5. A combination of the terms, "stratified reproduction," was coined by Shellee Colen to describe how reproduction is structured across social and cultural boundaries, empowering privileged women and disempowering less privileged women. Shellee Colen, *"With Respect and Feelings": Voices of West Indian Child Care Workers in New York City, in* All American Women: Lines That Divide, Ties That Bind 46–70 (J.B. Cole ed.) (1986). *See also* Lorraine Cully, Nicky Hudson, & Floor Van Rooij, Marginalized Reproduction: Ethnicity, Infertility and Reproductive Technologies (2009).

6. Diane B. Paul, Controlling Human Heredity: 1865 to the Present (1995), at 3.

7. *Id.* at 4–5.

8. Francis Galton, Inquiries and Human Faculty and Its Development 17 (1883).

9. *See* Judith Daar, Reproductive Technologies and the Law 285 (2d ed. 2013).

10. *See* Michael J. Malinowski, *Choosing the Genetic Makeup of Children: Our Eugenics Past—Present, and Future?,* 36 Conn. L. Rev. 125, 134, *citing* Daniel J. Kevles, In the Name of Eugenics 41–43 (1985).

11. Paul, *supra* note 6, at 18.

12. Paul, *supra* note 6, at 8.

13. Funding for the Eugenics Records Office was initially provided by Mary Harriman, then the recent widow of railroad magnate E. H. Harriman. Between 1910 and 1918, Harriman contributed nearly $650,000 to endow the ERO. *See* Lombardo, *supra* note 1, at 31.

14. Malinowski, *supra* note 10, at 136.

15. Lombardo, *supra* note 1, at 33–34.

16. *See* Paul A. Lombardo, *Medicine, Eugenics, and the Supreme Court: From Coercive Sterilization to Reproductive Freedom,* 13 J. Contemp. Health L. & Pol'y 1, 3 (1996).

17. Paul, *supra* note 6, at 18.

18. *See* Malinowski, *supra* note 10, at 137, *quoting* Nancy L. Gallagher, Breeding Better Vermonters: The Eugenics Project in the Green Mountain State 4 (1999). For a piercing analysis of the range of opinions that existed on the efficacy of eugenic sterilization in the early 1920s, as told through Harvard University's decision to decline a bequest to support teaching eugenics on campus, *see* Paul A. Lombardo, *When Harvard Said No to Eugenics,* 57 Persp. Biology & Med. 374 (2015).

19. Lombardo, *supra* note 16, at 4. Lombardo attributes these tenets to American eugenicist Harry Laughlin, whom Charles Davenport named as the superintendent of

the Eugenics Record Office. The ERO, under Laughlin's direction and authorship, published its research results in the form of bulletins about eugenics. *See, e.g.,* Harry H. Laughlin, *Report of the Committee to Study and to Report on the Best Practical Means of Cutting Off the Defective Germ-Plasm in the American Population,* Eugenics Rec. Off. Bull. No. 10A (1914).

20. *See* Malinowski, *supra* note 10, at 137. *See also* Dr. William Allen, *The Relationship of Eugenics to Public Health,* 21 Eugenical News 73–75 (July–Aug. 1936) (adopting the powerful language of public health law to characterize unchecked procreation among the "socially inadequate" as an epidemic force), as cited in Lombardo, *supra* note 16, at 2.

21. As noted below, the category of negative eugenics—the suppression of reproduction by undesirables—was largely the product of public eugenics (enacted law and judicial interpretation) and thus will be incorporated into the coverage of this latter category.

22. *See* Wilkinson & Garrard, *supra* note 2, at 3–4.

23. *See, e.g.,* Arizona v. U.S., 132 S. Ct. 2492 (2012) (federal government's broad power over immigration preempts state's authority to enact laws regulating the treatment and status of unauthorized aliens within state borders).

24. For example, the Chinese Exclusion Act of 1882 suspended the entry of laborers and prohibited all foreign-born Chinese from acquiring citizenship. In 1907, the "Gentlemen's Agreement" with Japan called for the "voluntary" restriction of immigration in return for an end to the segregation of Japanese students in San Francisco public schools. Finally, in 1917, an Asiatic Barred Zone was created, excluding laborers from the rest of Asia. Paul, *supra* note 6, at 97–98.

25. Paul, *supra* note 6, at 8; *see generally* Alan M. Kraut, Silent Travelers: Germs, Genes and the "Immigrant Menace" (1994).

26. Immigration Act, ch. 190, 43 Stat. 153 (1924).

27. *See* Kevles, *supra* note 10, at 97.

28. Lombardo, *supra* note 16, at 5. According to Paul, "As it turns out, the assumption of high immigrant fertility was wrong." Paul, *supra* note 6, at 103. Assertion of immigrant populations' hyper-fertility as compared with that of native residents remains an active tactic in American politics. In 2013 while delivering a speech on immigration policy, former Florida governor Jeb Bush told the audience that "immigrants are more fertile" than women born in the United States. *See* Bill Chappell, *"Immigrants Are More Fertile," Jeb Bush Says in Reform Speech,* NPR, June 14, 2013, *available at* http://www .npr.org/sections/thetwo-way/2013/06/14/191776099/immigrants-are-more-fertile-jeb -bush-says-in-reform-speech (last visited Oct. 13, 2015).

29. *Quoted* in Kevles, *supra* note 10, at 97.

30. *See* Lombardo, *supra* note 16, at 1, *citing* Allan Chase, The Legacy of Malthus: The Social Costs of the New Scientific Racism 15, 19–20 (1977); Mark H. Haller, Eugenics: Hereditarian Attitudes in American Thought 155–56 (1963); James W. Trent Jr., Inventing the Feeble Mind: A History of Mental Retardation in the United States 173, 292 n.3 (1994).

31. Paul, *supra* note 6, at 102.

32. *Id.*

33. Lombardo, *supra* note 1, at 32, quoting a letter Theodore Roosevelt wrote to Charles Davenport, Jan. 3, 1913. Charles B. Davenport Papers, American Philosophical Society, Phila., Pa.

34. Kevles, *supra* note 10, at 147.

35. Paul, *supra* note 6, at 103.

36. Scholars have debated the likelihood, merit, and drawbacks of assessing legal liability against physicians who assist in the conception of a child likely to be born with disabilities. *See, e.g.,* Kristen Smolensky, *Creating Children with Disabilities: Parental Tort Liability for Preimplantation Genetic Intervention,* 60 Hastings L.J. 299 (2008).

37. *See* Ctrs. for Disease Control & Prevention, U.S. Dep't of Health & Hum. Servs., Unmarried Childbearing (2012), *available at* http://www.cdc.gov/nchs/fastats/unmarried-childbearing.htm (last visited Aug. 26, 2014) (reporting that 40.7 percent of U.S. births in 2012 were to unmarried women). In 2013, the rate declined slightly, with 40.6 percent of total U.S. births to unmarried women. *See* Joyce A. Martin et al., *Births: Final Data for 2013,* 64 Nat'l Vital Stat. Reps. 1 (Jan. 15, 2015), *available at* http://www.cdc.gov/nchs/data/nvsr/nvsr64/nvsr64_01.pdf (last visited Oct. 15, 2015).

38. *See generally* Peggy Pascoe, What Comes Naturally: Miscegenation Law and the Making of Race in America (2009).

39. Paul, *supra* note 6, at 112.

40. *Id.* at 111.

41. The eugenics period also saw other types of marriage restrictions put in place, each with the aim to prevent birth of offspring from undesirable couplings. In 1894, Connecticut enacted a law prohibiting epileptics, imbeciles, and feebleminded persons from marrying or having extramarital relations before age forty-five. *See* Act of July 4, 1895, 1895 Conn. Pub. Acts ch. 325. Other states embraced and even extended these prohibitions, barring marriage by those with transmissible diseases or alcoholism. *See, e.g.,* Act of March 6, 1905, 1905 Ind. Pub. Acts ch. 126, § 3.

42. Paul Lombardo, *Miscegenation, Eugenics, and Racism: Historical Footnotes to Loving v. Virginia,* 21 U.C. Davis L. Rev. 421, 428 (1988) (describing the work of Dr. Walter Plecker, the registrar at the Virginia Bureau of Vital Statistics who wrote publications warning of racial inbreeding as a public health problem).

43. The Virginia Racial Integrity Act, Act of March 20, 1924 ch. 371, 1924 Va. Acts 534.

44. Va. Code Ann. § 20–54-59 (1950).

45. 388 U.S. 1 (1966).

46. *See* Lombardo, *supra* note 42, at 450 (quoting Judge Leon Bazile, Caroline County Circuit Court, Va. Briefs and Records, No. 6163 at 14, Loving v. Virginia [1958]).

47. Loving v. Virginia, 388 U.S. 1, 12 (1966) (quoting language from Skinner v. Oklahoma, 316 U.S. 535, 539–40 [1942]).

48. Alabama repealed its anti-miscegenation law in 2000, two years after South Carolina. *See* Darren Rosenblum, *Loving Gender Balance: Reframing Identity-Based*

Inequality Remedies, 76 Fordham L. Rev. 2873, 2877, n. 26, *citing Alabama Removes Ban on Interracial Marriage,* USA Today, Nov. 7, 2000.

49. *See, e.g.,* DeBoer v. Snyder, 772 F.3d 388 (6th Cir. 2014), *rev'd by* Obergefell v. Hodges, 135 S. Ct. 2584 (2015) (upholding state ban on same-sex marriage reasoning in part that the "biological reality" is that such unions do not produce offspring).

50. *See* Lombardo, *supra* note 1, at 24–25.

51. Lombardo, *supra* note 1, at 293–94 (charting the adoption and repeal of sterilization laws); *see also* John J. Michalczyk, Nazi Medicine: In the Shadow of the Reich (First Run Features 1997).

52. Paul A. Lombardo, *Disability, Eugenics, and the Culture Wars,* 2 St. Louis J. Health L. & Pol'y 57, 62 (2008).

53. Lombardo, *supra* note 1, at 294 (listing Washington and Mississippi as having intact sterilization laws as of 2008). Thanks to Lombardo for alerting me that the Mississippi Sexual Sterilization Act was repealed in 2008, leaving only Washington's law intact.

54. *See* California Healthline, *Senate Committee Seeks Inmate Sterilization Audit, Legislation,* Aug. 14, 2013, *available at* http://www.californiahealthline.org/articles/2013/8/14/senate-committee-seeks-inmate-sterilization-audit-legislation (last visited Aug. 16, 2013).

55. Harry Laughlin, *Report of the Committee to Study and to Report on the Best Practical Means of Cutting Off the Defective Germ-Plasm in the American Population,* Eugenics Records Office Bulletin No. 10A, at 54–55 (1914).

56. Robert J. Cynkar, Buck v. Bell: *Felt Necessities v. Fundamental Values,* 80 Colum. L. Rev. 1418, 1429 (1981). According to Cynkar, "Some eugenicists hoped to build enough custodial institutions so that by 1980 they would be able to care for 1,500 feebleminded per 100,000 of the population." *Id.*

57. Harry Laughlin, The Legal Status of Eugenical Sterilization 65 (1929).

58. Lombardo, *supra* note 1, at 11.

59. *See* Cynkar, *supra* note 56, at 1433.

60. For a list of the cases overturning forced sterilization laws on constitutional grounds, *see id.* at 1434, n.79.

61. 1924 Va. Acts 569 (repealed by Act of Apr. 2, 1974, ch. 296).

62. Buck v. Bell, 274 U.S. 200, 207 (1927).

63. Lombardo, *supra* note 1, at x.

64. 274 U.S. at 205–6. Today we better understand the history and impetus for the Virginia law. Virginia mental health agency records reveal that the sterilization law was originally written to protect one physician, Dr. Albert Priddy, who had been performing unconsented surgeries and longed for legal immunity after a malpractice claim put a temporary end to his freelance sterilizations. Dr. Priddy lobbied for a law based on the work of prominent eugenical activist Harry Laughlin, who had written a model sterilization law he believed would withstand legal challenges. *See* Lombardo, *supra* note 1, at xii.

65. Lombardo, *supra* note 1, at xi.

66. *See* Paul A. Lombardo, *Facing Carrie Buck,* 33 Hastings Ctr. Rep. 14 (2003).

67. *See generally* Albert W. Alschuler, Law Without Values: The Life, Work and Legacy of Justice Holmes (2002).

68. 274 U.S. at 207.

69. 316 U.S. 535 (1942).

70. Lombardo offers this analysis on the question of whether *Skinner v. Oklahoma* overturned *Buck v. Bell*: "There is a common misconception that the Supreme Court decision in *Skinner* all but overruled *Buck* and that the postwar revelation of Nazi practices led to a general rejection of eugenics. But eugenically based assumptions about heredity as a basis for law survived well beyond *Skinner,* just as they outlived the Third Reich. Years after the case, Justice Douglas himself reiterated that there was no desire by the *Skinner* court to overrule *Buck.* Douglas was 'very clear' on the case's constitutional validity. The eugenic foundations of *Buck* were safe because of the procedural protections that the Virginia law included." Lombardo, *supra* note 1, at 232.

71. Lombardo, *supra* note 1, at xii.

72. Malinowski, *supra* note 10, at 156.

73. Lombardo, *supra* note 1, at xii.

74. *See* Malinowski, *supra* note 10, at 160–64, describing the Nuremberg Code—ten principles developed to judge the actions of the Nazi doctors in the absence of pre-existing codified guidance. The Code emphasized patient informed consent, including in the clinical and research settings.

75. *See supra* note 18; *see also* Wendy Kline, Building a Better Race: Gender, Sexuality, and Eugenics from the Turn of the Century to the Baby Boom 78 (2001).

76. Kline, *supra* note 75, at 86–87, *citing* Sterilization patient #398, Papers of Dr. Ezra S. Gosney, 17.8.

77. *See* Heywood Campbell Broun & Margaret Leech, Anthony Comstock 265 (1927).

78. This attitude was hardly unanimous, as told by Wendy Kline. She writes, "The National Woman's Party and the League of Women Voters refused to support birth control because it 'clashed with their conceptions of femininity, maternity, and progress.' " Kline, *supra* note 75, at 64, *citing* Carole R. McCann, Birth Control Politics in the United States, 1916–1945, 51 (1994).

79. Kline, *supra* note 75, at 63–72.

80. As Daniel Kevles explains, positive eugenics aims "to foster greater representation in a society of people whom eugenicists [consider] socially valuable." Daniel Kevles, "Eugenics," in 2 Encyclopedia of Bioethics 848 (3d ed. 2004).

81. *See* David E. Bernstein & Thomas C. Leonard, *Excluding Unfit Workers: Social Control Versus Social Justice in the Age of Economic Reform,* 72 Law & Contemp. Probs. 177 (2009) (discussing the development and popularization of the concept of race suicide during the early twentieth century).

82. For a critique of the use of the terms "positive" and "negative" eugenics, *see* Alexandra Stern, *Making Better Babies: Public Health and Race Betterment in Indiana, 1920–1935,* 92(5) Am. J. Pub. Health 742 (2002).

83. *See id.* at 748.

84. *Id., citing generally* Annette K. Vance Dorey, Better Baby Contests: The Scientific Quest for Perfect Childhood Health in the Early Twentieth Century (1999).

85. African Americans did hold their own Better Baby contests between 1924 and 1934. Overseen by the NAACP, these contests were designed to raise money for the organizations' social justice movement, as well as promote "assimilationist" eugenics as discussed by W. E. B. Du Bois. *See* Gregory Michael Dorr & Angela Logan, *Quality, Not Mere Quantity, Counts: Black Eugenics and the NAACP Baby Contests in* A Century of Eugenics in America (Paul A. Lombardo ed.) 68–92 (2011).

86. *Id.* at 742, *citing* James H. Madison, Indiana Through Tradition and Change: A History of the Hoosier State and Its People, 1920–1945, 322 (1982). The contests had other beneficial health impacts, including lowering the percentage of underweight contestant babies from 10 percent in 1920 to 2 percent in 1929. *Id.* at 749.

87. *See Judge the Parents, Too,* Kansas City Star, Aug. 18, 1920 (published in anticipation of the first Fitter Family contest, urging "better breeding as well as better feeding").

88. *Human Stock at the Kansas Free Fair,* Eugenical News 111 (Oct. 1922).

89. *See* Erica Bicchieri Boudreau, *"Yea, I Have a Goodly Heritage": Health Versus Heredity in the Fitter Family Contests, 1920–1928,* 30 J. Family Hist. 366–87 (2005).

90. *Id.*

THREE   The High Cost of Assisted Reproduction

1. Gina Kolata, *The Heart's Desire,* N.Y. Times, May 11, 2004, at F1.

2. *See* Deborah Spar, The Baby Business: How Money, Science, and Politics Drive the Commerce of Conception (2006).

3. Rosalind Berkowitz King & Joan Davis, *Introduction: Health Disparities in Infertility,* 85 Fertility & Sterility 842 (2006).

4. According to the American Society for Reproductive Medicine, the average cost for a single cycle of IVF in the United States is $12,400. American Society for Reproductive Medicine (ASRM), *Is IVF Expensive?, available at* http://www.asrm.org/detail .aspx?id=3023 (last visited Oct. 15, 2015). A typical IVF cycle involves ovarian stimulation using a variety of drugs, surgical retrieval of mature oocytes, insemination followed within three to five days by embryo transfer, and finally pregnancy testing. *See* Soc'y for Assisted Reprod. Tech., *ART: Step-by-Step Guide, available at* http://www.sart.org/ detail.aspx?id=1903 (last visited Feb. 9, 2015). A recent study looking at out-of-pocket expenditures for IVF pegged the average cost per cycle at $19,234. *See* Alex Wu et al., *Out-of-Pocket Fertility Patient Expense: Data from a Multicenter Prospective Infertility Cohort,* 191 J. Urology 427 (2014).

5. ICSI involves injection of a single sperm into the egg in order to achieve fertilization. Developed in the early 1990s, ICSI was initially reserved for cases involving male infertility (low sperm count, for example). Today two-thirds of all IVF cycles involve ICSI. *See* Ctrs. for Disease Control & Prevention, U.S. Dep't of Health & Hum. Servs., 2010 Assisted Reproductive Technology, National Summary Report 4 (2012), *available*

at http://www.cdc.gov/art/ART2010/NationalSummary_download.html (last visited Sept. 5, 2014).

6. This figure derives from the total number of IVF cycles performed for immediate reproductive purposes (thus, excluding egg banking cycle) (163,209) and the total number of deliveries that yielded live births (54,323) in 2013. *See* Ctrs. for Disease Control & Prevention, U.S. Dep't of Health & Hum. Servs., 2013 Assisted Reproductive Technology: Fertility Clinic Success Rates Report 5 (2015), *available at* http://www.cdc .gov/art/pdf/2013-report/art-2013-fertility-clinic-report.pdf (last visited Oct. 15, 2015).

7. *See* Peter J. Neumann, Soheyla D. Gharib, & Milton C. Weinstein, *The Cost of a Successful Delivery with In Vitro Fertilization,* 331 New Eng. J. Med. 239 (1994).

8. *See* Anjani Chandra et al., Infertility and Impaired Fecundity in the United States, 1982–2010: Data from the National Survey of Family Growth, National Health Statistics Reports, No. 67 (Aug. 14, 2013), at 1. An additional 12 percent of married women experience impaired fecundity, defined as "physical difficulty in either getting pregnant or carrying a pregnancy to live birth." *Id.*

9. *See* Ctrs. for Disease Control & Prevention, U.S. Dep't of Health & Hum. Servs., 2011 Assisted Reproductive Technology: Fertility Clinic Success Rates Report 3 (2013), *available at* http://www.cdc.gov/art/ART2011/index.htm (last visited Sept. 5, 2014).

10. Chandra, *supra* note 8.

11. *Id.* Measuring the incidence of infertility and fertility care treatment-seeking can vary according to the metrics employed by the inquiring researchers. For example, according to the CDC, between 3.3 and 4.7 million men and 6.7 million women are infertile in the United States today, bringing the total infertile U.S. population to 10 million. *See* Ctrs. for Disease Control & Prevention, U.S. Dep't of Health & Hum. Servs., Reproductive Health, *Infertility FAQs, available at* http://www.cdc.gov/reproductive health/infertility/ (last visited Apr. 14, 2016), and Ctrs. for Disease Control & Prevention, U.S. Dep't of Health & Hum. Servs., Nat'l Ctr. for Health Stats., *Infertility, available at* http://www.cdc.gov/nchs/fastats/infertility.htm (last visited Apr. 14, 2016). Further, it is estimated that about one-fifth of those with infertility—roughly two million—seek treatment each year. *See Fertility, Infertility, available at* http://www.fertilitytoday.org/ infertility.html (last visited Nov. 6, 2014). This estimate of treatment-seeking is slightly higher than the figure reported by Chandra, *supra* note 8.

12. RESOLVE, a national nonprofit infertility advocacy organization, reports that 44 percent of women with infertility have sought medical assistance. *See* William M. Mercer, *Infertility as a Covered Benefit* (1997) (a study commissioned by RESOLVE to study treatment-seeking for infertility), *available at* http://www.resolve.org/about/fast -facts-about-fertility.html (last visited Sept. 5, 2014).

13. Lawrence M. Kessler et al., *Infertility Evaluation and Treatment Among Women in the United States,* 100 Fertility & Sterility 1025 (2013).

14. *See* Georgina M. Chambers et al., *The Impact of Consumer Affordability on Access to Assisted Reproductive Technologies and Embryo Transfer Practices: An International Analysis,* 101 Fertility & Sterility 191 (2014) (finding a decrease in cost of one percentage point of disposable income predicts a 3.2 percent increase in utilization).

15. *See* Deborah Lynn Steinberg, *A Most Selective Practice: The Eugenic Logic of IVF*, 20(1) Women's Studies Int'l Forum 33 (1997). *See also* Ann V. Bell, *"It's Way Out of My League": Low Income Women's Experiences of Medicalized Infertility*, 23 Gender & Society 688 (2009) (documenting infertility journey of poor and working-class women, 60 percent of whom were minorities).

16. Not all sperm donors are or need be paid. A man can agree to provide his sperm without charge, though even in cases of "directed donation" a woman might seek medical assistance to screen for infectious diseases or genetic markers. In still other cases the woman might require IUI or IVF, thus adding the expense of processing the "free" sperm.

17. *See* California Cryobank, *Sperm Bank Costs, available at* https://www.cryobank.com/Services/Pricing/ (last visited Sept. 8, 2014).

18. In 2005, the Food and Drug Administration (FDA) issued comprehensive regulations requiring tissue banks to test donors and donated tissues for a host of diseases including HIV, hepatitis, and syphilis. In addition, tissue banks are now required to ask donors a series of questions to determine their risk factors for particular diseases. While the FDA regulations are not aimed exclusively or directly at ART clinics, they do have an impact on the practice of reproductive medicine when donor gametes are used. *See* Human Cells, Tissues, and Cellular and Tissue-Based Products, 21 C.F.R. § 1271, *available at* http://www.accessdata.fda.gov/scripts/cdrh/cfdocs/cfcfr/CFRSearch.cfm?CFRPart=1271 (last visited Aug. 2, 2010).

19. *See* California Cryobank, *Directed Donor, available at* https://www.cryobank.com/Services/Directed-Donor/ (last visited Apr. 14, 2016).

20. *See, e.g.,* Stephanie M. Lee, *Insemination Rules Will Be Eased by New Law*, S.F. Chron., Dec. 27, 2012 (reporting on a newly enacted California law that expands opportunity for FDA waivers in cases of directed donation).

21. Kan. Stat. Ann. § 23–2208.

22. *See* Chandrika Narayan, *Kansas Court Says Sperm Donor Must Pay Child Support*, CNN Justice, Jan. 24, 2014, *available at* http://www.cnn.com/2014/01/23/justice/kansas-sperm-donation/ (last visited Sept. 8, 2014).

23. Martha Frase-Blunt, *Ova-Compensating? Women Who Donate Eggs to Infertile Couples Earn a Reward—But Pay a Price*, Wash. Post, Dec. 4, 2001, at F1.

24. *See* Sharon Covington & William Gibbons, *What Is Happening to the Price of Eggs?*, 87 Fertility & Sterility 1001 (2007).

25. *See* www.thedonorsource.com.

26. *See* Ctrs. for Disease Control & Prevention, U.S. Dep't of Health & Hum. Servs., 2013 Assisted Reproductive Technology: National Summary Report 3–4 (2015), *available at* http://www.cdc.gov/art/pdf/2013-report/national-summary/art_2013_national_summary_report.pdf (last visited May 4, 2016) [hereinafter 2013 ART National Report].

27. *Id.* at 46.

28. *See* Tamar Lewin, *Coming to the U.S. for Baby, and Womb to Carry It*, N.Y. Times, July 6, 2014, at A1. *See also* Kiran M. Perkins, Sheree L. Boulet, Denise J. Jamieson

& Dmitry M. Kissin, *Trends and Outcomes of Gestational Surrogacy in the United States,* Fertility & Sterility (2016) (reporting birth of 18,400 infants via gestational surrogacy between 1999 and 2013).

29. For a breakdown of one agency's cost estimates, *see* Center for Surrogate Parenting, Inc., *Estimated Costs for Gestational Surrogacy (In Vitro Fertilization), available at* https://www.creatingfamilies.com/intended-parents/?Id=44#.VA5BfSvn9rQ (last visited Apr. 14, 2016).

30. *See* Brian Melly, *Idaho Woman Who Owned Egg-Donor Company Gets 1 1/2 Years in Prison for Scamming Would-Be Parents,* U.S. News & World Rep. (Sept. 28, 2015), *available at* http://www.usnews.com/news/us/articles/2015/09/28/idaho-woman-gets -1-year-term-for-california-egg-donor-fraud (last visited Oct. 16, 2015).

31. *See* Alan Zarembo, *Scam Targeted Surrogates as Well as Couples,* L.A. Times, Aug. 13, 2011, *available at* http://articles.latimes.com/2011/aug/13/local/la-me-baby -ring-20110814 (last visited Apr. 14, 2016); Alan Zarembo & Kimi Yoshino, *Surrogacy Makes for a Perilous Path to Parenthood,* L.A. Times, Mar. 29, 2009, *available at* http:// articles.latimes.com/2009/mar/29/local/me-surrogate29 (last visited Feb. 9, 2015).

32. The Kaiser Family Foundation, *The Uninsured: A Primer—Key Facts About Health Insurance on the Eve of Coverage Expansion,* Oct. 23, 2013, *available at* http://kff .org/uninsured/report/the-uninsured-a-primer-key-facts-about-health-insurance-on -the-eve-of-coverage-expansions/ (last visited Sept. 9, 2014) (reporting 55.7 percent of nonelderly Americans receive employer-sponsored health insurance).

33. Patient Protection and Affordable Care Act, Pub. L. No. 111–148, 124 Stat. 119 (2010). Some of the statutory provisions of the Affordable Care Act were subsequently amended by the Health Care and Education Reconciliation Act of 2010, Pub. L. No. 111– 152, 124 Stat. 1029 (Mar. 30, 2010).

34. Surprisingly, infertility services are covered under Medicaid and Title X, although there is little information available on the amount of public funds actually spent on infertility treatment. See 42 C.F.R. § 59.5(a)(1).

35. For a comprehensive analysis of ERISA, see Barry R. Furrow, Thomas L. Greaney, Sandra H. Johnson, Timothy Stoltzfus Jost, & Robert L. Schwartz, Health Law 418–60 (2d ed. 2000).

36. *ERISA Preemption Primer, available at* http://www.nashp.org/sites/default/ files/ERISA_Primer.pdf (last visited Sept. 15, 2014).

37. *See* Michelle Andrews, *Health Insurance Rules May Decide Whether Infertility Treatment Is Essential,* Wash. Post, Jan. 24, 2011.

38. For a comprehensive analysis of the ACA and its impact on infertility care coverage, *see* RESOLVE, *The Affordable Care Act and Infertility, available at* http:// www.resolve.org/get-involved/the-center-for-infertility-justice/public-policy/the -affordable-care-act-and-infertility.html (last visited Sept. 8, 2014).

39. Barry R. Furrow et al., Health Law 529 (5th ed. 2004).

40. Andrea D. Gurmankin, Arthur L. Caplan, & Andrea M. Braverman, *Screening Practices and Beliefs of Assisted Reproductive Technology Programs,* 83 Fertility & Sterility 61 (2005).

41. *Id.* at 65.

42. *Id.* at 63 (52 percent of practices collect data on patients' financial stability).

43. California Cryobank, *General Sperm Donor Requirements, available at* https://www.spermbank.com/sperm-donor-faqs (last visited Sept. 11, 2014).

44. *See How Much More Do College Graduates Earn Than Non-College Graduates?,* Study.com, *available at* http://education-portal.com/articles/How_Much_More_Do_College_Graduates_Earn_Than_Non-College_Graduates.html (last visited Sept. 11, 2014) (reporting those with college degrees earn 66 percent more than workers with high school diplomas).

45. *See* Barefoot Student, http://www.barefootstudent.com/baton_rouge/jobs/opportunity/egg_donor_needed_generous_compensation_103795 (last visited Sept. 11, 2014).

46. *See* http://fertilityhelp.com/index.php?option=com_comprofiler&task=reg isters (last visited Sept. 11, 2014).

47. *See* Center for Surrogate Parenting, Inc., *Typical Surrogate Mom Profile, available at* http://www.creatingfamilies.com/surrogate-mothers/?typical-surrogate-profile -56#.VBIa3Svn9rQ (last visited Sept. 11, 2014).

48. Rayven Perkins, *Why Can't a Surrogate Mother Be on Public Assistance?, available at* http://directory.distributeyourarticles.com/2ca09d666e39/why_cant_a_ surrogate_mother_be_on_government_assistanceij (last visited Sept. 11, 2014).

49. *See* http://www.allaboutsurrogacy.com/forums/index.php?showtopic=57395 (last visited Sept. 11, 2014).

50. Johnson v. Calvert, 851 P.2d 776, 785 (Cal. 1993).

51. In 2015, the CDC reported that just under 1 percent (0.9) of all births from ART cycles using fresh nondonor eggs or embryos were triplets or more, compared with 2.6 percent in 2004. 2013 ART National Report, *supra* note 26, at 58.

52. The case for avoiding multiple pregnancy is often made in medical terms. As one recent medical journal article explains, "There are well-documented increases in maternal morbidity and mortality from gestational diabetes, hypertension, cesarean delivery, pulmonary emboli, and postpartum hemorrhage in addition to fetal, neonatal, and childhood complications from neurologic insults, ocular and pulmonary damage, learning disabilities, and retardation, and congenital malformations." R. Stillman, K. Richter, N. Banks, & J. Graham, *Elective Single Embryo Transfer: A 6-Year Progressive Implementation of 784 Single Blastocyst Transfers and the Influence of Payment Method of Patient Choice,* 92 Fertility & Sterility 1895, 1900 (2009).

53. *See* Practice Comm. of the Society for Assisted Reprod. Tech. and Practice Comm. of the Am. Soc'y for Assisted Reprod. Med., *Guidelines on the Number of Embryos Transferred,* 86 Fertility & Sterility S51 (2006). The rate of embryo transfer per cycle is improving. In 2013, patients under age thirty-five averaged 1.8 embryos per cycle, while ASRM practice guidelines recommend patients with a "favorable prognosis should be offered a single-embryo transfer and no more than two embryos . . . should be transferred." Practice Comm. of the Soc'y for Assisted Reprod. Tech. and Practice Comm. of the Am. Soc'y for Assisted Reproductive Med., *Criteria for Number of Embryos to Transfer: A Committee Opinion,* 99 Fertility & Sterility 44 (2013).

54. *See* Deborah L. Forman, *When "Bad" Mothers Make Worse Law: A Critique of Legislative Limits on Embryo Transfer,* 14 U. Pa. J.L. & Soc. Change 273, 297–98 (2011). *See also* Tara Siegel Bernard, *Insurance Coverage for Fertility Treatments Varies Widely,* N.Y. Times, July 25, 2014 (reporting patient desires to exceed recommended embryo transfer guidelines to save money on later cycles).

55. Jill Stark & Rachel Browne, *Multiple Births to Cash-Strapped IVF Mums on Rise,* BrisbaneTimes.com, *available at* http://www.brisbanetimes.com.au/lifestyle/life/multiple-births-to-cashstrapped-ivf-mums-on-rise-20100501-u0a6.html (last visited May 2, 2010).

56. *See* Norbert Gleicher et al., *New Debate: A Formal Comparison of the Practice of Assisted Reproductive Technologies Between Europe and the USA,* 21 Hum. Reprod. 145, 145 (2006).

57. M. P. Vélez et al., *Universal Coverage of IVF Pays Off,* 29 Hum. Reprod. 1313 (2014).

58. Tarun Jain, Bernard L. Harlow, & Mark D. Hornstein, *Insurance Coverage and Outcomes of In Vitro Fertilization,* 347 New Eng. J. Med. 661 (2002). The researchers opined, "Although the rates of pregnancy and live births from in vitro fertilization are higher in states that do not require insurance coverage, so are the rates of pregnancies with three or more fetuses, probably because more embryos are transferred per cycle in these states than in states that require complete insurance coverage. It is also possible that because patients must pay out of pocket in states without mandated coverage, physicians are under pressure to obtain a 'successful' outcome the first time and therefore transfer more embryos per cycle." *Id.* at 665.

59. *Id.*

60. See Camille M. Davidson, *Octomom and Multi-fetal Pregnancies: Why Federal Legislation Should Require Insurers to Cover In Vitro Fertilization,* 17 Wm. & Mary J. Women & L. 135, 167 (2010).

61. *Id., citing* Mackenzie Carpenter, *Blue Cross Draws Line on In-Vitro Fertilization Procedure,* Pittsburgh Post-Gazette, June 27, 1993, at A1.

62. *See* Edward G. Hughes & Mita Giacomini, *Funding In Vitro Fertilization Treatment for Persistent Subfertility: The Pain and the Politics,* 76 Fertility & Sterility 431 (2001) (reporting providing infertility coverage for all privately insured employee-based health plans would raise annual premiums about $3.00).

FOUR Race and Ethnicity as Barriers to ART Access

1. Inst. of Med., Nat'l Res. Council, Board on Population Health & Public Health Practice, U.S. Health in International Perspective: Shorter Lives, Poorer Health (Steven H. Woolf & Laudan Aron eds., 2013).

2. Inst. of Medicine of the Nat'l Academies, Unequal Treatment: Confronting Racial and Ethnic Disparities in Health Care 80–214 (2003).

3. Dayna Bowen Matthew, *A New Strategy to Combat Racial Inequality in American Health Care Delivery,* 9 DePaul J. Health Care L. 793, 794 (2006).

4. 42 U.S.C. § 263a-1 et seq.

5. *See, e.g.,* Melissa F. Wellons et al., *Race Matters: A Systematic Review of Racial/ Ethnic Disparity in Society for Assisted Reproductive Technology Reported Outcomes,* 98 Fertility & Sterility 406 (2012) (finding 65 percent of IVF cycles reported contained the race and/or ethnicity of the treated patient).

6. *See* Bernadette V. Blanchfield & Charlotte J. Patterson, *Racial and Sexual Minority Women's Receipt of Medical Assistance to Become Pregnant,* 34 Health Psychol. 571 (2015), *citing* Marianne Bitler & Lucie Schmidt, *Health Disparities and Infertility: Impacts of State-Level Insurance Mandates,* 85 Fertility & Sterility 858 (2006). Thanks to my colleague and RESOLVE board member Lee Collins for offering a critical and thorough assessment of these reported wide disparities among black, Hispanic, and white women. She cautions that, from her read, at times the authors compare dissimilar data and as a result overstate the distinctions in the incidence of infertility among women in the three groups. She urges greater reliance on the National Survey of Family Growth data, which shows that black women are 1.8 times more likely (as opposed to 3 times more likely) to have infertility than either Hispanic or white women. *See* email from Lee Rubin Collins to Judith Daar, June 22, 2015 (on file with author).

7. Anjani Chandra et al., Infertility and Impaired Fecundity in the United States, 1982–2010: Data from the National Survey of Family Growth, National Health Statistics Reports, No. 67 (Aug. 14, 2013), at 18.

8. Marcia C. Inhorn & Michael Hassan Fakid, *Arab Americans, African Americans, and Infertility: Barriers to Reproduction and Medical Care,* 85 Fertility & Sterility 844, 845–46 (2006).

9. Tanzina Vega, *Infertility, Endured Through a Prism of Race,* N.Y. Times, Apr. 26, 2014, at A12.

10. Tarun Jain, Socioeconomic and Racial Disparities Among Infertility Patients Seeking Care, 85 Fertility & Sterility 876 (2006).

11. Ctrs. for Disease Control & Prevention, U.S. Dep't of Health & Hum. Servs., Sexually Transmitted Disease Surveillance (2004).

12. Jain, *supra* note 10, at 879.

13. Am. Soc'y for Reprod. Med., Age and Fertility: A Guide for Patients (2012), *available at* https://www.asrm.org/uploadedFiles/ASRM_Content/Resources/Patient_Resources/Fact_Sheets_and_Info_Booklets/agefertility.pdf (last visited Sept. 17, 2014).

14. Arthur L. Greil, Julia McQuillan, & Karina M. Shreffler, *Race-Ethnicity and Medical Services for Infertility: Stratified Reproduction in a Population-Based Sample of U.S. Women,* 52 J. Health & Soc. Behav. 1 (2011).

15. Jain, *supra* note 10 (4.3 years for black women versus 3.3 years for whites).

16. D.A. Grainger et al., *Racial Disparity in Clinical Outcomes from Women Using Advanced Reproductive Technology (ART): Analysis of 80,196 ART Cycles from the SART Database 1999 and 2000,* 82 Fertility & Sterility S37 (2004).

17. Lynn White, Julia McQuillan, & Arthur Greil, *Explaining Disparities in Treatment Seeking: The Case of Infertility,* 85 Fertility & Sterility 853 (2006). Different studies show different ordering of the minority woman when measuring for different aspects of

ART, but the general conclusion that women of color fare worse than white women is universally supported by research.

18. K.S. Richter et al., *Racial/Ethnic Disparities in Assisted Reproductive Technology (ART) Outcomes: An Analysis of 10,413 Patients from a Single Fertility Practice,* 96 Fertility & Sterility S64 (2011).

19. Victor Fujimoto et al., *Racial and Ethnic Disparities in Assisted Reproductive Technology Outcomes in the United States,* 93 Fertility & Sterility 382 (2010). A more recent article concludes that racial and ethnic disparities in access to ART treatment and outcomes not only exist, but may be increasing. *See* Molly Quinn & Victor Fujimoto, *Racial and Ethnic Disparities in Assisted Reproductive Technology Access and Outcomes,* 105 Fertility & Sterility 1119 (2016).

20. *See* Eve C. Feinberg et al., *Comparison of Assisted Reproductive Technology Utilization and Outcomes Between Caucasian and African American Patients in an Equal-Access-to-Care Setting,* 85 Fertility & Sterility 888 (2006) (reporting miscarriage rates for black and white patients at 25 percent versus 15.9 percent, and live birth rates at 29.6 percent and 35.8 percent, respectively).

21. *See* Ctr. for Uterine Fibroids, *About Uterine Fibroids, available at* http://www.fibroids.net/fibroids.html (last visited Apr. 14, 2016).

22. Dorothy E. Roberts, *Race and the New Reproduction,* 47 Hastings L.J. 935 (1996).

23. *Id.* at 940.

24. Kaiser Family Foundation, *Health Coverage by Race and Ethnicity: The Potential Impact of the Affordable Care Act,* Mar. 13, 2013, *available at* http://kff.org/disparities-policy/issue-brief/health-coverage-by-race-and-ethnicity-the-potential-impact-of-the-affordable-care-act/ (last visited Sept. 19, 2014).

25. Rakesh Kochhar, Richard Fry, & Paul Taylor, *Wealth Gaps Rise to Record Highs Between Blacks, Whites, Hispanics,* Pew Research, July 28, 2011, *available at* http://www.pewsocialtrends.org/2011/07/26/wealth-gaps-rise-to-record-highs-between-whites-blacks-hispanics/ (last visited Sept. 19, 2014).

26. Council of Economic Advisors for the President's Initiative on Race (2009), *Economic Report of the President, available at* http://www.gpo.gov/fdsys/browse/collection.action?collectionCode=ERP (last visited Sept. 14, 2014).

27. In addition to the cost of treatment, ART care can include time away work and travel costs to distant clinics for regular monitoring. Since IVF clinics tend to be located in more affluent urban areas, minority women may face a geographic barrier that adds to their treatment costs.

28. Tarun Jain & Mark D. Hornstein, *Disparities in Access to Infertility Services in a State with Mandated Coverage,* 84 Fertility & Sterility 221 (2005).

29. Marianne Bitler & Lucie Schmidt, *Health Disparities and Infertility: Impacts of State-Level Insurance Mandates,* 85 Fertility & Sterility 858 (2006). In this study, researchers used a woman's level of education as a proxy for socioeconomic status, finding that women with higher levels of education sought out infertility services at greater rates than women with lower levels of education.

30. *See, e.g.,* Md. Ins. Code Ann. § 15–810, Md. Health-Gen. Code Ann. § 19–701 (2000) (requires a history of infertility of at least two years' duration); Haw. Rev. Stat. §§ 431:10A-116.5(4) (requiring a patient and the patient's spouse to have a history of infertility of at least five years' duration for insurance coverage to apply).

31. *See* Casey E. Copen et al., First Marriage in the United States: Data from the 2006–2010 National Survey of Family Growth, National Health Statistics Reports, No. 49 (Mar. 22, 2012), *available at* http://www.cdc.gov/nchs/data/nhsr/nhsr049.pdf (last visited Sept. 21, 2014).

32. Maine Legislature, LD 943 (SP 334), *available at* http://legislature.maine.gov/LawMakerWeb/summary.asp?paper=SP0334&SessionID=11 (last visited Oct. 29, 2015).

33. *See, e.g., Our View: Fertility Bill Would Be Misuse of State Power,* Portland [Maine] Press Herald, Apr. 20, 2015, *available at* http://www.pressherald.com/2015/04/20/our -view-infertility-bill-would-be-misuse-of-state-power/ (last visited Oct. 29, 2015); Jeff Guo, *Maine Wants to Help You Get Fertility Treatment—Unless It Was an STD That Made You Infertile,* Wash. Post, Apr. 21, 2015, *available at* https://www.washingtonpost .com/blogs/govbeat/wp/2015/04/21/maine-wants-to-help-you-get-fertility-treatments -unless-it-was-an-std-that-made-you-infertile/ (last visited Oct. 29, 2015).

34. Feinberg, *supra* note 20, at 889.

35. This is greater than their proportional representation in the total U.S. population at 12.3 percent (compared with 75 percent Caucasian, 12.6 percent Hispanic, 3.7 percent Asian, and 5.5 percent other). *Id.* at 890.

36. *Id.* at 893, *citing* P. Lukoschek, *African Americans' Beliefs and Attitudes Regarding Hypertension and Its Treatment: A Qualitative Study,* 14 J. Health Care Poor Underserved 556 (2003).

37. Tara M. Cousineau & Alice D. Domar, *Psychological Impact of Infertility,* 21(2) Psychol. Issues Obstetrics & Gynecology 293 (2007).

38. *See, e.g.,* B.D. Peterson, C.R. Newton, K.H. Rosen, & G.E. Skaggs, *Gender Differences in How Men and Women Who Are Referred for IVF Cope with Infertility Stress,* 21(9) Hum. Reprod. 2443 (2006); J. McQuillan, A. Greil, L. White, & M. Jacob, *Frustrated Fertility: Infertility and Psychological Stress Among Women,* 65(4) J. Marriage & Family 1007 (2004); S. Fassino, A. Piero, S. Boggio, V. Piccioni, & L. Garzaro, *Anxiety, Depression and Anger Suppression in Infertile Couples: A Controlled Study,* 17(11) Hum. Reprod. 2986 (2002).

39. Dorothy Roberts, Killing the Black Body: Race, Reproduction and the Meaning of Liberty 259 (1997).

40. S. Molock, *Racial, Cultural, and Religious Issues in Infertility Counseling,* in Infertility Counseling: A Comprehensive Handbook for Clinicians 249 (L. Burns & S. Covington eds., 1999). In support of the notion that black couples are less likely than white couples to use ART, Roberts observes, "Black people may be more reluctant to seek a technological fix for natural circumstances beyond their control." Dorothy E. Roberts, *The Nature of Blacks' Skepticism About Genetic Testing,* 27 Seton Hall L. Rev. 971, 973 (1997). She also cites research that links the contrasting responses of infertile black women to their spiritual or psychological outlook on adversity, attributing the infertility to God's will rather than seeking to address it in science. Roberts, *supra,* at 973–74.

41. Ziba Kashef, *Miracle Babies: One in Ten Black Women Will Face the Anguish of Being Unable to Conceive, but Today's Fertility Treatments Are Improving the Odds*, 28 Essence 80 (Jan. 1998).

42. Vega, *supra* note 9. Studies indicate the unique sense of shame that black women feel as a result of infertility. Researchers document the "imperative to be an African American mother" as influenced "by an interplay of gendered, racial, and religious mandates." Rosario Ceballo, Erin T. Graham, & Jamie Hart, *Silent and Infertile: An Intersectional Analysis of the Experiences of Socioeconomically Diverse African American Women with Infertility*, Psychol. Women Q. 1–15 (2015).

43. Regina Townsend, *Voice Behind the Egg, available at* http://thebrokenbrownegg .org/about/mrs-tiye/ (last visited Oct. 1, 2014). *See also* James McIntosh, *Many African-American Women "Silent and Alone" with Infertility*, Med. News Today, June 8, 2015.

44. Inhorn & Fakid, *supra* note 8, at 846–47.

45. Roberts, *supra* note 22, at 940.

46. Jain, *supra* note 10, at 880. *See also* Vega, *supra* note 9 (reporting one black woman's frustration over unsuccessful attempts to get a referral to an infertility specialist).

47. Townsend, *supra* note 9.

48. *See* James H. Jones, Bad Blood: The Tuskegee Syphilis Experiment (1981).

49. *See* Jean Heller, *Syphilis Victims in U.S. Study Went Untreated for 40 Years; Syphilis Victims Got No Therapy*, N.Y. Times, July 26, 1972, at A1.

50. The aftermath of the Tuskegee syphilis experiment saw passage of the National Research Act, 42 U.S.C. § 28g1–1 (1974), and establishment of the National Commission for the Protection of Human Subjects of Biomedical and Behavioral Research, which ultimately issued The Belmont Report: Ethical Principles and Guidelines for the Protection of Human Subjects of Biomedical and Behavioral Research (1979).

51. *See, e.g.,* Susan Reverby, Examining Tuskegee: The Infamous Syphilis Study and Its Legacy (2009); Jeff Stryker, *Tuskegee's Long Arm Still Touches a Nerve*, N.Y. Times, Apr. 13, 1997, at D4 (reporting that "[so] great is the mistrust that grew out of the [Tuskegee syphilis] study that it is continuing to interfere with attempts to fight AIDS in certain black neighborhoods"); S. Thomas & S. Quinn, *The Tuskegee Syphilis Study, 1932 to 1972: Implications for HIV Education and AIDS Risk Education Programs in the Black Community*, 81 Am. J. Pub. Health 1498 (1991).

52. Rhea Boyd, *Dying While Black: The Case of Jahi McMath*, S.F. Chron., Jan 31, 2014, *available at* http://www.sfgate.com/opinion/article/Dying-while-black-the-case -of-Jahi-McMath-5194176.php (last visited Dec. 1, 2014).

53. *See, e.g.,* Feinberg, *supra* note 20, at 893; Lukoschek, *supra* note 36.

54. Roberts, *supra* note 39, at 974.

55. *Id., citing* Mark R. Farfel & Neil A. Holtzmann, *Education, Consent and Counseling in Sickle-Cell Screening Programs: Report of a Survey*, 74 Am. J. Pub. Health 373 (1984).

56. Michelle Oberman, *Thirteen Ways of Looking at* Buck v. Bell: *Thoughts Occasioned by Paul Lombardo's Three Generations, No Imbeciles*, 59 J. Legal Ed. 357, 377 (2010).

57. Roberts, *supra* note 39, at 172–75 (relaying statistics from 1990).

58. Michele Goodwin, *Issues of Access to Advanced Reproductive Technologies: Prosecuting the Womb*, 76 Geo. Wash. L. Rev. 1657, 1667 (2008).

59. Oberman, *supra* note 56, at 378.

60. Ctrs. for Disease Control & Prevention, U.S. Dep't of Health & Hum. Servs., 2013 Assisted Reproductive Technology: National Summary Report 7 (2015), *available at* http://www.cdc.gov/art/pdf/2013-report/national-summary/art_2013_national _summary_report.pdf (last visited May 4, 2016).

61. Nearly 50 percent of all ART procedures are performed in just six states (mostly in the Northeast), and the majority of clinics are located in the eastern United States or in or near major cities. *See* S. Sunderam, D.M. Kissin, I. Flowers, et al., *Assisted Reproductive Technology Surveillance: United States, 2009*, 61 Morbidity & Mortality Wkly. Rev.: Surveill. Summ. 1 (2009).

62. A.K. Nangia, D.S. Likosky, & D. Wang, *Access to Assisted Reproductive Technology Centers in the United States*, 93 Fertility & Sterility 745 (2010).

63. *See Infertility Resources*, http://www.ihr.com/infertility/provider/ivf-fertility -clinics-california-los-angeles.html (last visited Oct. 8, 2014).

64. *Mapping L.A. Neighborhoods*, L.A. Times, *available at* http://maps.latimes .com/neighborhoods/ (last visited Oct. 8, 2014).

65. Jim Hawkins, *Selling ART: An Empirical Assessment of Advertising on Fertility Clinics' Websites*, Ind. L.J. 1147 (2013).

66. Kimberly D. Krawiec, *Altruism and Intermediation in the Market for Babies*, 66 Wash. & Lee L. Rev. 203, 312–14 (2009).

67. Ariel Weissman et al., *Use of the Internet by Infertile Couples*, 73 Fertility & Sterility 1179 (2000).

68. Hawkins, *supra* note 65, at 1169.

69. *Id.* at 1170.

70. *Id., citing* Leslie Bender, *Genes, Parents, and Assisted Reproductive Technologies: ARTs, Mistakes, Sex, Race & Law*, 12 Colum. J. Gender & L. 1 (2003).

71. Marcia C. Inhorn, Rosario Ceballo, & Robert Nachtigall, *Marginalized, Invisible, and Unwanted: American Minority Struggles with Infertility and Assisted Conception*, in Marginalized Reproduction 185 (Lorraine Culley, Nicky Hudson, & Floor van Rooij eds., 2009).

72. Hawkins, *supra* note 65, at 1170.

73. *See, e.g.*, Robert D. Nachtigall et al., *The Challenge of Providing Infertility Services to a Low-Income Immigrant Latino Population*, 92 Fertility & Sterility 116 (2009) (describing significant language barriers in delivering fertility care to Spanish-only speaking patient population).

74. Hawkins, *supra* note 65, at 1170–71.

75. Agency for Healthcare Research & Quality, National Healthcare Disparities Report (2004).

76. Ruqaiijah Yearby, *Breaking the Cycle of "Unequal Treatment" with Health Care Reform: Acknowledging and Addressing the Continuation of Racial Bias*, 44 Conn. L. Rev. 1281 (2012).

77. *Id.* at 1287.

78. *Id.* at 1320–23 (arguing for expanded enforcement of Title VI of the Civil Rights Act of 1964, which prohibits health care entities receiving government funding from using racial bias to determine who receives quality health care).

79. *See* Am. Soc'y for Reprod. Med., *Protect Your Fertility, available at* http://www .asrm.org/Protect_Your_Fertility_Campaign/ (last visited Oct. 10, 2014).

80. Am. Soc'y for Reprod. Med., *Infertility Prevention Campaign, at* http://www .fertilitycommunity.com/fertility/asrms-infertility-prevention-campaign.html (last visited Oct. 10, 2014).

81. *See* Malls and Movie Theaters Say Infertility Is Not for Them, *at* http://www .fertilitycommunity.com/fertility/asrms-infertility-prevention-campaign.html (last visited Oct. 10, 2014).

82. John A. Robertson, Children of Choice 23 (1994).

83. *Id.*

84. Roberts, *supra* note 22, at 947.

85. *Id.*

FIVE   Social Infertility and the Quest for Parenthood

1. According to the Centers for Disease Control and Prevention, between 3.3 million and 4.7 million men and 6.7 million women are infertile in the United States today. *See* Ctrs. for Disease Control & Prevention, U.S. Dep't of Health & Hum. Servs., *Reproductive Health, Infertility FAQs, available at* http://www.cdc.gov/reproductivehealth/ infertility/ (last visited Apr. 14, 2016), and *FastStats, Infertility, available at* http://www .cdc.gov/nchs/fastats/infertility.htm (last visited Apr. 14, 2016). It is estimated that about one-fifth of those with infertility—roughly two million—seek treatment each year. *See Fertility, Infertility, available at* http://www.fertilitytoday.org/infertility.html (last visited Nov. 6, 2014).

2. A transgender individual may also experience social infertility even if part of an opposite-sex relationship. For example, a trans man (defined as a female to male transsexual) may retain ovaries and a uterus but would require donor sperm to become pregnant.

3. *See* Diane English, *Speaking of Dan Quayle and "Murphy Brown" . . . [Blowback]*, L.A. Times, Mar. 27, 2013, *available at* http://articles.latimes.com/2013/mar/27/ news/la-ol-dan-quayle-murphy-brown-blowback-20120327 (last visited Nov. 6, 2014). Discussion and support for Dan Quayle's position continue to appear in the public domain. *See, e.g.,* Isabel Sawhill, *20 Years Later, It Turns Out Dan Quayle Was Right About Murphy Brown and Unmarried Moms,* Wash. Post, May 25, 2012, *available at* https:// www.washingtonpost.com/opinions/20-years-later-it-turns-out-dan-quayle-was -right-about-murphy-brown-and-unmarried-moms/2012/05/25/gJQAsNCJqU_story .html (last visited Oct. 30, 2015).

4. *See* Ctrs. for Disease Control & Prevention, U.S. Dep't of Health & Hum. Servs., Unmarried Childbearing (2012), *available at* http://www.cdc.gov/nchs/fastats/

unmarried-childbearing.htm (last visited Aug. 26, 2014) (reporting 40.7 percent of U.S. births in 2012 to unmarried women).

5. DeBoer v. Snyder, 772 F.3d 388 (6th Cir. 2014), *cert. granted* (Jan. 16, 2015). The decision in DeBoer was reversed by the U.S. Supreme Court in Obergefell v. Hodges, 135 S. Ct. 2584 (2015), in which the Court held that the right to marry is a fundamental right inherent in the liberty of the person, and under the Due Process and Equal Protection Clauses of the Fourteenth Amendment, couples of the same sex may not be deprived of that right and that liberty.

6. DeBoer v. Snyder, *supra* note 5, at 405–6.

7. A transgender man with a fully intact female reproductive system would also likely require medical assistance with self-insemination if he has been taking hormone therapy that interacts with his endocrine system.

8. *Moving Upstream: Sperm Banks in the U.S. Industry,* Apr. 11, 2012, *available at* http://www.prweb.com/releases/2012/4/prweb9389275.htm (last visited Nov. 7, 2014).

9. *See* Mikki Morrisette, *Redefining Family: Single Women and Lesbian Couples Who Choose Parenthood Are Transforming the Donor Insemination Industry,* Minnesota Women's Press, *available at* http://www.womenspress.com/main.asp?SectionID=1&SubSectionID=1&ArticleID=2391&TM=57580.26 (last visited June 19, 2009).

10. *See* Nanette K. Gartrell et al., *Satisfaction with Known, Open-Identity, or Unknown Sperm Donors: Reports from Lesbian Mothers of 17-Year-Old Adolescents,* 103 Fertility & Sterility 242 (2015).

11. *See* Inst. for Science, Law & Tech. Working Group, *ART into Science: Regulation of Fertility Techniques,* 281 Science 651 (1998) (reporting sixty thousand AID births annually); *see also* Ctrs. for Disease Control & Prevention, U.S. Dep't of Health & Hum. Servs., 2012 Assisted Reproductive Technology Fertility Clinic Success Rates Report (Aug. 2014) (reporting births of 65,160 infants via ART), *available at* http://www.cdc.gov/art/ART2012/PDF/ART_2012_Clinic_Report-Full.pdf (last visited Oct. 15, 2014).

12. *Home Insemination Success Rates, available at* http://www.fertilityauthority.com/home-insemination-success-rates (last visited Nov. 7, 2014).

13. *See* Tony Dokoupil, *"Free Sperm Donors" and the Women Who Want Them,* Newsweek, Oct. 2, 2011, *available at* http://www.newsweek.com/free-sperm-donors-and-women-who-want-them-68233 (last visited Feb. 11, 2015).

14. *See, e.g.,* R.S. Ross, M. Elgas, & M. Roggendorf, *HIV-1 Transmission Through Artificial Insemination,* 351 Lancet 1812 (1998); Barry J. Maron et al., *Implications of Hypertrophic Cardiomyopathy Transmitted by Sperm Donation,* 302 JAMA 1681 (2009).

15. *See* Chandrika Narayan, *Kansas Court Says Sperm Donor Must Pay Child Support,* CNN Justice, Jan. 24, 2014, *available at* http://www.cnn.com/2014/01/23/justice/kansas-sperm-donation/ (last visited Sept. 8, 2014).

16. *See U.S. Sperm Donation Laws by State, available at* http://knowndonor registry.com/component/content/article/166-legal/private-donation-laws/114-us-sperm-donation-laws-by-state (last visited Nov. 7, 2014).

17. 44 Cal. 4th 1145, 189 P.3d 959, 81 Cal. Rptr.3d 708 (2008).

18. *Id.* at 1149.

19. *Id.* at 1151. The Unruh Civil Rights Act is codified in Cal. Civ. Code § 51(a). While the text of the statute did not list sexual orientation as a prohibited basis for discrimination in 1999 and 2000, California case law did describe the statute as prohibiting sexual orientation discrimination. The act was amended in 2005 to expressly prohibit sexual orientation discrimination. Currently, the statute also includes marital status as a protected classification.

20. *Id.* at 1149. The Unruh Act applies to business establishments that offer to the public "accommodations, advantages, facilities, privileges or services" that have been deemed to include a medical group providing medical services to the public. *Id.* at 1153.

21. *Id.* at 1159. In his concurring opinion, Justice Baxter questions whether such advice would work for a solo practitioner—a good point indeed. *Id.* at 1162–63.

22. *See* Lisa Leff, *California Court Hears Lesbian Insemination Case,* USA Today, May 28, 2008.

23. *See* Letter Issued by Jennifer C. Pizer, Lambda Legal Senior Counsel, *available at* http://www.lambdalegal.org/sites/default/files/legal-docs/downloads/benitez_ca_2090929_joint-statement-upon-settlement.pdf (last visited Nov. 10, 2014).

24. Leff, *supra* note 22.

25. *See, e.g.,* Ferguson v. McKiernan, 940 A.2d 1236 (Pa. 2007) (in dispute between known sperm donor and birth mother, court mentions in footnote that IVF practice involved in the case limited treatment to "women in stable marriages").

26. Andrea D. Gurmankin, Arthur L. Caplan, & Andrea M. Braverman, *Screening Practices and Beliefs of Assisted Reproductive Technology Programs,* 83(1) Fertility & Sterility 61 (2005).

27. *Id.* at 64.

28. *Id.* (64 percent of respondents agreed or strongly agreed with this statement).

29. Dorothy A. Greenfield, *Gay Male Couples and Assisted Reproduction: Should We Assist?,* 88 Fertility & Sterility 18 (2007), *citing* J. Bigner & R. Jacobsen, *Adult Responses to Child Behavior and Attitudes Toward Fathering: Gay and Non-Gay Fathers,* 23 J. Homosexuality 99 (1992).

30. *See* Ctrs. for Disease Control & Prevention, U.S. Dep't of Health and Hum. Servs., 2006 Assisted Reproductive Technology Success Rates: National Summary and Fertility Clinic Reports 89 (2008), *available at* http://www.cdc.gov/art/Archived-PDF-Reports/2006ART.pdf (last visited Nov. 13, 2014).

31. *See* Ctrs. for Disease Control & Prevention, U.S. Dep't of Health & Hum. Servs., 2013 Assisted Reproductive Technology: National Summary Report 5 (2015), *available at* http://www.cdc.gov/art/pdf/2013-report/national-summary/art_2013_national_summary_report.pdf (last visited May 4, 2016).

32. Another cohort that experiences widespread discrimination in the provision of reproductive assistance services is transgender persons. *See* Sarah Elizabeth Richards, *The Next Frontier in Fertility Treatment,* N.Y. Times, Jan. 12, 2014, at A19. In a study published in 2015, a majority of trans people surveyed indicated negative experiences in attempting to access assisted reproductive services. *See* S. James-Abra et al., *Trans*

People's Experiences with Assisted Reproduction Services: A Qualitative Study, 30 Hum. Reprod. 1365 (2015).

33. *See* Greenfield, *supra* note 29; G. Mallon, Gay Men Choosing Parenthood (2004); Ethics Comm., Am. Soc'y for Reprod. Med., *Access to Fertility Treatment by Gays, Lesbians and Unmarried Persons: A Committee Opinion,* 100 Fertility & Sterility 1524 (2013) (collecting data on concerns about child welfare in nontraditional families).

34. Ethics Comm., *supra* note 33, at 1525.

35. *See, e.g.,* Am. Acad. Child & Adolescent Psychiatry, Facts for Families: Children with Lesbian, Gay, Bisexual and Transgender Parents (2011) (current research shows that children with LGBT parents do not differ from children with heterosexual parents); Am. Psychol. Ass'n, Sexual Orientation, Parents & Children (2004) (finding no scientific evidence that parenting effectiveness is related to parental sexual orientation); F. Maccallum & S. Golombok, *Children Raised in Fatherless Families from Infancy: A Follow-Up of Children of Lesbian and Single Heterosexual Mothers at Early Adolescence,* 45 J. Child Psychol. Psychiatry 1407 (2004) (being raised in fatherless home does not have negative consequences for children).

36. *See* Greenfield, *supra* note 29, at 18.

37. *See* Dale Carpenter, *A "Reality Check" for the Regnerus Study on Gay Parenting,* Wash. Post, May 10, 2015, *available at* https://www.washingtonpost.com/news/volokh -conspiracy/wp/2015/05/10/new-criticism-of-regnerus-study-on-parenting-study/ (last visited Oct. 30, 2015) (reporting on a 2012 study published by University of Texas sociologist Mark Regnerus concluding children of gay parents fare worse than children raised by married opposite-sex parents. Further examination by researchers showed significant methodological problems with the original research, calling into question the study's fundamental conclusion).

38. Gurmankin, *supra* note 26, at 64.

39. Ethics Comm., *supra* note 33, at 1524.

40. Pedro Acién, *Access to Fertility Treatment,* 93 Fertility & Sterility e23 (2010).

41. *See generally* Paul A. Lombardo, Three Generations, No Imbeciles (2008).

42. Civil Rights Act of 1964, 42 U.S.C. § 2000d et seq. (2014).

43. *See, e.g.,* The Federal Fair Housing Act of 1968, 42 U.S.C. § 3600 et seq. (2014) (prohibits discrimination in the sale, rental, and financing of housing based on race, color, national origin, religion, sex, familial status, and disability); the federal Pregnancy Discrimination Act of 1978, 42 U.S.C. § 2000e(k) (2014) (prohibits discrimination because of or on the basis of pregnancy, childbirth, or related medical conditions); Title VII of the Civil Rights Act of 1964, 42 U.S.C. § 2000e-2(a)(1) (2014) (prohibits discrimination against individuals with respect to compensation, terms, conditions, or privileges of employment because of race, color, religion, sex, or national origin).

44. *See* Sara Rosenbaum & Joel Teitelbaum, *Civil Rights Enforcement in the Modern Healthcare System: Reinvigorating the Role of the Federal Government in the Aftermath of* Alexander v. Sandoval, 3 Yale J. Health Pol'y L. & Ethics 215 (2003).

45. Dayna Bowen Matthew, *A New Strategy to Combat Racial Inequality in American Health Care Delivery,* 9 DePaul J. Health Care L. 793, 796 (2006).

46. Age Discrimination Act of 1975, 42 U.S.C. § 6101 et seq. (1975).

47. Americans with Disabilities Act of 1991, 42 U.S.C. § 12101 et seq. (1991).

48. Pregnancy Discrimination Act of 1978, 42 U.S.C. § 2000(e).

49. Family and Medical Leave Act of 1993, 29 U.S.C. § 2601.

50. *See* 42 U.S.C. § 2000e-2(a)(1) (2014). The Equal Employment Opportunity Commission (EEOC), the federal agency that enforces the prohibitions against employment discrimination under Title VII, states that an LGBT person can state a sex discrimination claim under the law. *See* http://www.eeoc.gov/federal/otherprotections.cfm (last visited Nov. 13, 2014).

51. The Civil Service Reform Act of 1978 has been interpreted to prohibit personnel actions (such as firing) to be based on non-employment-related characteristics such as marital status. *See* http://www.eeoc.gov/facts/qanda.html (last visited Nov. 13, 2014).

52. 42 U.S.C. § 2000e-2(a)(1) (2014).

53. *See* Mark Joseph Stern, *EEOC Rules Workplace Sexual Orientation Discrimination Already Illegal Under Federal Law,* Slate, July 16, 2015, *available at* http://www.slate.com/blogs/outward/2015/07/16/sexual_orientation_discrimination_at_work_eeoc _says_it_s_illegal_under_federal.html (last visited Oct. 30, 2015) (reporting on EEOC's decision that sexual orientation is "associational discrimination on the basis of sex").

54. Herx v. Diocese of Ft. Wayne-South Bend, Inc., 2014 WL 4373617 (N.D. Ind. 2014). In December 2014, a jury awarded Mrs. Emily Herx $1.75 million for her Title VII claims, a sum that was later reduced by the judge to around $500,000. *See* Kelly Knaub, *Catholic Teacher Seeks Fees After IVF Firing Award Slashed,* Law 360, Jan. 14, 2015, *available at* http://www.law360.com/articles/611469/catholic-teacher-seeks-fees-after -ivf-firing-award-slashed (last visited Oct. 30, 2015).

55. *See, e.g.,* Saks v. Franklin Covey, 117 F. Supp. 2d 318 (2000), *aff'd* 316 F.3d 337 (2d Cir. 2003) (dismissing all of plaintiff's claims).

56. Cal. Civ. Code § 51(a).

57. *See* Leach v. Drummond Medical Group, Inc., 144 Cal. App. 3d 362 (1983) (medical group providing services to the public held to be business establishment for purposes of Unruh Civil Rights Act).

58. *See* Judith Daar, *Accessing Reproductive Technologies: Invisible Barriers, Indelible Harms,* 23 Berkeley J. Gen. L. & Justice 18, 65 fn.175 (2008) (listing states that protect against marital status and sexual orientation discrimination). A 2013 survey of state civil rights laws lists eighteen states plus the District of Columbia as having protection in public accommodations against sexual orientation discrimination (California, Connecticut, Washington, D.C., Hawaii, Illinois, Iowa, Maine, Maryland, Massachusetts, Minnesota, New Hampshire, New Jersey, New Mexico, New York, Oregon, Rhode Island, Vermont, Washington, Wisconsin). *See* Inst. of Real Estate Mgmt., Laws Prohibiting Discrimination Based on Sexual Orientation and Gender Identity (Aug. 2013), *available at* http://www.irem.org/File%20Library/Public%20Policy/Anti-discrimination.pdf (last visited Nov. 18, 2014).

59. Institute of Real Estate Mgmt., *supra* note 58.

60. *See* Kimberly M. Mutcherson, *Welcome to the Wild West: Access to Cross Border Fertility Care in the United States,* 22 Cornell J.L. & Pub. Pol'y 349 (2012); Fertility

Treatment Bans in Europe Draw Criticism (Apr. 13, 2012), *available at* http://www.fox news.com/world/2012/04/13/fertility-treatment-bans-in-europe-draw-criticism/ (last visited Nov. 19, 2014).

61. *See* Mary Beth Schneider, *Assisted Reproduction Bill Dropped,* Ind. Star, Oct. 6, 2005, at 2B.

62. *Id.*

63. *See* Hunter, *Indiana's R's Seek to Criminalize "Unauthorized Reproduction,"* Daily Kos, Oct. 5, 2005, *available at* http://www.dailykos.com/story/2005/10/05/154434/ -Indiana-R-s-Seek-to-Criminalize-Unauthorized-Reproduction-UPDATED (last visited Nov. 19, 2014).

64. *See* Lombardo, *supra* note 41, at 24–25.

65. *Id.*

66. H.B. 187, 2006 Reg. Sess. (Va. 2006).

67. Va. Code Ann. § 2.2–3900.

68. *See* Ark. Code Ann. §§ 23–85-137; 23–86-118; Haw. Rev. Stat. §§ 431:10A-116.5, 432:1–604; Md. Code Ann., Ins. § 15–810; R.I. Gen. Laws § 27–19-23; Tex. Ins. Code Ann. § 1366.005. The legislative desire to limit IVF coverage to married individuals seems not to have dissipated. In 2015, a Maine bill that would have mandated insurance coverage for infertility care in the state limited coverage to married patients. *See* An Act to Provide Access to Infertility Treatment, Maine Legislature, LD 943 (SP 334), *available at* http:// legislature.maine.gov/LawMakerWeb/summary.asp?paper=SP0334&SessionID=11 (last visited Oct. 29, 2015).

69. R.I. Gen. Laws § 27–19-23.

70. *Id.*

71. *See* Ark. Rules & Regulation, In Vitro Fertilization, § 5.A.

72. Md. Code Ann., Ins. § 15–810(c)(2).

73. *See, e.g.,* Jessie R. Cardinale, *The Injustice of Infertility Insurance Coverage: An Examination of Marital Status Restrictions Under State Law,* 75 Alb. L. Rev. 2133 (2011–12).

74. Tex. Ins. Code Ann. § 1366.005(3).

75. *See, e.g.,* Haw. Rev. Stat. §§ 431:10A-116.5(4) (listing medical conditions that permit a married couple to seek IVF before waiting five years).

76. Cal. Health & Safety Code § 1374.55.

77. Cal. Health & Safety Code § 1374.55(g). A similar statutory fix to an existing law that ruled out coverage for married couples of the same sex was enacted in Maryland in 2015. Maryland's IVF coverage statute requires that the "patient's oocytes are fertilized with the patient's spouse's sperm," thus limiting coverage to opposite-sex married couples. A bill enacted by the legislature requires insurers to offer fertility treatment coverage without regard to a patient's sexual orientation. *See* Josh Hicks, *New LGBT Protections to Take Effect Without Gov. Hogan's Signature,* Wash. Post, May 24, 2015, *available at* https:// www.washingtonpost.com/local/md-politics/new-lgbt-protections-to-become-law-in -md-without-gov-hogans-signature/2015/05/24/1c11e57a-018a-11e5–833c-a2de05b6b2a4 _story.html (last visited Oct. 30, 2015).

78. *See* Seema Mohapatra, *Achieving Reproductive Justice in the International Surrogacy Market,* 21 Annals Health L. 191, 193 (2012) (asserting gestational surrogacy has "all but replaced" traditional surrogacy).

79. *See* Tamar Lewin, *Coming to the U.S. for Baby, and Womb to Carry It,* N.Y. Times, July 6, 2014, at A1.

80. *See* Judith Daar, Reproductive Technologies and the Law 439 (2013) (listing Arkansas, Connecticut, Florida, Illinois, Iowa, Nevada, New Hampshire, Texas, Utah, Virginia, and West Virginia as authorizing surrogacy by statute).

81. *Id.* (listing Arizona, Washington, D.C., Indiana, Kentucky, Louisiana, Michigan, Nebraska, New York, North Dakota, and Washington as banning surrogacy).

82. Conn. Gen. Stat. Ann. § 7–48a. The law was enacted in response to a Connecticut Supreme Court decision that upheld the parental status of a biological father and his same-sex domestic partner who entered a surrogacy agreement. The court held that the state's statutory law "allows an intended parent who is a party to a valid gestational surrogacy agreement to become a parent without first adopting the children." Raftopol v. Ramey, 299 Conn. 681, 12 A.3d 783 (2011).

83. Fla. Stat. Ann. § 742.15.

84. *Id.*

85. Tex. Fam. Code Ann. § 160.756.

86. Utah Code Ann. § 78B-15–706.

87. A.G.R. v. D.R.H. & S.H., N.J. Super. Ct., Ltr. Op. (Dec. 13, 2011), *available at* http://www.docstoc.com/docs/document-preview.aspx?doc_id=108833252 (last visited Nov. 25, 2014). The men were legally married in California and registered domestic partners under the laws of New Jersey.

88. In the Matter of Baby M, 109 N.J. 396, 537 A.2d 1227 (1988).

89. *See* Joanna L. Grossman, *The Complications of Surrogacy: A New Jersey Court Refuses to Uphold a Surrogacy Arrangement but Awards Full Custody to the Intended Father,* Verdict, Jan. 12, 2012, *available at* http://verdict.justia.com/2012/01/10/the-compli cations-of-surrogacy (last visited Nov. 25, 2014).

90. A.G.R. v. D.R.H. & S.H., N.J. Super. Ct., Op. (Dec. 23, 2009), *available at* http://graphics8.nytimes.com/packages/pdf/national/20091231_SURROGATE.pdf (last visited Nov. 25, 2014).

SIX Disability and Procreative Diminishment

1. *See Blind Woman Loses Federal Discrimination Lawsuit Against Fertility Clinic,* USA Today, Nov. 12, 2003, *available at* http://usatoday30.usatoday.com/news/nation/ 2003–11-21-fertility-lawsuit_x.htm (last visited Dec. 3, 2014). According to published reports, the dispute arose when clinic personnel demanded Ms. Chambers hire an occupational therapist to evaluate the safety of her home. When the patient refused, claiming no such expert existed, treatment was discontinued.

2. National Council on Disabilities, Rocking the Cradle: Ensuring the Rights of Parents with Disabilities and Their Children 205 (2012) [hereinafter NCD Report], *available at* http://www.ncd.gov/publications/2012/Sep272012/ (last visited Dec. 3, 2014).

3. *Id.*

4. Harry Laughlin, The Legal Status of Eugenical Sterilization 65 (1929).

5. Measured from a statutory perspective, the eugenics era may not be totally in our past. According to the National Council on Disabilities, the following states retain dangerous and offensive statutory language that authorizes a court to order the involuntary sterilization of a person with a disability: Arkansas (Ark. Code Ann. § 20–49-101), Colorado (Colo. Rev. Stat. § 27–10.5–130), Delaware (16 Del. C. § 5712), Georgia (Ga. Code. Ann. § 31–20-3), Maine (34-B M.R.S.A. § 7010), North Carolina (N.C.G.S.A. § 35A-1245), Oregon (O.R.S. § 436.205), Utah (U.C.A. 1953 § 62A-6–102), Vermont (18 V.S.A. § 8705 et seq.), Virginia (Va. Code Ann. § 54.1–2975 et seq.), and West Virginia (W.Va. Code, § 27–16-1 et seq. [uses especially offensive language regarding the best interests of society]). NCD Report, *supra* note 2, at 44.

6. Americans with Disabilities Act, 42 U.S.C. § 12102 (1990), amended by the Americans with Disabilities Amendments Act, Pub. L. No. 110–325 (2008).

7. Bragdon v. Abbott, 524 U.S. 624 (1998) (holding that reproduction is a major life activity and that HIV interferes with reproduction by posing risk of transmission to sexual partner and child).

8. Skinner v. Oklahoma, 316 U.S. 535, 541 (1942).

9. U.S. Census Bureau, *Nearly 1 in 5 People Have a Disability in the U.S., Census Bureau Says,* July 25, 2012, *available at* https://www.census.gov/newsroom/releases/archives/miscellaneous/cb12–134.html (last visited Dec. 3, 2014) (reporting 56.7 million Americans with one or more disabilities). This survey used the following definition of disability: "Difficulty with any of the six types of disability collected in the American Community Survey: vision, hearing, ambulatory, cognitive, self-care, and independent living. It covers functional limitations in the three domains of disability (communication, mental, and physical), activities of daily living (ADLs), and instrumental activities of daily living (IADLs)."

10. NCD Report, *supra* note 2, at 49.

11. *See* Margaret A. Nosek, *Overcoming the Odds: The Health of Women with Physical Disabilities in the United States,* 81 Archives Physical Med. & Rehabilitation 135 (2000).

12. NCD Report, *supra* note 2, at 219–22.

13. Ora Prilletensky, *A Ramp to Motherhood: The Experiences of Mothers with Physical Disabilities,* 21(1) Sexuality & Disability 22–23 (2003). The myth of asexuality among persons with disabilities (PWD) is further explored in Maureen S. Milligan & Aldred H. Neufeldt, *The Myth of Asexuality: A Survey of Social and Empirical Evidence,* 19 Sexuality & Disability 91 (2001) (confirming PWD are sexually disenfranchised by inaccurate perceptions they are asexual; calling for changes in professional practice, research, societal attitudes, and the lives of PWD).

14. Joan Rothschild, The Dream of the Perfect Child 105 (2005).

15. Alicia Ouellette, *Selection Against Disability: Abortion, ART, and Access,* 43 J.L. Med. & Ethics 211, 213 (2015), *citing* S. Linton, Claiming Disability: Knowledge and Identity 11 (1998).

16. *Id.* at 214.

17. *See, e.g.,* Ella Callow, Kelly Buckland, & Shannon Jones, *Parents with Disabilities in the United States: Prevalence, Perspectives, and a Proposal for Legislative Change to Protect the Right to Family in the Disability Community,* 17 Tex. J. Civ. Liberties & Civ. Rts. 9 (2011). In addition to fertility treatment denials, disabled parents also experience greater rates of child removal than parents who are not disabled. According to Callow, Buckland, and Jones, in many cases, these removals are unnecessary and cause trauma and loss of familial integrity.

18. *See* Am. Med. Ass'n, Code of Medical Ethics, Op. 8.20(1) (treatments that have no medical indication and offer no possible benefit to the patient should not be used) and Op. 8.121 (ethical duty to study and prevent error and harm in health care).

19. *See* Carl H. Coleman, *Conceiving Harm: Disability Discrimination in Assisted Reproductive Technologies,* 50 UCLA L. Rev. 17, 30 (2002) (reporting treatment denials to prospective patients with severe lupus, uncontrolled diabetes, and uncontrolled hypertension based on risk to women's health and to potential child from pregnancy complications).

20. *See* Ethics Comm., Am. Soc'y for Reprod. Med., *Child-Rearing Ability and the Provision of Fertility Services: A Committee Opinion,* 100 Fertility & Sterility 50 (2013) (approving treatment denials in cases where treatment poses a substantial risk of harm to resulting offspring). In some cases, risk of harm from ART treatment is posed equally to mother and child. One example is Eisenmenger syndrome, in which the specific heart defect associated with the disease causes maternal and fetal death in half of all pregnancies. *See, e.g.,* S.M. Yentis, P.J. Steer, & F. Plaat, *Eisenmenger's Syndrome in Pregnancy: Maternal and Fetal Mortality in the 1990's,* 105 Brit. J. Obstetrics & Gynaecology 921 (1998).

21. *See* Ethics Comm., *supra* note 20, at 50 ("Fertility programs may withhold services from prospective patients on the basis of well-substantiated judgments that those patients will be unable to provide minimally adequate or safe care for offspring").

22. *See* Ctrs. for Disease Control & Prevention, U.S. Dep't of Health & Hum. Servs., *Achievements in Public Health: Reduction of Perinatal Transmission of HIV Infection—United States, 1985–2005,* 55 Morbidity & Mortality Wkly. Rep. 592 (2006) [hereinafter CDC Report].

23. Callow, *supra* note 17, at 18–20.

24. PGD can be performed either on Day 3, in which one of the embryo's four to eight cells—called blastomeres—can be removed, or on Day 5, in which around ten to twenty cells are removed from the trophectoderm or outer layer of the developing embryos—called a blastocyst. *See* Ruthi B. Lathi et al., *Outcomes of Trophectoderm Biopsies on Cryopreserved Blastocysts: A Case Series,* 25 Reprod. Biomed. Online 504 (2012), *available at* http://www.rbmojournal.com/article/S1472–6483(12)00414–2/abstract (last visited Dec. 5, 2014).

25. Using PGD, physicians can count and visualize the chromosomes within the cell to determine the embryo's gender (XX—girl or XY—boy) and to detect if the embryo has extra or missing chromosomes, a condition known as aneuploidy. Examples of

aneuploidic conditions include Down syndrome (three chromosomes in pair 21, sometimes called trisomy 21), Patau syndrome (three chromosomes in pair 13), Klinefelter syndrome (a male with two X chromosomes, XXY), and Turner syndrome (a female with only one X chromosome, XO). PGD can also be used to detect disease-causing genes that are located at specific places on a chromosome. Single-gene disorders include cystic fibrosis, Tay-Sachs disease, Huntington's disease, muscular dystrophy, and sickle cell anemia. *See* Judith Daar, Reproductive Technologies and the Law 313–14 (2d ed. 2013).

26. *See* Human Fertilisation and Embryology Authority, http://www.hfea.gov.uk/preimplantation-genetic-diagnosis.html (last visited Dec. 8, 2014).

27. *See, e.g.,* RESOLVE, *The Costs of Infertility Treatment, available at* http://www.resolve.org/family-building-options/making-treatment-affordable/the-costs-of-infertility-treatment.html (last visited Dec. 5, 2014).

28. *See* Mark Sauer, *American Physicians Remain Slow to Embrace the Reproductive Needs of Human Immunodeficiency Virus–Infected Patients,* 85 Fertility & Sterility 295 (2006).

29. *See* CDC Report, *supra* note 22.

30. *See* Mark Sauer et al., *Providing Fertility Care to Men Seropositive for Human Immunodeficiency Virus: Reviewing 10 Years of Experience and 420 Consecutive Cycles of In Vitro Fertilization and Intracytoplasmic Sperm Injection,* 91 Fertility & Sterility 2455 (2009).

31. Bergero v. University of Southern California Keck School of Medicine, Cal. Ct. of App., Case No. B200595 (2009), *available at* http://www.fearnotlaw.com/articles/article27303.html (last visited Dec. 8, 2014).

32. Andrea D. Gurmankin, Arthur L. Caplan, & Andrea M. Braverman, *Screening Practices and Beliefs of Assisted Reproductive Technology Programs,* 83(1) Fertility & Sterility 61, 64 (2005).

33. *Id.* (64 percent of respondents agreed or strongly agreed with this statement).

34. Richard F. Storrow, *The Bioethics of Prospective Parenthood: In Pursuit of the Proper Standard for Gatekeeping in Infertility Clinics,* 28 Cardozo L. Rev. 2283 (2007) (arguing clinics should be able to screen for parental fitness but not to assess the best interests of the child, as that standard is used in custody disputes).

35. In one unpublished case, a woman unsuccessfully sued an academic medical center for disability discrimination based on the clinic's imposing eligibility criteria for access to IVF. The plaintiff alleged the clinic screened out individuals with disabilities via tests for HIV, genetic screening, and psychological evaluation. Since the plaintiff had not been denied infertility treatment, her claim was dismissed for failure to state a claim. Sheils v. University of Pennsylvania Medical Center, 1998 WL 134230 (E.D. Pa. 1998).

36. Storrow, *supra* note 34, at 2286.

37. *Id.* (*citing* Gurmankin, *supra* note 32, at 63).

38. Gurmankin, *supra* note 32, at 65.

39. *See* Paul A. Lombardo, *Facing Carrie Buck,* 33 Hastings Ctr. Rep. 14 (2003) (describing his personal interview with Carrie Buck and review of many historic docu-

ments surrounding her case, all showing Carrie, her mother, and her daughter to be of average, even above average, intelligence).

40. NCD Report, *supra* note 2, at 216.

41. *See supra* note 1.

42. Chapter 12 of the NCD Report, *supra* note 2, explores and is titled, "The Impact of Disability on Parenting." The authors note the sparse literature on the topic, which itself can lead to presupposing negative effects of the parents' disabilities on their children. One researcher clarifies the existing research, concluding, "Despite the lack of appropriate resources for most disabled parents and their children as well as persistent negative assumptions about these families, the vast majority of children of disabled parents have been shown to have typical development and functioning and often enhanced life perspectives and skills." NCD Report, *supra* note 2, at 230, *citing* Paul Preston, *Parents with Disabilities,* International Encyclopedia of Rehabilitation (J.H. Stone & M. Blouin eds., 2011), *available at* http://cirrie.buffalo.edu/encyclopedia/en/article/36/ (last visited Oct. 23, 2015).

43. The concept of nondirectiveness is borrowed from the field of genetic counseling in reproductive ethics, in which the goal is to allow patients to make fully informed autonomous decisions surrounding their genetic information. *See* Barbara Bowles Biescecker, *Reproductive Ethics: The Ethics of Reproductive Genetic Counseling:* Nondirectiveness, *in* Encyclopedia of Ethical, Legal and Policy Issues in Biotechnology (2003).

44. *See generally* Susan H. McDaniel, *The Psychotherapy of Genetics,* 44 Family Process 25 (2005).

45. The list of genetic disorders detectible through PGD published by Genesis Genetics contains more than 250 entries. *See* http://genesisgenetics.org/pgd/what-we -test-for/ (last visited Dec. 11, 2014).

46. *See, e.g.,* Michael J. Malinowski, *Choosing the Genetic Makeup of Children: Our Eugenics Past, Present and Future?,* 36 Conn. L. Rev. 125 (2003).

47. *See, e.g.,* John Harris, Enhancing Evolution: The Ethical Case for Making People Better (2007) (arguing not only is it morally desirable to enhance ourselves, but in some cases it is morally obligatory).

48. For an argument that parents have a duty to use PGD in certain situations, *see* Judith Daar & Janet Malek, *The Case for a Parental Duty to Use Preimplantation Genetic Diagnosis for Medical Benefit,* 12 Am. J. Bioethics 3 (2012).

49. Ouellette, *supra* note 15, at 214, *citing* Erik Parens & Adrienne Asch, *The Disability Rights Critique of Prenatal Genetic Testing: Reflections and Recommendations,* 29 Hastings Ctr. Rep. S1 (1999).

50. M. Saxton, *Disability Rights and Selective Abortion, in* Abortion Wars: A Half Century Struggle, 1950–2000 (Rickie Solinger ed.), 374 (1997).

51. *See* Liz Mundy, *A World of Their Own,* Wash. Post, Mar. 31, 2002, at W22.

52. John Sproston, *Like Mother, Like Child,* Letters, Wash. Post, June 9, 2002, at W2.

53. Further popular ire accompanied the women's decision to deny their son, at age four months, the use of a hearing aid, which doctors said could improve his ability

to lip read. Reportedly, the mothers said if he wanted a hearing aid later, they would allow him to have one. Mundy, *supra* note 51.

54. *See* Joel Feinberg, *The Child's Right to an Open Future, in* Whose Child? Children's Rights, Parental Authority, and State Power 124 (W. Aiken & H. LaFollette eds., 1980); *see also* Dena S. Davis, *Genetic Dilemmas and the Child's Right to an Open Future,* 28 Rutgers L.J. 549 (1997).

55. *See* Kristen Rabe Smolensky, *Creating Children with Disabilities: Parental Tort Liability for Preimplantation Genetic Interventions,* 60 Hastings L.J. 336 (2008) (arguing children should be able to successfully sue their parents who engage in certain direct genetic interventions); Jacob M. Appel, *Genetic Screening and Child Abuse: Can PGS Rise to the Level of Criminality?,* 80 UMKC L. Rev. 373 (2011) (analyzing child abuse charges against either parents or fertility clinics who use IVF intentionally to produce severely impaired infants). *But see* Brigham A. Fordham, *Disability and Designer Babies,* 45 Valparaiso U. L. Rev. 1473 (2011) (arguing parents who make genetic choices in favor of disability should not face liability).

56. Richard Gray, *Couples Could Win Right to Select Deaf Baby,* The Telegraph, Apr. 13, 2008, *available at* http:// www.telegraph.co.uk /news /uknews /1584948 /Couples -could-win-right-to-select-deaf-baby.html (last visited Dec. 11, 2014).

57. Darshak M. Sanghavi, *Wanting Babies Like Themselves, Some Parents Choose Genetic Defects,* N.Y. Times, Dec. 5, 2006, at F5.

58. *Id.*

59. *Id.*

60. Susannah Baruch, David Kaufman, & Kathy L. Hudson, *Genetic Testing of Embryos: Practices and Perspectives of U.S. In Vitro Fertilization Clinics,* 89 Fertility & Sterility 1053 (2008).

61. *Id.* at 1056.

62. Ouellette, *supra* note 15, at 218.

63. Skinner v. Oklahoma, 316 U.S. 535, 541 (1942). While *Skinner* did render the Oklahoma criminal sterilization statute at issue and other similar laws unconstitutional, it must be noted that other forms of compulsory sterilizations (of the "feeble-minded," mentally disabled, etc.) continued after the Court's decision and probably continue to this day. It is estimated that over one-third of all compulsory sterilizations in the United States took place after *Skinner v. Oklahoma. See* Bonnie F. Fremgen, Just the Facts 101: Medical Law and Ethics (3d ed. 2014).

SEVEN   The Harms of Procreative Deprivation

1. Buck v. Bell, 274 U.S. 200, 207 (1927).

2. *Id.* at 207.

3. Paul A. Lombardo, *Facing Carrie Buck,* 33 Hastings Ctr. Rep. 14 (2003).

4. *Id.*

5. Paul A. Lombardo, Three Generations, No Imbeciles (2008), at ix.

6. One victim of forced sterilization recalls the events in graphic form. "They cut me open like a hog," exclaims Elaine Riddick, sterilized in 1968 at age thirteen. Another

survivor describes her lifelong anguish, "When you go through something like that, you don't get over it." *Victims of NC Forced Sterilization Program Tell Their Stories,* wral.com, June 22, 2011, *available at* http://www.wral.com/news/state/nccapitol/story/9761898/ (last visited Dec. 18, 2014). *See also* Alexandra Minna Stern, Eugenic Nation: Faults and Frontiers of Better Breeding in Modern America (2005).

7. North Carolina became the first state to legislate a program of reparations to eugenics victims. In October 2014, North Carolina governor Pat McCrory announced disbursement of initial payments to the surviving members of the state's 7,600 forced sterilization victims. Acknowledging that "no money could undo the wrong that was done to these victims," the state's chief executive added, "I hope these payments bring some solace in their acknowledgment that the actions of the Eugenics Board were wrong." The state set aside $10 million for eligible applicants. *Payments Begin for Eugenics Victims, available at* http://www.governor.state.nc.us/newsroom/press-releases/20141027/payments-begin-eugenics-victims (last visited Dec. 16, 2014). Official apologies for eugenic harms began in the early 2000s. Governors and legislators in Virginia, Oregon, North Carolina, South Carolina, California, Indiana, and Georgia have made proclamations of apology, adopted resolutions of regret, and voiced general repudiations of past eugenic laws and other efforts aimed at achieving race and social purity. *See* Gregory Michael Dorr & Angela Logan, *"Quality, Not More Quantity, Counts": Black Eugenics and the NAACP Baby Contests, in* Paul A. Lombardo, A Century of Eugenics in America 68 (2011).

8. Portions of this chapter's discussion of harms to patients, providers, children, and society are based in an earlier work by the author. *See* Judith Daar, *Accessing Reproductive Technologies: Invisible Barriers, Indelible Harms,* 23 Berkeley J. Gen. L. & Justice 18, 48–73 (2008).

9. John A. Robertson, Children of Choice: Freedom and the New Reproductive Technologies 4 (1994).

10. A. Galhardo, J. Pinto-Goveia, M. Cunha, & M. Matos, *The Impact of Shame and Self-Judgment on Psychopathology in Infertile Patients,* 26 Hum. Reprod. 2408 (2011).

11. Harriet Vickers, *Involuntary Childlessness Has a Significant Impact,* BioNews (Aug. 23, 2010) (reporting on study by Swedish researcher Marianne Johansson), *available at* http://www.bionews.org.uk/page_68973.asp (last visited Dec. 17, 2014).

12. *Id.*

13. Lucy Freem, *Childlessness Resulting from Failed IVF Is Associated with Decreased Lifespan,* BioNews (last visited Dec. 12, 2012) (women who remained childless were four times more likely to die early compared with women who did conceive; childless infertile men were twice as likely to die early compared with men who went on to have children), *available at* http://www.bionews.org.uk/page_224477.asp (Dec. 17, 2014).

14. Lisa Leff, *California Court Hears Lesbian Insemination Case,* USA Today, May 28, 2008.

15. Brian Dakass, *Blind Woman Suing Fertility Clinic,* CBS News, Nov. 3, 2003, *available at* http://www.cbsnews.com/news/blind-woman-suing-fertility-clinic/ (last visited Dec. 18, 2014).

16. Jane Gerster, *Transgender Man Seeks Reasons from Facility That Refused to Impregnate Him,* Toronto Star, Jan. 20, 2014, *available at* http://www.thestar.com/news/gta/2014/01/20/transgender_man_seeks_reasons_from_facility_that_refused_to_impregnate_him.html (last visited Dec. 18, 2014).

17. Ellen Waldman, *The Parent Trap: Uncovering the Myth of "Coerced Parenthood" in Frozen Embryo Disputes,* 53 Am. U. L. Rev. 1021, 1056–59 (2004).

18. According to adoption experts, discrimination against single individuals and same-sex couples can be a factor in state-sponsored adoption even if the state permits unmarried and LGBT prospective parents to be considered as adopting parents. Waldman recounts state agencies often limit placement of "desirable" children—that is, healthy newborns—to married couples. Single individuals, typically women, must be willing to accept children with special needs, such as physical or mental handicaps, or children who are older or behaviorally hard to handle. *Id.* Attorney Heather Cullen, who advises clients about adoption, acknowledges that while state laws might protect against marital status and/or sexual orientation discrimination, "Social workers who are uncomfortable with homosexuality may find the prospective adoptive parents unsuitable for other reasons." *Adoption and Same-Sex Couples: Types of Adoption, available at* http://family.findlaw.com/adoption/adoption-and-same-sex-couples-types-of-adoption.html (last visited Dec. 18, 2014). An analysis by the Human Rights Campaign (HRC), an LGBT civil rights organization, on the impact of marriage equality on same-sex couples' adoption rights counsels, "The reality will persist that adoption agencies and professionals in the adoption field have different levels of experience with, and openness, to same-sex couples. In some states, publicly funded adoption agencies are allowed to discriminate against same-sex couples. So even with marriage equality, it will remain important to research agencies that have proven track records in working with same-sex couples, and explicit inclusive and welcoming policies." *See* Hum. Rts. Campaign, *What Will Marriage Equality Mean If We Want to Adopt?, available at* http://hrc-assets.s3-website-us-east-1.amazonaws.com//files/documents/MarriageEquality-Adoption-QandA.pdf (last visited Oct. 23, 2015).

19. According to the HRC, same-sex couples are prohibited from adopting in Mississippi and Utah. Miss. Code Ann. § 93–17-3(2) (2013) (adoption by couples of the same gender prohibited); Utah Code Ann. § 78–30-1(3)(b) (2013) (prohibiting adoption "by a person who is cohabiting in a relationship that is not legally valid and binding marriage"). The Utah Supreme Court essentially nullified the ban on same-sex adoption in October 2014 when it permitted the Department of Health to issue birth certificates to same-sex adopting couples. This legal action came within weeks of the legalization of same-sex marriage in the state. *See* Jennifer Dobner, *Utah Supreme Court Lifts Same-Sex Adoption Stay,* Salt Lake Tribune, Oct. 23, 2014, *available at* http://www.sltrib.com/news/1739377–155/utah-court-families-legal-marriage-sex (last visited Oct. 23, 2015). The HRC also notes that four states have laws or policies that permit discrimination in adoption placement (Arizona, Michigan, Montana, and Virginia). *See* Hum. Rts. Campaign, Maps of State Laws & Policies, *available at* http://www.hrc.org/state_maps (last visited Oct. 23, 2015).

20. I. Glenn Cohen & Daniel L. Chen, *Trading-Off Reproductive Technology and Adoption: Does Subsidizing IVF Decrease Adoption Rates and Should It Matter?*, 95 Minn. L. Rev. 485 (2010).

21. Skinner v. Oklahoma, 316 U.S. 535 (1942).

22. *Id.* at 541.

23. *Id.*

24. Robertson, *supra* note 9, at 23.

25. Planned Parenthood of Southeastern Pennsylvania v. Casey, 505 U.S. 833 (1992).

26. *Id.* at 846.

27. *Id.* at 878.

28. *See* Stenberg v. Carhart, 530 U.S. 914 (2000) (declaring unconstitutional Nebraska statute banning "partial birth abortion" as unduly burdening right to choose abortion); Gonzales v. Carhart, 127 S. Ct. 1610 (2007) (upholding federal Partial-Birth Abortion Ban Act of 2003 as not imposing a substantial obstacle to late-term abortion because alternative methods, not banned by the act, are available).

29. *But see* Caitlin E. Borgmann, *Roe v. Wade's 40th Anniversary: A Moment of Truth for the Anti-Abortion-Rights Movement?*, 24 Stan. L. & Pol'y Rev. 245 (2013) (calling the undue burden standard an "abortion-specific test").

30. *See* Ark. Code Ann. §§ 23–85-137; 23–86-118; Haw. Rev. Stat. §§ 431:10A–116.5, 432:1–604; Md. Code Ann., Ins. § 15–810; R.I. Gen. Laws § 27–19-23; Tex. Ins. Code Ann. § 1366.005.

31. Eisenstadt v. Baird, 405 U.S. 438, 453 (1972).

32. In *Eisenstadt*, Justice Brennan set the constitutional standard that must be met for the government to justify a law restricting access to contraceptives. "'Compelling,'" he wrote, "is of course the key word; where a decision as fundamental as that whether to bear or beget a child is involved, regulations imposing a burden on it may be justified only by compelling state interests, and must be narrowly drawn to express only those interests." 405 U.S. at 686. The compelling state interest requirement was extended to reproduction in *Roe v. Wade*, where Justice Blackmun wrote, "Where certain 'fundamental rights' are involved, the Court has held that regulation limiting these rights may be justified only by a 'compelling state interest' . . . and that legislative enactments must be narrowly drawn to express only the legitimate state interests at stake." 410 U.S. 113, 155 (1973).

33. The distinction between private conduct and state action is admittedly presented in this paragraph in a highly simplified manner. It may be possible for a private physician to be considered a state actor, for example, if she is employed by a university medical center funded and operated by the state. *See, e.g.*, Chudacoff v. University Medical Center, 649 F.3d 1143 (9th Cir. 2011) (finding county hospital's board of trustees to be state actors in claim by physician alleging violation of due process rights).

34. North Coast Women's Care Med. Group v. Super. Ct., 44 Cal. 4th 1145, 189 P.3d 959, 81 Cal. Rptr.3d 708 (2008).

35. At the time Lupita and Joanne sought IVF near their home in San Diego, there were approximately eight ART clinics in the greater San Diego area.

36. *See* Andrea D. Gurmankin, Arthur L. Caplan, & Andrea M. Braverman, *Screening Practices and Beliefs of Assisted Reproductive Technology Programs,* 83(1) Fertility & Sterility 61 (2005) (reporting only 28 percent of ART programs reported having a formal policy describing on what grounds they might turn away a given candidate).

37. *See* Ethics Comm., Am. Soc'y for Reprod. Med., *Cross-Border Reproductive Care: A Committee Opinion,* 100 Fertility & Sterility 645 (2013).

38. Gerster, *supra* note 16.

39. Jacob M. Appel, *May Doctors Refuse Infertility Treatments to Gay Patients?,* 36 Hastings Ctr. Rep. 20, 21 (2006) (asserting, "If any physician opting out of performing certain procedures on certain patients publicize their decision adequately, it appears unlikely that prospective patients will be highly inconvenienced. They will simply go elsewhere").

40. A.K. Nangia, D.S. Likosky, & D. Wang, *Access to Assisted Reproductive Technology Centers in the United States,* 93 Fertility & Sterility 745 (2010).

41. Arthur L. Greil, Julia McQuillan, & Karina M. Shreffler, *Race-Ethnicity and Medical Services for Infertility: Stratified Reproduction in a Population-Based Sample of U.S. Women,* 52 J. Health & Soc. Behav. 1 (2011).

42. Mary Beth Foglia & Karen I. Fredriksen-Goldsen, *Health Disparities Among LGBT Older Adults and the Role of Nonconscious Bias,* 44 Hastings Ctr. Rep. S40 (2014). These same findings of refusal of treatment by health care staff, verbal abuse, and disrespectful behavior, as well as many other forms of failure to provide adequate care, were noted in a 2011 report by the Institute of Medicine. *See* Inst. of Med., The Health of Lesbian, Gay Bisexual, and Transgender People: Building a Foundation for Better Understanding 62 (2011).

43. *See* Sarah Elizabeth Richards, *The Next Frontier in Fertility Treatment,* N.Y. Times, Jan. 12, 2014, at A19.

44. Kate O'Hanlan, *Lesbian Health and Homophobia: Perspectives for the Treating Obstetrician/Gynecologist,* 18 Curr. Probs. Obstetrics & Gynecology 93, 136 (1995).

45. Susan Cochran et al., *Cancer-Related Risk Indicators and Preventive Screening Behaviors Among Lesbian and Bisexual Women,* 91 Am. J. Pub. Health 591, 596 (2001).

46. Cait McDonagh, *Lesbian Couple Sue Hospital After Being "Refused IVF,"* Bio-News, Nov. 18, 2013, *available at* http://www.bionews.org.uk/page_364841.asp (last visited Oct. 29, 2015).

47. 42 U.S.C. § 2000a (2013).

48. Heart of Atlanta Motel, Inc. v. U.S., 379 U.S. 241, 250 (1964) (quoting from the Senate Commerce Committee's report on the bill that became the Civil Rights Act of 1964).

49. *Id.* at 259. Numerous commentators have documented the depth of dignitary harm that arises when goods and services are withheld from individuals or couples based on personal characteristics. *See, e.g.,* Holning Lau, *Transcending the Individualist Paradigm in Sexual Orientation,* 94 Cal. L. Rev. 1271 (2006) ("Exclusions [based on sexual orientation] suggests that the business refuses to recognize the couple's legitimacy, striking a blow at the couple's collective dignity and self-respect"); Christopher A.

Bracey, *Dignity in Race Jurisprudence*, 7 U. Pa. J. Const. L. 669 (2005) ("Dignity remains the core aspirational value in the struggle for racial justice").

50. Title II limits places of public accommodation to specific locales, including hotels, restaurants, theaters, and places of "exhibition or entertainment." 42 U.S.C. § 2000a(b) (2013). A later part of the Civil Rights Act, Title VI, prohibits discrimination on the basis of race, color, and national origin in programs and activities receiving federal financial assistance. 42 U.S.C. § 2000d (2013). Clearly, this section captures hospitals or health care facilities that received federal funding (generally via the Medicare or Medicaid programs), but does not appear to apply when a provider is financed exclusively by private entities, such as patients and private health insurance carriers. Thus, it would appear that Title VI would not reach independent, non-university-based fertility clinics that do not receive any form of federal financial assistance.

51. For example, the Americans with Disabilities Act of 1990, 42 U.S.C. § 12101 et seq. (2013), prohibits discrimination of the basis of disability "in the full and equal enjoyment of the goods, services, facilities, privileges, advantages, or accommodations of any place of public accommodation." *Id.* at § 12182(a). Further, the term "public accommodation" is defined in the ADA to include the "professional office of a health care provider." *Id.* at § 12181(7)(F). Public funding is not a requisite for action under the ADA, which has been interpreted to apply to the disability of "substantial limitations" on the "major life activity" of reproduction. *See* Bragdon v. Abbott, 524 U.S. 624, 637–38 (1998).

52. *But see* Dayna Bowen Matthew, *A New Strategy to Combat Racial Inequality in American Health Care Delivery*, 9 DePaul J. Health Care L. 793, 820 (2006) (explaining the difficulty individual plaintiffs experience in bringing Title VI claims on the basis of racial discrimination in the provision of health care services). Under Supreme Court precedent, private individuals can sue to enforce Title VI's prohibition against intentional discrimination (intent often difficult to prove), but the Court has denied a private right of action to claim that an activity has a disparate impact (less difficult to prove) on the basis of race. Alexander v. Sandoval, 532 U.S. 275 (2001).

53. *See, e.g.,* Richard S. Saver, *Medical Research and Intangible Harm*, 74 U. Cincinnati L. Rev. 941 (2006) (arguing for recognition of dignitary harm in the context of human subject research).

54. 105 N.E. 92, 93 (N.Y. 1914). Judge Cardozo penned the oft-quoted refrain that "[every] human being of adult years and sound mind has a right to determine what shall be done with his own body." *Id.*

55. Saver, *supra* note 53, at 957.

56. The Supreme Court has spoken about the personal dignity attached to procreative decision-making, calling the decision about whether to bear a child one of "the most intimate and personal choices a person may make in a lifetime, choices central to personal dignity and autonomy." Planned Parenthood of Southeastern Pa. v. Casey, 505 U.S. 833, 851 (1992).

57. Am. Med. Ass'n, AMA Policies on LGBT Issues, E-9.12, *available at* http://www.ama-assn.org/ama/pub/about-ama/our-people/member-groups-sections/glbt-advisory-committee/ama-policy-regarding-sexual-orientation.page? (last visited

Dec. 19, 2014). For a discussion of the complex and arguably contradictory nature of the AMA ethics opinions as applied to physician refusals based on religious objections, *see* Richard F. Storrow, *Medical Conscience and the Policing of Parenthood,* 16 Wm. & Mary J. Women & Law 369 (2009–10).

58. Disability discrimination poses another source of denials but is covered by the Americans with Disabilities Act.

59. *See* Unruh Civil Rights Act, Cal. Civ. Code § 52(a) (West 2007).

60. Am. Med. Ass'n, Principles of Medical Ethics IX (adopted June 1957, revised 1980, 2001), *available at* http://www.ama-assn.org/ama/pub/physician-resources/medical-ethics/code-medical-ethics/principles-medical-ethics.page? (last visited Dec. 22, 2014).

61. *Id.* at VI, stating, "[A] physician shall, in the provision of appropriate patient care, except in emergencies, be free to choose whom to service, with whom to associate, and the environment in which to provide medical care."

62. *See* Lawrence M. Kessler et al., *Infertility Evaluation and Treatment Among Women in the United States,* 100(4) Fertility & Sterility 1025 (2013).

63. *See* Arthur L. Greil, Julia McQuillan, & Karina M. Shreffler, *Race-Ethnicity and Medical Services for Infertility: Stratified Reproduction in a Population-Based Sample of U.S. Women,* 52 J. Health & Soc. Behav. 1 (2011).

64. *See, e.g.,* Marianne Bitler & Lucie Schmidt, *Health Disparities and Infertility: Impacts of State-Level Insurance Mandates,* 85 Fertility & Sterility 858 (2006); Eve C. Feinberg et al., *Comparison of Assisted Reproductive Technology Utilization and Outcomes Between Caucasian and African American Patients in an Equal-Access-to-Care Setting,* 85 Fertility & Sterility 888 (2006); Tarun Jain & Mark D. Hornstein, *Disparities in Access to Infertility Services in a State with Mandated Coverage,* 84 Fertility & Sterility 221 (2005).

65. *See* Eric Blyth, *Sperm Donation: Time to Look Forward, Not Back,* BioNews, Mar. 22, 1999, *available at* http://bionews.org.uk/commentary.lasso?storyid'3190 (*citing* K. Daniels & O. Lalos, *The Swedish Insemination Act and the Availability of Donors,* 10 Hum. Reprod. 1871–74 [1995]).

66. This perception proved accurate, as a follow-up study in 2000 revealed that 89 percent of parents had not disclosed their use of AID to their children. *See* Claus Gottlieb et al., *Disclosure of Donor Insemination to the Child: The Impact of Swedish Legislation on Couples' Attitudes,* 15 Hum. Reprod. 2052 (2000).

67. *See supra* note 61.

68. Barry R. Furrow et al., Health Law 529 (5th ed. 2004).

69. *See, e.g.,* Civil Rights Act of 1964, 42 U.S.C. § 2000d (2013) (providing that "no person in the United States shall, on the ground of race, color, or national origin, be excluded from participation in, be denied the benefits of, or be subjected to discrimination under any program or activity receiving Federal financial assistance").

70. Americans with Disabilities Act, 42 U.S.C. § 12182 (2013).

71. *See* Institute of Real Estate Management, *Laws Prohibiting Discrimination Based on Sexual Orientation and Gender Identity,* Aug. 2013, *available at* http://www.irem.org/File%20Library/Public%20Policy/Anti-discrimination.pdf (last visited Nov. 18, 2014).

72. North Coast Women's Care Med. Group, Inc. v. San Diego County Super. Ct., 189 P.3d 959 (Cal. 2008).

73. *See, e.g.,* Elane Photography, LLC v. Willock, 309 P.3d 53 (New Mex. 2013) (company's refusal to photograph same-sex wedding on basis of sexual orientation violated state civil rights law); McCready v. Hoffius, 459 Mich. 131 (1998) (landlords discriminated against unmarried couples in violation of state civil rights laws; assertion of religious freedom did not supersede tenants' claims); Swanner v. Anchorage Equal Rights Commission, 874 P.2d 274 (Alaska 1994) (landlord who discriminated based on marital status because of religious belief violated prohibition on discrimination).

74. Burwell v. Hobby Lobby, 573 U.S. __ (2014).

75. *See, e.g.,* Priscilla J. Smith, *Who Decides Conscience? RFRA's Catch 22,* 22 J. Law & Pol'y 727 (2014).

76. *See* Elizabeth Sepper, *Taking Conscience Seriously,* 98 Va. L. Rev. 1501 (2012) (explaining that conscience legislation has been extended to include refusals to perform sterilization, prescribe contraception, and provide futile end-of-life care).

77. *See, e.g.,* N.J. Stat. Ann. § 2A:65A-3 (2012) ("The refusal to perform, assist in the performance of, or provide abortion services or sterilization procedures shall not constitute grounds for civil or criminal liability, disciplinary action or discriminatory treatment").

78. Judith F. Daar, *A Clash at the Bedside: Patient Autonomy v. a Physician's Professional Conscience,* 44 Hastings L.J. 1241, 1247 (1993).

79. Am. Congress of Obstetricians & Gynecologists, Comm. on Ethics, *The Limits of Conscientious Refusal in Reproductive Medicine,* No. 385 (Nov. 2007, reaffirmed 2013), *available at* http://www.acog.org/Resources-And-Publications/Committee-Opinions/Committee-on-Ethics/The-Limits-of-Conscientious-Refusal-in-Reproductive-Medicine (last visited Dec. 24, 2014).

80. *See, e.g.,* Thaddeus Mason Pope, *Legal Briefing: Conscience Clauses and Conscientious Refusal,* 21 J. Clin. Ethics 163 (2010).

81. *See id.* (reporting that almost all states allow health care providers to refuse end-of-life treatment to which they have conscientious objections); *see also* Tex. Health & Safety Code § 166.045 (permitting physician who refuses to comply with end-of-life treatment decision to transfer patient to another physician or health care facility willing to comply with treatment request).

82. *See, generally,* Seana Valentine Shiffrin, *Wrongful Life, Procreative Responsibility, and the Significance of Harm,* 5 Legal Theory 117 (1999).

83. *Id.*

84. Becker v. Schwartz, 386 N.E.2d 807, 811 (N.Y. 1978). According to Shiffrin, only three states recognize a cause of action for wrongful life—California, New Jersey, and Washington. Shiffrin, *supra* note 82, at 118 n.4.

85. Anjani Chandra et al., Infertility and Impaired Fecundity in the United States, 1982–2010: Data from the National Survey of Family Growth, National Health Statistics Reports, No. 67 (Aug. 14, 2013), at 6.

86. *See* T. Wertman, *How Infertility Is Impacting My Child*, Apr. 8, 2013, *available at* http://www.sheknows.com/parenting/articles/988611/how-secondary-infertility-impacts-children (last visited Apr. 14, 2016).

87. *Id.*

88. *Id.* (quoting Claudia Pascale, director of mental health services at the Institute for Reproductive Medicine and Science at Saint Barnabas, New Jersey).

89. *See, e.g.,* Katrina Clark, *My Father Was an Anonymous Sperm Donor,* Wash. Post, Dec. 17, 2006, at B1 (personal narrative describing author's anger and confusion over being a donor-conceived child).

90. The most often used website connecting donors and donor-conceived persons is the Donor Sibling Registry. As of December 2014, the DSR reports attracting twelve thousand visitors to its website each month. *See* https://www.donorsiblingregistry.com/ (last visited Dec. 26, 2014).

91. One particularly interesting scenario involved a Florida woman who used an Israeli anonymous sperm donor to conceive a daughter. When she returned three years later to use frozen sperm from the same donor to birth a whole-blood sibling, she was told the donor had changed his mind and withdrawn his gametes from the clinic. The Israeli High Court of Justice favored the man's autonomy, rejecting the woman's claim of ownership over the frozen sperm she had paid to maintain in storage for her later use. *See* Ronny Linder-Ganz, *His or Hers? Who Owns a Donor's Sperm?*, Haaretz, Feb. 24, 2013, *available at* http://www.haaretz.com/israel-news/his-or-hers-who-owns-a-donor-s-sperm-1.505332 (last visited Oct. 23, 2015).

92. Elizabeth S. Anderson & Richard H. Pildes, *Expressive Theories of Law: A General Restatement*, 148 U. Pa. L. Rev. 1503, 1504 (2000) (explaining that expressivism is a method of evaluating action, "an internal account of existing normative practices, but one with sufficient critical capacity to exert leverage over those practices and to indicate where they ought to be reformed").

93. *See* Mary B. Mahowald, *Aren't We All Eugenicists? Commentary on Paul Lombardo's "Taking Eugenics Seriously,"* 30 Fla. St. U. L. Rev. 219 (2003) (explaining how the expressivist argument sends the message to people with disabilities that their lives are not worth living).

94. Alan Strudler, *The Power of Expressive Theories of Law*, 60 Md. L. Rev. 492, 492 (2001).

95. *See* Anderson et al., *supra* note 92, at 1504 (arguing that "most of the purposes, beliefs, attitudes, intentions, and other mental states that individuals can have on their own can also be properly attributed to groups, including the State").

96. As Strudler explains, not all stigma is unwarranted. Stigmatizing people who commit crimes, for example, serves a legitimate law enforcement goal. Stigmatizing tortfeasors expresses society's empathy for victims of wrongdoing. *See* Strudler, *supra* note 94, at 494–95.

97. *Id.* at 495.

EIGHT The New Eugenics

1. *See, e.g.,* Gina Kolata, *Robert G. Edwards Dies at 87: Changed Rules of Conception with First "Test Tube Baby,"* N.Y. Times, Apr. 11, 2013, at A1; Martin H. Johnson, *Sir Robert Edwards Obituary,* The Guardian, Apr. 10, 2013.

2. Osagie K. Obasagie, *The Eugenics Legacy of the Nobelist Who Fathered IVF,* Scientific American, Oct. 4, 2013, *available at* http://www.scientificamerican.com/article/eugenic-legacy-nobel-ivf/ (last visited Jan. 6, 2015).

3. *Id.*

4. Kara Swanson writes about medical paternalism and eugenic tendencies surrounding the provision of artificial insemination by donor when the technique was first emerging. Famed reproductive health physician Alan Guttmacher advocated that donor insemination should be available only to "deserving, exceptional couples," defined as opposite-sex married couples in which the female is medically infertile. Once these two factors were met, Dr. Guttmacher insisted, "The doctor needed to 'acquaint himself with the couple and satisfy himself as much as is humanly possible of the permanence of their marriage, of the emotional stability of the individuals involved and of their ability to grasp all the psychic implications' of the therapy. Only then should he treat the woman as she requested." Kara Swanson, *The Doctor's Dilemma: Paternalisms in the Medicolegal History of Assisted Reproduction and Abortion,* 43 J. Law Med. & Ethics 312 (2015), *citing* A. F. Guttmacher, *Practical Experience with Artificial Insemination,* 3 J. Contraception 75–76 (1938).

5. Paul Ramsey, *Shall We "Reproduce?,"* 220 JAMA 1346 (1972). *See also* Leon R. Kass, *Babies by Means of In Vitro Fertilization: Unethical Experiments on the Unborn?,* 285 New Eng. J. Med. 1174 (1971) (urging a "voluntary moratorium on any attempts to create a child through IVF and embryo transfer until the safety of the procedures could be assessed").

6. Obasagie, *supra* note 2 (attributing this statement to Edwards in 1993).

7. *See, e.g.,* Sonia M. Suter, *A Brave New World of Designer Babies?,* 22 Berkeley Tech. L.J. 897, 922 (2007) (defining neoeugenics as "a voluntary 'improvement' of the human race at the individual level").

8. *See. e.g., The First IVF Baby Born Following MALBAC-Based Whole Genome Screening,* Peking University, *available at* http://english.pku.edu.cn/News_Events/News/Research/11626.htm (announcing successful use of whole genome amplification method to survey genetics of preimplantation embryos) (last visited Jan. 14, 2015).

9. *See* Hum. Fertilisation & Embryology Authority, *Pre-implantation Genetic Diagnosis, available at* http://www.hfea.gov.uk/preimplantation-genetic-diagnosis.html (last visited Apr. 14, 2016).

10. *See, e.g.,* Maxwell J. Mehlman, *Will Directed Evolution Destroy Humanity, and If So, What Can We Do About It?,* 3 St. Louis U. J. Health L. & Pol'y 93, 97 (2009) (asserting the "destruction of humanity as a result of ill-informed, overzealous, genetic manipulation would undeniably be a dreadful calamity").

11. *See* Catechism of the Catholic Church, Part Three, Life in Christ, as discussed by Jim Graves, *Church Teaching on In Vitro Fertilization,* Catholic World Report, Nov. 29,

2012, *available at* http://www.catholicworldreport.com/Item/1774/church_teaching_on
_in_vitro_fertilization.aspx (last visited Jan. 14, 2015).

12. Address of His Holiness Benedict XVI to Members of "The New Family Movement," Nov. 3, 2007, *available at* http://www.catholic-church.org/ejtyler/catholic_life/
MarriageInBenedictXVI.html (last visited Jan. 14, 2015).

13. The Holy See, *Congregation for the Doctrine of the Faith, Instruction, Dignitas Personae on Certain Bioethical Questions, available at* http://www.vatican.va/
roman_curia/congregations/cfaith/documents/rc_con_cfaith_doc_20081208_dignitas
-personae_en.html (last visited Jan. 14, 2015).

14. *Id.*

15. *Id.* (*citing* John Paul II, Encyclical Letter *Evangelium Vitae,* Mar. 25, 1995)
available at http://www.vatican.va/holy_father/john_paul_ii/encyclicals/documents/
hf_jp-ii_enc_25031995_evangelium-vitae_en.html (last visited Jan. 16, 2015).

16. *See generally* Nicholas Agar, Liberal Eugenics: In Defence of Human Enhancement (2004).

17. *See, e.g.,* Bonnie Steinbock, *Preimplantation Genetic Diagnosis and Embryo Selection, in* A Companion to Genetics 147–57 (C. Burley & J. Harris eds., 2002).

18. *See* Eugenics, Stanford Encyclopedia of Philosophy (2014), *available at* http://
plato.stanford.edu/entries/eugenics/ (last visited Jan. 16, 2015).

19. *See* Suter, *supra* note 7.

20. Michael J. Malinowski, *Choosing the Genetic Makeup of Children: Our Eugenics Past—Present, and Future?,* 36 Conn. L. Rev. 125, 132–33 (2003).

21. *See* Suter, *supra* note 7, at 936.

22. *Id.*

23. Am. Med. Ass'n, Council on Ethical & Judicial Affairs, CEJA Report A-A-91:
Ethical Issues in Carrier Screening of Cystic Fibrosis and Other Genetic Disorders
(1991).

24. Julian Savulescu, *Procreative Beneficence: Why We Should Select the Best Children,* 15 Bioethics 413 (2001). *See also* Julian Savulescu & Guy Kahane, *The Moral Obligation to Create Children with the Best Chance of the Best Life,* 23 Bioethics 274 (2009).

25. Allen Buchanan, Dan Brock, Norman Daniels, & Daniel Wikler, From Chance
to Choice: Genetics and Justice 302 (2000).

26. John Harris, Enhancing Evolution: The Ethical Case for Making People Better
20 (2007).

27. *See, e.g.,* Michael Sandel, *The Case Against Perfection: Ethics in the Age of Genetic Engineering* (2007) (arguing that choosing our children's genetic traits reflects a
lack of humility with respect to our ability to control the world around us and a failure
to appreciate the giftedness of life); Leon Kass, *Ageless Bodies, Happy Souls,* 1 The New
Atlantis 9 (2003) (warning we should resist the temptation to advance new biotechnology because to do so "runs the risk of losing the human import and significance of the
undertakings").

28. *See* Ctrs. for Disease Control & Prevention, U.S. Dep't of Health & Hum. Servs.,
2013 Assisted Reproductive Technology: National Summary Report 5 (2015), *avail-*

able at http://www.cdc.gov/art/pdf/2013-report/national-summary/art_2013_national
_summary_report.pdf (last visited May 6, 2016) [hereinafter 2013 ART National Report].

29. *See* Elizabeth S. Ginsburg et al., *Use of Preimplantation Genetic Diagnosis and Preimplantation Genetic Screening in the United States: A Society for Assisted Reproductive Technology Writing Group Paper,* 96 Fertility & Sterility 865 (2011).

30. *See, e.g.,* Melinda B. Henne & Kate Bundorf, *Insurance Mandates and Trends in Infertility Treatments,* 89 Fertility & Sterility 66 (2008) (documenting increased IVF utilization in mandated versus nonmandated states).

31. *See* Edward G. Hughes & Mita Giacomini, *Funding In Vitro Fertilization Treatment for Persistent Subfertility: The Pain and the Politics,* 76 Fertility & Sterility 431 (2001) (reporting providing infertility coverage for all privately insured employee-based health plans would raise annual premiums about $3.00).

32. Tarun Jain, Bernard L. Harlow, & Mark D. Hornstein, *Insurance Coverage and Outcomes of In Vitro Fertilization,* 347 New Eng. J. Med. 661 (2002) (documenting higher incidence of high-order multiple births in states without IVF insurance mandates).

33. The Family Act, S 881, H.R. 1851 (introduced in May 2013 by Senator Kirsten Gillibrand [D-N.Y.] and Congressman John Lewis [D-Ga.]). The bill failed to pass during the 2013–14 congressional session and would need to be reintroduced to be considered by a later Congress.

34. *See* Federal Tax Credit for Infertility Would Increase IVF by Thirty Percent, *available at* https://www.fertilityauthority.com/articles/federal-tax-credit-infertility -would-increase-ivf-thirty-percent (last visited Jan. 21, 2015).

35. *See* Kaylen Silverberg, Dennis Meletiche, & Gina Del Rosario, *An Employer's Experience with Infertility Coverage: A Case Study,* 92 Fertility & Sterility 2103 (2009) (describing Southwest Airlines' self-funded infertility benefit plan for its employees, providing a lifetime maximum of $10,000 with corresponding copayments of 50 percent).

36. *See, e.g.,* Tom Wilemon, Insurance Plans Give Fertility Treatments Short Shrift, USA Today, Mar. 5, 2013 (detailing lower fees at one Nashville clinic), *available at* http:// www.usatoday.com/story/news/nation/2013/03/05/health-insurance-fertility/1964341/ (last visited Jan. 23, 2015).

37. *See* New York Fertility Services, *Need-Based Grant Help with the Cost of Infertility, available at* http://www.newyorkfertilityservices.com/patient-center/affordable -ivf/ (last visited Jan. 23, 2015).

38. *Id.*

39. *See* S. Silber, N. Barbey, M. DeRosa, J. Pineda, & K. Lenahan, *Use of a Novel Minimal Stimulation In Vitro Fertilization ("Mini-IVF") Protocol for Low Ovarian Reserve and for Older Women,* 100 Fertility & Sterility S18 (2013) (reporting the mini-IVF cycles yielded three to six eggs versus twelve with standard IVF but cost half as much); *but see* N. Gleicher, *A Pilot Study Raising Concern About Utilization of Low Intensity IVF (LI-IVF) in Place of Standard IVF (S-IVF),* 96 Fertility & Sterility S185 (2011) (showing reduced pregnancy rates in mini-IVF, erasing potential cost advantages because patients usually undergo more cycles).

40. *Low-Cost Fertility Treatment: Maybe Babies,* The Economist, July 19, 2014, *available at* http://www.economist.com/news/international/21607881-vitro-fertilisa

tion-once-seen-miraculous-now-mainstream-rich-countries-soon (last visited Jan. 23, 2015).

41. *See* Kate Johnson, *New Vaginal Device Acts as Incubator for IVF Embryos,* Medscape Med. News, Oct. 24, 2014 (explaining how embryos are formed in the laboratory by combining eggs and sperm, and when two to four hours old are transferred to a tampon-sized capsule and inserted into the vagina for three to five days, after which the embryos are transferred into the uterus), *available at* http://www.medscape.com/view article/833834 (last visited Jan. 24, 2015). Novel strategies for reducing IVF costs continue to be investigated and show promise. *See* Richard Paulson, Bart Fauser, Lan Voung & Kevin Doody, *Can We Modify Assisted Reproductive Technology Practice to Broaden Reproductive Care Access?,* 105 Fertility & Sterility 1138 (2016).

42. The language appears on the INCIID tax return filed for tax year 2012, *available at* http://inciid.org/sites/default/files/INCIID_2012_990.pdf (last visited Jan. 23, 2015).

43. *Id.*

44. The INCIID website currently lists twelve participating ART physicians nationwide. *See* http://www.inciid.org/professional-services (last visited Jan. 23, 2015).

45. INCIID, *The INCIID Scholarship, available at* http://inciid.org/scholarship -faq (last visited Jan. 23, 2015) (requiring all applicants to make an annual $55 donation and limiting services to applicants who are medically infertile).

46. The Tinina Q. Cade Foundation was established in 2005 "to provide information support and financial assistance to help needy interfile families overcome infertility." To date, the foundation has provided thirty-one families with financial support for adoption and fertility treatment. Cade Foundation, *Family Building Grant, available at* http://www.cadefoundation.org/Grants/family-building-grant (last visited Apr. 25, 2016). Baby Quest Foundation (est. 2011) also provides financial assistance to "those who cannot afford the high costs of procedures such as egg and sperm donation, egg freezing, artificial insemination, in vitro fertilization, embryos donation, and gestational surrogacy." To date, the foundation has awarded twenty-one grants. Baby Quest Foundation, *Our Recipients, available at* http://babyquestfoundation.org/our-recipients/ (last visited Apr. 25, 2016).

47. *See Fertile Hope Launches First-Ever Financial Assistance Program for Cancer Patients Facing Infertility,* PR Newswire, Sept. 29, 2001, *available at* http://www.prnews wire.com/news-releases/fertile-hope-launches-first-ever-financial-assistance-program -for-cancer-patients-facing-infertility-73972262.html (last visited Jan. 24, 2015).

48. For example, the California State Bar Foundation is a nonprofit organization affiliated with the state bar of California, which collects voluntary donations from licensed California lawyers (via the annual bar membership invoice) and other donors. The foundation distributes grants to nonprofit organizations and awards scholarships to law students committed to public service. *See* California Bar Foundation, http://www .calbarfoundation.org/about-us.html (last visited Jan. 24, 2015).

49. For example, there is only one reproductive endocrinologist serving Montana, Wyoming, and western North Dakota. She appears to see patients in two Montana

cities, Bozeman and Billings, but not in Wyoming or North Dakota. *See* Billings Clinic, Reprod. Med. & Fertility Care, *available at* http://www.billingsclinic.com/services -specialties/womens/reproductive-medicine/ (last visited Jan. 26, 2015). There are no ART clinics in Wyoming. *See* 2013 ART National Report, *supra* note 28, at 7.

50. *See, e.g.*, San Diego Fertility Ctr., *Sample IVF Calendar*, *available at* http:// www.sdfertility.com/ivfcalendar.htm (last visited Jan. 26, 2015).

51. *See* Mike Janssen, *Obamacare to Impact Medical Office Space Growth?*, Nat'l Real Estate Investor, Apr. 11, 2012, *available at* http://www.nuwireinvestor.com/articles/ obamacare-to-impact-medical-office-space-growth-59046.aspx (last visited Jan. 26, 2015).

52. *See, e.g.*, Susan DeVore, *The Changing Health Care World: Trends to Watch in 2014*, Health Affairs, Feb. 10, 2014, *available at* http://healthaffairs.org/blog/2014/02/10/ the-changing-health-care-world-trends-to-watch-in-2014/ (last visited Jan. 26, 2015).

53. *See generally* Sunil Kripalani, Jada Bussey-Jones, Marra G. Katz, & Inginia Genao, *A Prescription for Cultural Competence in Medical Education*, 21 J. Gen. Internal Med. 1116 (2006); Susan J. Landers, *Mandating Cultural Competency: Should Physicians Be Required to Take Courses?*, Am. Med. News (Oct. 19, 2009), *available at* http://www .amednews.com/article/20091019/profession/310199971/4/ (last visited Jan. 30, 2015); Ass'n of Am. Med. Colleges, Cultural Competence Education for Medical Students (2005), *available at* https://www.aamc.org/download/54338/data/culturalcomped.pdf (last visited Jan. 30, 2015).

54. Brian Wu, *Physicians and Cultural Competency*, The Student Doctor Network, Jan. 19, 2015, *available at* http://www.studentdoctor.net/2015/01/physicians-and -cultural-competency/ (last visited Jan. 30, 2015).

55. *Id.*

56. For example, in New Jersey, physicians are required to earn six Continuing Medical Education (CME) credits in cultural competency training over two years, in addition to the one hundred CME credits already required for licensure. California law requires that all CME courses contain "clinically relevant cultural and linguistic infor-mation, such as how symptoms of various diseases may present themselves differently in specific groups." Landers, *supra* note 53.

57. Kripalani, *supra* note 53.

58. *See* J. Weissman, J. Betancourt, E. Campbell, et al., *Resident Physicians' Pre-paredness to Provide Cross-Cultural Care*, 294 J. Am. Med. Ass'n. 1058 (2005) (reporting little training, formal evaluation, or role modeling of cultural competency training in resident programs, affecting preparedness).

59. *See, e.g.*, Kaiser Permanente Nat'l Diversity Council, A Provider's Handbook on Culturally Competent Care: Lesbian, Gay, Bisexual and Transgender Population (2d ed. 2004), *available at* http://kphci.org/downloads/KP.PHandbook.LGBT.2nd .2004.pdf (last visited Jan. 30, 2015).

60. Stacey A. Missmer, David B. Seifer, & Tarun Jain, *Cultural Factors Contribut-ing to Health Care Disparities Among Patients with Infertility in Midwestern United States*, 95 Fertility & Sterility 1943 (2011); Robert D. Nachtigall et al., *The Challenge of Providing*

Infertility Services to a Low-Income Immigrant Latino Population, 92 Fertility & Sterility 116 (2009).

61. Am. Soc'y for Reprod. Med., Preliminary Program, 2014 Annual Meeting, *available at* http://www.asrm.org/uploadedFiles/ASRM_Content/Events/2014_Annual _Meeting/PreliminaryProgram.pdf (last visited Jan. 30, 2015).

62. *See* Judy E. Stern, Catherine P. Cramer, Andrew Garrod, & Ronald M. Green, *Access to Services at Assisted Reproductive Technology Clinics: A Survey of Policies and Practices*, 184 Am. J. Obstetrics & Gynecology 591 (2001) (survey results showing only 40 percent of respondent ART clinics reported having written policies on access to service).

63. Zouves Fertility Ctr., http://www.goivf.com/about-us/success-rates/ (last visited Jan. 26, 2015).

64. *See* Judy E. Stern, Catherine P. Cramer, Andrew Garrod, & Ronald M. Green, *Attitudes on Access to Services at Assisted Reproductive Technology Clinics: Comparisons with Clinic Policy*, 77 Fertility & Sterility 537 (2001) (concluding that individual physician attitudes are generally more conservative than clinic policies of the practice).

65. *Id.*

66. The author was and remains a member of this ASRM/SART ad hoc committee.

67. *See* Susan L. Crockin & Judith Daar, *American Society for Reproductive Medicine Updates Consent Forms for Egg Donation*, 16 Virtual Mentor 302 (2014), *available at* http://journalofethics.ama-assn.org/2014/04/pdf/corr1–1404.pdf (last visited Jan. 30, 2015).

68. *See* Hector Cordero-Guzman, *The "Majority-Minority" America Is Coming, So Why Not Get Ready?*, *available at* http://www.msnbc.com/melissa-harris-perry/the -majority-minority-america-coming-so-why-not-get-ready (last visited Jan. 31, 2015).

Index

abortion, 5, 111, 158, 173–75, 177
Abram (biblical figure), 207 n. 2
achondroplasia (dwarfism), 145, 149–50
adoption, 83, 90, 155–57, 205
Affordable Care Act (ACA; 2010), 64, 65, 69, 101, 103, 173, 193, 199
age discrimination, 118
A.G.R. v. D.R.H & S.H. (2009), 130–31
Alaska, 96, 162
American Academy of Family Physicians, 115
American Academy of Pediatrics, 115
American Congress of Obstetricians and Gynecologists (ACOG), 174
American Eugenics Society, 51
American Gynecological Society, 48
American Medical Association (AMA), 50, 167, 168, 169, 172, 190
American Psychiatric Association, 115
American Society for Reproductive Medicine (ASRM), 21, 75, 82, 102, 114–15, 116, 198, 203–4
Americans with Disabilities Act (ADA), 119, 134
amyotrophic lateral sclerosis, 145

aneuploidy, 241–42 n. 25
Arkansas, 66
Armstrong, Lance, 197
artificial insemination by donor (AID), 8, 9, 10, 175, 179; anonymous, 59, 107, 171; cost of, 58–60; do-it-yourself, 106, 107–8; screening and, 72; statistics on, 11, 107
assisted reproductive technologies (ART), x; adoption and, 156–57; barriers to, xi–xii, 5, 6, 24, 25–27, 30, 41, 52–54, 74, 77, 78–103, 111–12, 124–25, 131, 141, 153, 157, 159, 162, 166, 169, 178, 179, 185–86, 192–93, 201, 205; cost of, 54–77, 153; current use in United States of, 10–23; definitions of, 10–13; democratizing, 205–6; destratifying, 100–103; eugenic aspects of, xiii–xiv, 2–3, 6, 27, 28–53, 57, 116, 184–206; international market for, 23–25, 205; opposition to, 2, 27; origins of, 5–9; proposals to advance, 192–204; racial and ethnic barriers to, 78–103, 166, 192, 201, 205; statistics on, 10–11, 13–16, 19; success rate of, 27; "whiteness" of, 83,